D0233948

Managing Hum... Resources

Is the Workplace ...d?

DATE DUE FOR RETURN

Bryan Downie and Mary Lou Coates
Editors

Industrial Relations Centre
Queen's University at Kingston
1995

IRC Press, Industrial Relations Centre
Queen's University, Kingston, Ontario
© 1995, IRC Press
Printed and bound in Canada

Canadian Cataloguing in Publication Data

Main entry under title:

Managing human resources in the 1990s and beyond :
is the workplace being transformed?

Proceedings of a conference held at the Industrial Relations Centre, Queen's University, Sept. 22-23, 1994.

Includes bibliographical references and index.

ISBN 0-88886-427-2

1. Personnel management - Congresses. I. Downie, Bryan M., 1938- . II. Coates, Mary Lou. III. Queen's University (Kingston, Ont.). Industrial Relations Centre.

HF5549.M35 1995 658.3 C95-932526-3
1001422145

Contents

Contributors

Jeffrey Pfeffer

Jeffrey Pfeffer is Thomas D. Dee II Professor of Organizational Behavior in the Graduate School of Business at Stanford University. He is the author of six books including *Managing with Power* (Harvard Business School Press, 1992) and *Competitive Advantage through People: Unleashing the Power of the Work Force* (Harvard Business School Press, 1994). In addition, he has written more than 90 articles and book chapters. He has taught executive seminars in Australia, New Zealand, Indonesia, Taiwan, Sweden, Malaysia, Belgium, Italy, Switzerland, Israel, South Africa, Thailand, and Singapore. He has directed the Executive Program and Management Development Program at the University of California at Berkeley and the Board of Directors Program at Stanford University.

Edward E. Lawler III

Edward Lawler III is Professor of Management and Organization in the Graduate School of Business Administration at the University of Southern California (USC). In 1979, he founded and became the director of USC's Center for Effective Organizations. He has consulted with over 100 organizations and four national governments on employee involvement, organizational change and compensation. He is the author of over 200 articles and 20 books, and his works have been translated into seven languages. His most recent books include *High Involvement Management, Strategic Pay* (Jossey-Bass, 1990), *Employee Involvement and Total Quality Management* (Jossey-Bass, 1992), and *Organizing for the Future* (Jossey-Bass, 1993).

Paul Osterman

Paul Osterman is Professor of Human Resources and Management in the Sloan School of Management at the Massachusetts Institute of Technology. He currently serves on the Board of Directors of the Work and Technology Institute and he has served as a consultant to numerous organizations including the White House Domestic Policy Council, the Equal Employment Opportunity Commission, the General Accounting Office, and the Ford Foundation. He is the author of numerous books, monographs and articles. His two most recent books are *Managers in Transition* (Oxford University Press, forthcoming) and (with Thomas Kochan) *The Mutual Gains Enterprise: Human Resources and National Policy* (Harvard Business School Press, 1994).

Gordon Betcherman

Gordon Betcherman is with EKOS Research Associates in Ottawa. The paper in this volume was prepared while he was Senior Research Fellow at the Industrial Relations Centre and School of Policy Studies at Queen's University and Director of the Human Resource Management Project of the Queen's-University of Ottawa Economic Projects. This project examined changing trends in managing human resources and workplace practices in Canada. Formerly, Dr. Betcherman was employed at the Economic Council of Canada where he was a Research Director responsible for labour market and human resource studies. He is the author of numerous articles and books. He has most recently published *Good Jobs, Bad Jobs* (Economic Council of Canada, 1990) and *The Canadian Workplace in Transition* (IRC Press, 1994).

Lee Dyer

Lee Dyer is Professor of Human Resource Management and Director of the Center for Advanced Human Resource Studies, at Cornell University. Professor Dyer has served as a consultant in the development of human resource strategies, policies, and planning processes in several major corporations (including IBM, Deloitte & Touche, Corning, NCR, Digital Equipment Corporation, Kodak, Mobil Oil, and the U.S. Navy) and has lectured widely on a variety of human resource management topics in the U.S., Canada, Europe, Venezuela, and Australia. He has published numerous articles and books on managing human resources including *Human Resources as a Source of*

Competitive Advantage (IRC Press, 1993) and *Personnel/Human Resource Management* (Richard D. Irwin, 1987) a widely used textbook now in its fourth edition.

Thomas A. Kochan

Tom Kochan is the George M. Bunker Professor of Management in the Sloan School of Management at the Massachusetts Institute of Technology. He is a well-known international scholar and co-author of the award winning book *The Transformation of American Industrial Relations* (Basic Books, 1986) which reshaped the study and practice of labour relations and human resource management. His most recent book (with Paul Osterman) is *The Mutual Gains Enterprise: Human Resources and National Policy* (Harvard Business School Press, 1994). He is also the author of more than 70 articles and book chapters on industrial relations and human resource management. He is currently President of the International Industrial Relations Association and member of President Clinton's Commission on the Future of Worker Management Relations.

Discussants

Ellen Glanz

Ellen Glanz is Senior Consultant at Conceptual Systems Inc. in Boston and was previously Human Resource Manager for human resources (worldwide) with Digital Equipment Corporation. She has had extensive experience in the fields of human resource development, organizational development, and education. Ellen has held positions in program management, research, consulting and teaching including policy development for the Governor of Massachusetts' Office of Educational Affairs, consultation to the Coordinating Committee for Boston (The 'Vault') around their investment in education, and management of multicultural awareness programs at the Education Collaborative for Greater Boston—a consortia of twenty school systems in this area. Her research efforts involve investigation into secondary school practice across the U.S. and educational reform. She is the author of several newspaper articles and many publications and is a frequent public lecturer and consultant to both academic and professional organizations.

Louise Piché

Louise Piché is Vice-President, Quality and Human Resources at Canadian National (CN). She has worked at CN since 1975. Her CN experience has encompassed all aspects of human resources work. She is now responsible for policies and programs in the areas of quality, labour relations, employment equity, personnel, occupational health services and pensions and benefits. She is a member of the Board of Directors of CANAC International Inc. and CANAPREV Inc. She also serves as a member of the Council of Human Resource Executives of the Conference Board of Canada and holds a number of offices in other groups and associations. Dr. Piché was a part-time professor of industrial and organizational psychology at l'Université de Montréal for several years.

Eileen Appelbaum

Eileen Appelbaum is Associate Research Director of the Economic Policy Institute in Washington, D.C. Formerly, she was Professor of Economics at Temple University and spent several summers as Guest Research Fellow in the Labor Markets and Employment section of the Wissenschaftszentrum Berlin. Dr. Appelbaum has studied and written about employee participation, and is co-author of *The New American Workplace*, on high performance work systems in the U.S. (ILR Press, 1994). She has published numerous articles on employment and labour market issues and on developments in the service sector of the economy. She has also published extensively on the labour market experiences of women, including the effects of technology on women's jobs and the reasons for the expansion of part-time and contingent work arrangements in the U.S.

Randall S. Schuler

Randall S. Schuler is Professor, Stern School of Business, New York University. His interests are international human resource management, human resource strategy, personnel and human resource management, entrepreneurship and the interface of competitive strategy and human resource management. He has authored or edited numerous books, contributed to several reading books, and published many articles in professional journals and academic proceedings. Presently, he is Associate Editor of the *Journal of Business and Economic Studies*, is on the Editorial Boards of *Organizational Dynamics, Human Resource Planning, Human Resource Management, The International Journal of Human Resources Management, Asia Pacific Journal of Human Resources*, and *Journal of High Technology Management Research* and is past Editor of the *Human Resource Planning* journal. He is a Fellow of the American Psychological Association.

Prem Benimadhu

Prem Benimadhu is the Vice-President, Human Resources Research Group and the Director of The Compensation Research Centre at The Conference Board of Canada. Prem has been with the Conference Board since 1984. Prior to joining the Board, Prem was a lecturer at

McMaster University and a project director at UNESCO and ACCT. He is the author of numerous articles and publications on human resources and industrial relations including *Implementing Employment Equity: A Canadian Experience* (1992), *Industrial Relations Outlook* (1990), and *Human Resource Management: Charting a New Course* (1989).

Ken Delaney

Ken Delaney is Research Director for the United Steelworkers of America in Canada where he is responsible for technical support for collective bargaining and work reorganization initiatives, the development of the Union's policy on economic and political matters and for providing the Union's locals with financial expertise when their employers are being restructured. He has extensive experience in designing and negotiating pension, benefit and profit sharing plans and workplace restructuring programs. His work on economic policy includes the Steelworker's paper *Empowering Workers in the Global Economy*. Mr. Delaney directed much of the Union's activities related to the worker buyout of Algoma Steel. He is a founding member of the Sectoral Skills Council and a member of the Trade and Human Resource committees of the Canadian Steel Trade and Employment Congress. He has been a member of several public policy advisory groups. He has also been the Labour Advisor in Residence at Queen's University.

1 Introduction

Bryan Downie and Mary Lou Coates

In the fall of 1994, the Industrial Relations Centre at Queen's University sponsored a conference entitled Managing Human Resources in the 1990s and Beyond: Is the Workplace Being Transformed? The overall concern of the conference was change—in the North American economy and in the workplace. Prominent scholars in the field were invited to identify key developments in the workplace, examine how human resources (HR) and industrial relations (IR) are being managed, and determine what effect this was having on organizations, employees, and the HR/IR function. Specifically, the intent of the conference was to set out (1) the argument for change in the workplace; (2) the type, extent, and diffusion of workplace change in Canada and the United States; (3) the barriers to change and its diffusion; (4) the role of strategic human resource management in adapting to or driving change; (5) the extent to which the human resource management function is playing a new role; and (6) the likely future developments in managing human resources and workplace change. At the core of the conference were papers by Jeffrey Pfeffer, Edward Lawler III, Paul Osterman, Gordon Betcherman, and Lee Dyer and Tom Kochan (see pp.vii–ix for brief biographical notes on each of the speakers).

To stimulate the dialogue, top practitioners and authorities in the field were invited as discussants of the major papers (see pp. x-xii for brief biographical notes on each of the discussants). The conference program is provided in Appendix A. The conference was by invitation only and 90 academics, senior executives from business, labour, and government and others whose interests are in managing human resources, industrial relations, and workplace change participated. Appendix B includes a list of participants.

In leading up to our discussion of the conference, it is first necessary to trace out the broad economic and workplace developments that gave rise to the papers that are presented in this volume. In the past two decades there has been rampant change in the economic, social, and public policy environment within which organizations operate. One of the most significant factors affecting organizations has been the widespread strengthening of competitive pressures, both nationally and internationally. Globalization, free trade, privatization, deregulation, and a difficult and protracted period of poor economic performance have intensified competitive forces. In a recent survey of Canadian establishments, almost 80 percent of respondents reported an increase in the degree of competition in their business environment (Betcherman et al. 1994).

The impression that exists in the popular press and, to some extent, in the academic literature, is that, because of these pressures, the workplace is being transformed. Much has been written about transformed workplace practices such as employee involvement/participation initiatives, teamwork, total quality management, job rotation, multiskilling and crosstraining, performance-based and other variable compensation schemes, and investment in training and skill development. If we believe reports, HR/IR management is also being impacted by such changes and the HR/IR function may be undergoing dramatic change as organizations look for new approaches to organizing, utilizing, managing, and rewarding employees.

Academics, practitioners, and policy makers have stressed that high levels of competitiveness and high standards of living and productivity depend on a highly skilled, educated, and motivated work force, as well as on human resource policies and practices that fully utilize those skills in the workplace. Traditional work systems for organizing and managing have tight divisions of labour, narrowly defined and specialized jobs, decision making by supervisors on how jobs are done, schedules of work, and performance evaluations. There tend to be limited employee involvement, detailed rules specified in a personnel policy or a collective agreement, and grievance procedures for complaints and an employee voice, and employers have the ability to adjust employment levels as desired.

It is argued that these systems are not well suited to the demands of today's environment and the needs of the organization for flexibility, efficiency, and improved quality and productivity. Instead, it is argued that because of increased global competition and new challenges, organizations need to adopt more flexible work practices and move to 'high-commitment/high-performance' work systems. These high-commitment/high-performance work systems have been characterized by higher levels of wages, skills, and training, fewer supervisors, fewer rules, more participation and decentralization, and fewer formal job classifications. There is more teamwork and greater information sharing, which can enhance flexibility, organizational performance, and productivity. Indeed, there has been growing evidence to suggest that there is a link between human resource management policies and practices and high-performance firms (Betcherman et al. 1994).

Responses to Competitive Pressures

Responses to this new 'industrial competitiveness era' (Walton, Cutcher-Gershenfeld, and McKersie 1994) have been many and varied. In the 1980s and 1990s, customer service, quality, flexibility, innovation, and cost-effectiveness emerged as key business strategies. In turn, many organizations discovered that developing organizational capabilities in these areas depended on the adaptability, flexibility, knowledge, skills, commitment, and attitudes of the work force. Consequently, it is argued, there has been a growing awareness of the need to place more emphasis on human resource management in terms of how work is organized and how people are managed.

Certainly, organizations have undertaken significant industrial restructuring and changes in corporate structure in an attempt to cut costs but also to improve efficiency, enhance financial performance, and, in some situations of crisis, to ensure survival (Downie and Coates 1994). Also, there has been a widespread application of new technology, a greater emphasis on the elimination of non-value-added tasks, and changes in traditional processes and work systems as organizations explore new ways to assemble, manufacture, or deliver products and service customers. Closures, relocations, and the sale of nonstrategic assets or unproductive businesses have taken place. Some companies have attempted to become more profit- and market-oriented and have created profit centres or strategic business units. Operations have been decentralized in order to get closer to the customer, focus on the particular needs of different markets of the business, and push accountability and decision making down to the lower levels. In other companies, there have been reorganizations aimed at centralizing activities to gain consistency and continuity in decision making and policy. There has also been a delayering of management structures and a rationalization of many administrative functions. At the same time, companies have been strengthening their businesses through mergers, acquisitions, or strategic alliances.

On the collective bargaining front, although cutting costs through wage and benefit concessions has not been as prevalent in Canada as in the United States over the past decade, employers have taken a firm stand against wage increases without commensurate improvements in productivity. Greater employment flexibility, contracting-out and work rule changes have also been important issues in contract negotiations. Bargaining structure, strategy, and processes have undergone changes, and there have been comprehensive management bargaining agendas, less pattern-setting, and settlements more 'individualized' to the economic situations of the particular company or industry. This has been the case in both the United States and Canada.

In the wake of many of these business strategies to lower costs and realize needed productivity gains, aggressive downsizing of the work force has also taken place. Immense economic, organizational, and personal change, uncertainty, and the fear of joblessness has eroded employee morale in many organizations.

Perhaps paradoxically, a rethinking of management style has also appeared to emerge. More and more, corporate leaders are articulating the old adage, 'our human resources are our most important asset.' They have espoused a need to build employee commitment, to involve employees more, encourage more participative approaches, and increase communications and information sharing, particularly on business issues. Mission, vision, and value statements have been developed outlining the objectives and strategies of the organization and often committing the organization to more consultation, relationship building and organizational effectiveness and development.

Management and labour have been urged to adopt more consensus-building approaches, to improve relationships and seek new alliances or partnerships in order to better meet the serious challenges of the new environment. Indeed, in both Canada and the United States, there have been examples of joint union-management initiatives at the workplace level, particularly on issues of mutual concern (e.g., health and safety, technological change, employee assistance programs, substance abuse). There have also been some attempts to go beyond traditional collective bargaining and experiment with alternative ways of resolving workplace issues (e.g., mutual gains bargaining). It also seems that in several organizations, management and labour have attempted to improve the labour relations climate through better and more communication, the sharing of information, and working together on areas of mutual interest.

The workplace and workplace relationships, therefore, on the surface at least, seem to be changing. A second development also seems to be significant. The increased importance of the 'people side' of the organization reflects a growing awareness that the management of human resources, and the relationship with employees and the union, could be an important aspect of an organization's competitive strategy. Achieving a competitive advantage through people places an increased emphasis on the need for organizations to take a more strategic approach to managing their employees (Kochan, Katz, and McKersie 1986; Lawler, Cohen, and Chang 1992, Pfeffer 1994). This has significant implications for the traditional role, responsibilities, and structure of the human resource management function.

The Role of Human Resource Management

The role of the human resource management function seems to be changing. But, the change has been evolutionary. Around the time of World War I, with increased demands for production and with labour shortages, the need arose in large organizations for the human resource or personnel specialist to handle employee matters such as recruiting, health and safety, and training. In the mid-1920s, formal personnel departments were established and gained a foothold in the 1930s when, in addition to handling wages, benefits, vacation, recruiting, training, and health and safety, organizations looked to the personnel department to counter union organizing efforts. Personnel policies and programs were developed, and in unionized companies, the personnel function handled the negotiation and administration of collective agreements. Responsibility for ensuring compliance with newly emerging government legislation and public policy (minimum wages, unemployment insurance, and so on) also fell to the personnel function.

Between the mid-1940s and 1970, more formal bureaucratic personnel policies and procedures, including job analysis and evaluation, employment testing, and performance appraisal were added to the roster. Besides these areas, the need for specialized managers to negotiate, interpret, and administer collective agreements increased, and the industrial relations function emerged. Its role was to curb the spread of unionism, deal with labour militancy, and stabilize labour relations at a time when strong demand for goods and services required uninterrupted production. Grievance and arbitration procedures, dues checkoffs, and other union security measures were developed.

By the 1960s, there tended to be a separate personnel function in organizations to deal with the nonunionized employees and an industrial relations function to handle matters pertaining to the unionized work force. Among the specialized areas of personnel at this time were compensation, recruitment, training and development, succession planning, and managerial reward systems. Throughout the

1960s and 1970s, the industrial relations function continued to grow. The influence of the personnel function began to expand, albeit gradually. This was largely due to a continued increase in government legislation (covering human rights, workers' compensation, employment standards, pensions, and the like), the rising number of managerial, professional, and technical workers and consequently, the need for appropriate personnel policies, and a growing interest in new forms of workplace organization. About this time, there was a change in nomenclature and 'personnel' departments began to become known as 'human resource' departments.

By the 1980s and 1990s, pressures from a rapidly altered environment began to put pressure on the human resource management function. Discussion of integrating corporate strategy and human resource strategy in order to enhance organizational effectiveness and competitiveness began to appear in the literature. The concept of 'strategic human resource management' (SHRM) seemed to symbolize, at least in theory, a shift away from traditional personnel management with its focus on administrative efficiency and low-priority activities towards a new human resource management with a focus on business considerations and a more strategic approach to organizing, utilizing, and managing the work force.

In addition to the imperative to forge stronger links between corporate strategy and human resource strategy, the new SHRM called for a greater integration of employee needs with organizational goals and the needs of the business, an interdependence between line management and human resource management, and a more strategic business partner role for the human resource function. Flexibility, employee commitment, and quality also became important dimensions of contemporary human resource management (Downie and Coates 1994).

In summary, what we seem to be witnessing are indications that a transformation in the workplace is taking place, as well as a possible metamorphosis in human resource management, both of which are in response to profound changes in the environment in which organizations operate. At the heart of these two components of change is the compelling need for flexibility/adaptability, quality, and efficiency, not only in methods of production and in workplace practices around which work is organized and managed but also in the work force itself. The skills and commitment of employees have become critical ingredients in enhancing productivity, organizational performance, and competitiveness.

Overall, in recent years, the changing nature of human resource management has become a subject of much debate and discussion.

While there tends to be a consensus that major changes need to take place and while there is much discussion of experimentation, the contour of that change and the degree of change are much less clear. It is also evident that while there are strong forces for change, there may be some important barriers to change as well.

These are many of the broad economic and workplace issues that were addressed by the speakers, discussants, and participants at the conference. For the convenience of those readers who do not have the time to read the entire volume of proceedings, the major themes of each of the papers presented at the conference are highlighted in the next section. Chapters 2 through 6 present the actual papers and the discussants' remarks. Chapter 7 provides a synopsis of the major themes and issues that surfaced during the conference.

An Overview of the Conference Papers

The conference began with Jeffrey Pfeffer's paper, which makes a strong argument for the high-commitment/-participation workplace. Following up on the theme of his recent book, *Competitive Advantage through People: Unleashing the Power of the Work Force* (1994), Pfeffer maintains that an organization's human assets are a source of competitive advantage in today's business environment and that high-commitment/-participation work systems are pivotal to achieving competitive success. He argues however, that these systems have not been widely diffused—that they are more rhetoric than reality. Why, then, have such management practices not been widely diffused? In answer to this question, Pfeffer tries to broaden our understanding of the issues of implementation by examining three major barriers to the adoption and implementation of workplace reform: social-psychological processes of management; organizational financial control and measurement systems; and the institutional and social environment of organizations.

In an expansion of his earlier work, Pfeffer presents the argument that among management, certain psychological processes (e.g., an overvaluation of work produced under their personal control; a perception that those monitored or supervised more closely are less trustworthy; resistance and opposition to changes in workplace practices among middle managers who fear giving up influence, power, or control) result in unwarranted levels of supervision and monitoring of employees, which curtails employee interest, motivation, initiative, and job performance and perpetuates the need for continued or closer monitoring. This prevents the adoption of high-commitment work practices. In addition to these social-psychological factors, Pfeffer also discusses the barriers that arise from financial capital markets and internal financial control and information systems.

The institutional and social environment can also be a barrier to the adoption of high-commitment work systems. For example, Pfeffer discusses such factors as the opposition of banks and investors to certain innovative work arrangements such as employee buyouts, worker or producer cooperatives, and other work practices that are 'not generally socially sanctioned' as well as social values that emphasize control, adversarial relations, and conflict.

In the second session of the conference, Edward Lawler III looked more closely at the other element of workplace change aside from transformed workplace practices, that is, strategic human resource management and building organizational capabilities as a way to move organizations to the high-performance model. Some of these organizational capabilities are the ability to focus on quality and innovation, the ability to get products to market quickly, a strong emphasis on customer service, the ability to manage change, and the ability to operate on a low-cost basis.

A critical element in those capabilities are the skills and competencies of individuals. However, aside from just having 'good people,' the challenge is to structure an organization in a way that provides the capability to use and deploy the sources of competitive advantage effectively. According to Lawler, that is the 'ultimate competitive advantage' by virtue of the fact that these capabilities are hard to duplicate, take a long time and much effort to establish, and require strong leadership. Lawler points out that organizational capabilities are not the same as the technical capabilities or core competencies of an organization that have been identified as competitive advantage in the literature (Hamel and Prahalad 1994). He states that organizational capabilities are the organizational learnings or performance capabilities which 'allow an organization to gain competitive advantage because they can organize and manage work better than their competitors' (Lawler, this volume).

It is through its ability to organize and manage the work force and understand the capabilities of the organization that the human resource function can play a strategic role and help move an organization to the high-performance model. Aside from performing its traditional role of just implementing strategy, Lawler states that the human resource function needs to be involved in the design and development of particular strategies.

Lawler clearly sees a need for redefining the role of the human resource function within organizations. Moreover, he believes that it is essential that the human resource function itself play a very active role in defining and developing that reconfiguration as well as being involved in the overall business strategy. The human resource function needs to be a major player in the change management activities that are going on in the organization. In Lawler's view, the human resource executive has not been and is not now a strategic partner—and significant change is required to move the function beyond its historically 'custodial administrative' role.

Following Jeffrey Pfeffer's discussion on the barriers to change and Edward Lawler's perspective on the role of the human resource function in the management of change, Paul Osterman's paper outlined the extent to which workplace change is happening in United States, in the context of two strategies that are being implemented in U.S. firms. First, organizations have undertaken massive restructuring in response to competitive forces, changes in the structure of financial markets, and the rise of new ideas about how to organize work. This restructuring has undermined the 'internal' system of work, which no longer embraces the principle of employment security. In addition, there has been an increase in the use of 'contingent' workers and indications that organizations are sacrificing commitment and training for flexibility. At the same time, a second and seemingly contradictory strategy is being followed as firms endeavour to implement high-commitment or high-performance work systems[1] which are characterized by the central principles of increased employee power and responsibility (e.g., work teams, problem-solving groups, flattening of organizational hierarchies, performance-based compensation, increased investment in training). In his paper, Osterman presents evidence on the strength of these two competing trends.

Turning to Canada, Gordon Betcherman presents new evidence on what has been taking place in this country. In his paper, he indicates that an understanding of the strategic orientation of the firm and its environment helps determine its human resource management systems and practices. Using data from a recent national survey of human resource practices of establishments in four major economic sectors, he finds that, in terms of business strategy responses to a more competitive environment, most Canadian firms have tended to pursue a cost-reduction strategy.

Betcherman's paper also identifies three human resource management (HRM) systems among the respondents—the traditional HRM system, the participation-based system, and the compensation-based system. The three are distinguished from one another by the priori-

1 Osterman also refers to these as 'mutual gain' systems (Kochan and Osterman 1994).

ty placed on human resources, the investments made to improve worker skills and commitment, and by HRM strategies. The participation-based and compensation-based systems are variations of the high-performance work system. In these systems, firms are doing more than just trying to compete by keeping their costs lower than those of their competitors. Instead, human resources are considered an important element of the firm's competitive strategy. The two high-performance models differ in terms of the practices emphasized. In the participation-based model, firms focus on intrinsic rewards such as employee participation, information sharing, and job design. In the compensation-based model, sophisticated compensation systems are used as extrinsic rewards to enhance productivity.

Based on the data, the majority of establishments can be described as fitting into the traditional system. Those firms in the traditional model were most likely to pursue a cost-reduction strategy, while those in the high-performance models focused on increasing employee skill levels. Firms in the traditional system were smaller and perceived their environments as less turbulent.

Betcherman outlines six elements of a high-performance workplace: a flexible work organization with adjustable work rules and job descriptions; minimal formal and informal hierarchies and increased employee discretion; a commitment to training; employee participation; information sharing; a work process design that improves health and reduces stress; and family friendly policies. He also discusses several barriers to the diffusion of high-performance workplace practices, including the lack of information on workplace reorganization, and how public policy can better support high-commitment strategies.

Lee Dyer provided a fitting wrap-up to the conference with his assessment of whether there is evidence of a new human resource management and of future directions.[2] In the paper, Dyer and Kochan present their discussion of what is happening in Canadian and American companies and the role of human resource functions against the background of two theoretical perspectives on strategic human resource management. The strategic human resource management perspective is comprised of two major components—the organizational environment and human resource strategy. One theory, the dominant model theory (DMT), starts with the human resource strategy and attempts to make it work in the organizational environment by eliminating any barriers that prevent diffusion of

2 The paper presented by Lee Dyer at the conference was coauthored by Lee Dyer and Thomas A. Kochan.

the model or strategy within or across firms. This model is associated with specific features, steps for successful implementation, and 'best practices.' Dyer and Kochan cite the work of Jeffrey Pfeffer (1994), Thomas Kochan and Paul Osterman (1994), and Edward Lawler III (1992) as examples of this approach.

The second theory, the multiple model theory (MMT), begins with the organizational environment and attempts to match the appropriate HR strategy to the environment for maximum effectiveness. The work of Dyer and Holder (1988) and Randall Schuler (1989) and proponents of total quality management and reengineering fall into this category. The prescriptive nature of organizational environments limits the range of options with respect to human resource strategies.

To illustrate the differences between the approaches of the DMT and MMT models, Dyer and Kochan discuss the extent to which these two perspectives are evident in practice by referring to several recent studies and surveys that have been conducted and discussed by many of the other speakers. Dyer and Kochan agree that although evidence is sparse, the diffusion of the two models has been limited, and they cite many of the factors that account for this result. In particular, Dyer follows up the presentation by Edward Lawler with a focus on the role of human resource management as a strategic business partner. Like Lawler, Dyer and Kochan envision this strategic business partner function to be an added, not a replacement, role for human resource management and suggest that the diffusion of this role is likely to be slow.

In conclusion, Dyer and Kochan indicate that, on the one hand, there is a new human resource management. Certain common themes have been embraced by many human resource theorists, researchers and practitioners, and these are outlined in the paper. On the other hand, they also point out that there continues to be confusion and not nearly the same level of agreement on the implications of this new human resource management, its basic constructs, major components, and future directions.

The conference proceedings were tape-recorded, and we have included the discussants' remarks after the Lawler, Osterman, and Betcherman papers at the end of Chapters 3, 4, and 5. At the end of each session, time was allowed for questions, answers, and remarks by participants. While there were several points of general agreement among the many speakers and discussants, there were also contrasting views. Chapter 7 attempts to pull together areas of consensus and divergence of thought on managing human resources in the 1990s, the various agendas for change suggested by the speakers and discussants, and future directions for managing human resources.

References

Betcherman, Gordon, Kathryn McMullen, Norm Leckie, and Christina Caron. 1994. *The Canadian workplace in transition*. Kingston, ON: IRC Press, Industrial Relations Centre, Queen's University.

Downie, Bryan and Mary Lou Coates. 1994. *Traditional and new approaches to human resource management*. HRM Project Series. Kingston, ON: IRC Press, Queen's University.

Dyer, Lee and Gerald W. Holder. 1988. A strategic perspective on human resource management. In *Human resource management: Evolving roles and responsibilities*, edited by Lee Dyer, pp.1–46. Washington, DC: Bureau of National Affairs.

Hamel, Gary and C.K. Prahalad. 1994. *Competing for the future*. Boston, MA: Harvard Business School Press.

Kochan, Thomas and Paul Osterman. 1994. *The mutual gains enterprise*. Cambridge, MA: Harvard Business School Press.

Kochan, Thomas, A. Harry C. Katz, and Robert B. McKersie. 1986. *The transformation of American industrial relations*. New York: Basic Books.

Lawler, Edward E., Susan G. Cohen, and Lei Chang. 1992. *Strategic human resource management*. Los Angeles, CA: Center for Effective Organizations, School of Business Administration, University of Southern California.

Pfeffer, Jeffrey. 1994. *Competitive advantage through people: Unleashing the power of the work force*. Boston, MA: Harvard Business School Press.

Schuler, Randall S. and Susan E. Jackson. 1989. Determinants of human resource management priorities and implications for industrial relations. *Journal of Management* 15(1):89–99.

Walton, Richard E., Joel E. Cutcher-Gershenfeld, and Robert B. McKersie. 1994. *Strategic negotiations: A theory of change in labor-management relations*. Boston, MA: Harvard Business School Press.

2 Managing Human Resources for Competitive Advantage: Barriers to Change

Jeffrey Pfeffer

For some time now—some would say decades—researchers and practitioners have been accumulating evidence that a set of practices for organizing the employment relation and managing the workplace are often associated with enhanced economic performance and productivity. There is substantial agreement as to what constitutes 'high-commitment' or control-oriented work practices and convincing evidence that high-commitment work systems tend to outperform the alternatives in a wide range of industries. I fully expect the other papers at this conference to continue the worthwhile effort of providing even more data on both the diffusion and the effects of value-adding human resource management techniques.

Without denying that many of these practices are diffusing over time (Osterman 1994; Lawler, Mohrman, and Ledford 1992), it seems clear that the adoption of these high-commitment work systems has proceeded more slowly than one might have expected given both their effectiveness and the increasing competitive pressures confronting organizations today. My own experience, mirrored, I suspect, by that of many others, is that the idea that high-commitment work practices are a source of competitive advantage is met with some skepticism by many of my academic colleagues in other fields. Proceeding from an assumption of efficient markets, these scholars suggest that if the presumed economic benefits of high-commitment work practices were, in fact, true, these practices would have diffused more fully under the stimulus of competitive pressure. Meanwhile, implementation in actual organizations often confronts some degree of resistance on the part of managers, unions, and even rank and file employees.

The purpose of this paper is to continue a task begun in my earlier work (Pfeffer 1994) to develop hypotheses and ideas that might first help us understand the barriers limiting the adoption of high-performance work practices and then, presumably, illuminate how to mitigate that resistance. I begin by briefly reviewing the evidence for the content and effectiveness of high-commitment or high-performance work systems and then spend the bulk of the paper developing ideas as to why these practices have not spread more quickly and easily in spite of their evident effectiveness.

Performance-Enhancing Work Systems

A number of different phrases have been used to characterize patterns for organizing and managing work—'control' and 'commitment' systems (Arthur 1994; Walton 1985); 'transformed' systems, salaried systems, and high-commitment organizations (Osterman 1994); high-performance work systems (Brown, Reich, and Stern 1993); quality of working life and employee-involvement programs (Gershenfeld 1987), lean production or flexible specialization (Womack, Jones, and Roos 1990; MacDuffie and Krafcik 1992), and participative decision making (Levine and Tyson 1990). Some of these terms are more encompassing and inclusive than others, in that they refer to systems of practices rather than just one, such as participative decision making, but often even phrases that refer to one specific practice implicate others. For the most part, the various management practices involved are fairly consistent across characterizations. Osterman (1994, 176) noted that 'many scholars who have written on the topic have the same broad set of practices in mind,' although 'different authors place primary emphasis on somewhat different sets of dimensions of those practices.' For instance, Table 1 compares the dimensions included in a number of the descriptions of more effective ways of organizing work and the employment relation.

High-commitment or high-performance work systems are characterized by higher levels of wages, skills, and training and a set of practices, including fewer supervisors, fewer rules and more participation and decentralization, fewer formal job classifications, the use of teams, and more sharing of information, that permits employees to be more creative and flexible in using those skills to enhance organizational performance and productivity.

The evidence is accumulating that these practices do enhance performance and various measures of productivity and efficiency, as well as often increasing employees' job satisfaction and reducing turnover. For instance, in a study of 30 minimills in the steel industry, Arthur (1994, 682) reported that high-commitment work practices were associated with lower scrap rates (lower waste) and a lower

Table 1
Interrelated Practices for Managing the Workforce

Jeffrey Arthur (1994)
Decentralization
Participation
General training
Skill level
Wage level
Bonus or incentives
Due process procedures
Span of control
Higher benefits
Social activities
Percent unionized

Jeffrey Pfeffer (1994)
Security of employment
Selective recruiting
High wages
Incentive pay
Employee ownership
Information sharing
Participation
The use of teams and job redesign
Training
Cross-utilization of people
Symbolic egalitarianism
Wage compression
Promotion from within
Long-term perspective
Measurement of human resource policies
Overarching philosophy

Womack, Jones, and Roos (1990)
Reduction of status differences
Contingent compensation
High levels of training
Commitment to retain employees
Emphasis on quality
Elimination of buffers/inventories
Multiskilled workers
Emphasis on flexibility
Emphasis on commitment of workers

MacDuffie (1992)
Use of inventory buffers
Work teams
Problem-solving groups
Suggestions made and implemented
Job rotation
Decentralization of quality tasks
Recruitment and hiring practices
Contingent compensation
Elimination of status barriers
Training

Osterman (1994)
Self-directed work teams
Job rotation
Employee problem-solving groups
Total quality management

Lawler, Mohrman, and Ledford (1992)
Sharing of information
Amount and type of training
Performance-based rewards
Alternative reward systems (all-salaried pay, skill-based pay)
Power-sharing practices
Job enrichment or redesign
Self-managing work teams
Employment security
Suggestion system
Flextime
Employee stock ownership

Ichniowski, Shaw, and Prennushi (1993)
Incentive pay
Selective recruiting and hiring
Teamwork and cooperation
Employment security
Flexible job assignment
Knowledge and skill training
Communication of information
Quality of labour relations

Walton (1985)
Frequent use of teams
Job design combines doing and thinking
Flat organizational structure
Minimum status differentials
Variable rewards; gain- or profit-sharing
Pay for skill
Business data widely shared
Attempt to ensure employment stability
Employee participation on many issues
Mutuality in labour relations

number of labour hours per ton of steel produced (higher productivity). He also reported that turnover was more than twice as high in mills using a control as contrasted with a commitment-oriented system. Arthur's data also demonstrate a positive relationship between quality and efficiency—he reported a correlation of .5 between the scrap rate and labour hours required to make a ton of steel in the various plants, indicating that lower quality was associated with lower labour productivity.

A study of integrated steel manufacturers, using the percentage of time a line actually operates as the dependent variable, demonstrated the positive effects of using high-commitment practices and showed furthermore that the effects were related to using a system of practices and were not simply the additive effects of the several separate practices employed (Ichniowski, Shaw, and Prennushi 1993). The difference in uptime between the most traditional, Taylorist human resource system and the most innovative system was about 11 percentage points (32). These results control for numerous technical factors. The study also produced data indicating that changes over time in the human resource system in the direction of a more innovative or progressive system were associated with significantly improved productivity.

MacDuffie (1992), using data from the MIT study of the world automobile assembly industry, observed a significant positive correlation between productivity and quality and a strong positive relationship between his measure of production organization and measures of quality and productivity. The production organization index included scales measuring the use of buffer inventories, work systems (including the use of work teams, problem-solving groups, the operation of suggestion systems, job rotation, and decentralization), and human resource management policies (including recruitment and hiring standards, contingent compensation, emphasis on training, and limited differentiation in status). Because these three constructs were themselves highly related, MacDuffie used only an overall measure of how production was organized and managed.

Kravetz (1988) studied 150 of the 500 largest companies listed by *Forbes* to assess the connection between human resources progressiveness and financial performance. Human resources progressiveness included the use of flexible work schedules, decentralization and less hierarchy, extensiveness of career development and training, participative management, and the degree of emphasis on people in the company culture (Fitz-enz 1990). The more progressive companies enjoyed 64 percent greater sales growth, four times as rapid an increase in profits, 61 percent higher profit margins, and a greater increase in earnings per share compared to the less progressive companies. Kravetz found that human resource practices varied systematically by industry, but that individual company characteristics nevertheless accounted for more of the variation in the progressiveness of human resource policies.

Macy and Izumi (1993) reviewed 131 field studies conducted in North America between 1961 and 1991 that assessed the effects of changes in work systems. They grouped 60 changes into the categories of structural, human resource, technological, and total quality 'action-levers,' although clearly the precise classifications are somewhat arbitrary. They examined effects on financial outcomes (such as quantity, quality, and costs), behavioural outcomes (such as turnover, absenteeism, accidents, work stoppages, suggestions, and so forth), and attitudinal outcomes (such as satisfaction, cohesiveness, and responses to leadership and job attribute scales). Their review of the evidence led them to conclude that 'there seem to be *large* overall performance improvements obtained from work innovation, organizational design, organizational transformation, and organizational development efforts' (265). The largest effects were for the financial outcome measures, with the smallest occurring for attitudinal consequences. Their review also demonstrated the superiority of an integrated, holistic approach to changing the way work is managed.

Pfeffer (1994) has reviewed other evidence on the effects of employment practices on organizations, and a comprehensive review would be well beyond the scope of this paper. But the clear conclusion is that there is convincing evidence, which is increasing all the time, that high-performance or high-commitment work practices do seem to be associated with positive outcomes. This leaves both the theoretical and practical conundrum as to why, in the face of this accumulated evidence and experience, diffusion of such management practices is not easier. I divide the discussion of barriers to implementation into three parts, the first treating the social-psychological processes that may inhibit implementation, the second focusing on organizational financial control and measurement systems, and the third dealing with the effects of the institutional and social environment of organizations.

The Social Psychology of Management

Much of the existing literature on systems for organizing and managing work has focused on the effects of control or commitment practices on those subject to the various systems. There has been, by contrast, little or no work on the effects of various control procedures or technologies on those who *exercise or administer* that control. Thus, for instance, the growing literature on the electronic monitoring of work provides evidence that monitored employees exhibit higher levels of psychological stress than non-monitored employees (Rogers, Smith, and Sainfort 1990; Irving, Higgins, and Safayeni 1986), that monitoring can reduce performance on a complex task because of social-facilitation effects (Aiello and Svec 1993), but that the adverse effects of computer monitoring depend on the context within which such monitoring is introduced, for instance, the amount of control provided, the incentive system, and the feedback and appraisal process (Chalykoff and Kochan 1989; Aiello 1993; Grant and Higgins 1989). The question of what effect computer monitoring has on those doing the monitoring remains unasked. The literature on rewards and incentives, and particularly that focusing on intrinsic and extrinsic motivation, has also emphasized the effects on the *targets* of the rewards (Lepper and Greene 1975; Deci 1972) as contrasted with the effects on those administering such rewards. The findings from the social psychology literature are quite consistent with the existing literature on high-commitment work practices: namely, the exercise of external control, particularly surveillance or behaviour-contingent reinforcement, diminishes intrinsic motivation and interest on the part of those subjected to it (Deci 1975; Enzle and Ross 1978; Lepper, Greene, and Nisbett 1973). These adverse consequences are particularly potent when the surveillance or monitoring is either not explained or is introduced with the stated intent to control behaviour (Enzle and Anderson 1993).

However, to understand why possibly ineffective practices persist, we must focus also on those who administer and determine those practices, not just on those subject to them. So the question becomes, What are the bases for the appeal of control (as contrasted with commitment-oriented) systems to managers and supervisors? One set of attractions arises from the social psychology of the management process, and it is these that I consider first.

Commitment and the Overvaluation of Output

Management requires time and effort, particularly when managerial activity is focused on controlling, monitoring, and directly supervising work processes. The psychology of commitment suggests that this investment in control will tend to bind the individual to that behaviour in a process of psychological attachment. The commitment literature (e.g., Salancik 1977; Cialdini 1988) states that when a course of action is chosen voluntarily by an individual, when that choice or the behaviour that results therefrom is public, and when it has explicit implications for subsequent behaviour, the behaviour is likely to persist—even in the face, for instance, of disconfirming evidence or evidence of failure (Staw 1976; Ross and Staw 1993). Managers who have invested time and effort in monitoring and supervision have only a limited number of ways of making sense of that behaviour. They can either believe they engaged in such activities in error, a judgment that is obviously self-punishing, or they can come to believe that such activity was both necessary and efficacious. The latter judgment is obviously more ego-enhancing and therefore likely to be preferred.

The commitment-investment argument suggests, first of all, that one reason why control and monitoring persist is that work produced under such regimes, to the extent there is any ambiguity associated with its evaluation, will be judged as being better than the same work produced with less managerial investment of effort and supervision. Preliminary results of an experimental study designed to test this argument reveal quite strong support. In a study being conducted with Robert Cialdini, Ben Hanna, and Kathleen Knopoff, we observed that work produced when a subject could not evaluate a project in process received a 3.5 (on a seven-point scale); when subjects could evaluate the work during the study, but could not provide feedback, the identical work product received an evaluation of 4.45; but when the subjects could evaluate the work and provide feedback to the presumed worker during the study, the evaluation was 5.8. The preliminary results also indicate that not only was the mean higher for this last condition, but the variation in evaluations was substantially reduced.

The commitment literature also suggests that supervising behaviour, once undertaken, will persist simply because of the behavioural commitment engendered by the investment in the activity. In that regard, supervising activity is no different from other activities for which commitment effects have been observed and will persist because of the investment and the consistency and self-perception implications of such investment. And, because of the commitment to oversight, it is even possible that those exercising the oversight will actually engage in behaviours that produce violations of control and then further justify additional surveillance. This effect was demonstrated experimentally by Lingle, Brock, and Cialdini (1977), who found that when subjects were personally more involved in the surveillance task, they engaged in more entrapment behaviour, which was actually more likely to provoke cheating. Thus, commitment effects may cause supervisors to overvalue work produced under their personal control, to engage in self-justification for the monitoring behaviour, and possibly to even provoke subordinates to engage in activities that then further demonstrate the need for the supervisory and surveillance activity.

Perceptions of Trust

Surveillance and the exercise of control not only commits those that have invested in the activity, it can also alter their perceptions of those over whom such control is exercised. This is nicely illustrated by Strickland's discussion of the dilemma of the supervisor:

> The supervisor, who presumably is concerned with the degree to which his subordinates will work without constant supervision, may become victimized by his own previous supervisory behaviour. If his interactions . . . have been largely confined to frequent monitoring . . . then the supervisor has, in effect, denied himself the opportunity to obtain relevant information concerning their unsupervised work efforts. His inferences about the motivation of the subordinates will be shaped by the mode and frequency of his past interaction . . . and he will tend to perceive the causal locus for the work efforts . . . as being 'outside' them. (1958, 201)

In a simulated work situation, in which the subject was randomly assigned to monitor one experimental confederate more closely than the other, Strickland observed that, although the actual work products of the two were the same, the subjects came to place more trust in the subordinate they supervised less often and in a second part of the experiment, attempted to increase their monitoring of the person they had monitored more closely in the first part of the experiment. In a subsequent experiment, Kruglanski (1970, 222) replicated Strickland's finding that 'the less frequently monitored worker' was judged to be more trustworthy.

An individual in position to monitor or control another has, almost by definition, power over that other individual. One might therefore ask, Does the mere possession of power over another affect one's interactions with and opinion of that other person? David Kipnis (1972) ran a study in which some subjects had the power to offer rewards or punishments to others in a simulated organization, while other subjects had no such power. The actual performance the 'managers' witnessed was, of course, identical in both conditions. Kipnis found that, not surprisingly, the subjects with power attempted to influence their subordinates about twice as frequently as those without power (37). Subjects with power tended to evaluate their subordinates less favourably than did those without; 72 percent of the subjects without power gave an appraisal of their workers above the median, while only 28 percent of those with power rated their workers above the median. At the end of the experiment, subjects without power expressed a much greater willingness to meet socially with those they presumably supervised than did the subjects who had more power during the study. Also as expected, only 28 percent of the subjects with power attributed the workers' efforts to their own motivation to do well, while 72 percent of the subjects without power attributed the workers' performance to their intrinsic motivation. Although subjects with power did not rate themselves as being more capable than did those without power, the other results are all consistent with the findings already discussed, that the ability to exercise control over another affects, mainly adversely, one's evaluation of that other individual. Certainly such evaluations, once formed, would then affect subsequent decisions about monitoring and supervising behaviour, and the exercise of various forms of control.

Expectation and Self-Fulfilling Prophecy Effects

Although it may be worthwhile analytically to focus attention either on those exercising control or those subject to it, in fact there is a cycle of behaviour that results from the interaction of both parties, and this cycle most often has a self-reinforcing or self-confirming character. Consequently, surveillance and control, once undertaken, is likely to produce behaviour on the part of those subjected to it that is quite consistent with the need for continued, or perhaps even more, close supervision. This interacting cycle of behaviour means that a set of supervisory practices, once in place, will be difficult to change because the practices themselves produce behaviour on the part of others consistent with their continued use.

The effects of expectations on performance levels have been demonstrated frequently—those expected to perform at a higher level do so, if we control for their actual level of ability (Livingston 1969; Eden 1984). There are a number of explanations for expectation effects—people expected to fail may not try as hard, fearing they will waste their effort; failure expectations may be anxiety-provoking and this tension can decrease performance; and people may fail to confirm the validity of others' (and their) perceptions of themselves. By contrast, high performance expectations may induce more motivated effort, cause people to operate in a more relaxed and stress-free condition, and cause people to attempt to validate the high expectations by succeeding.

Surveillance and monitoring may, by themselves, communicate low performance expectations to those subjected to such conditions.

After all, if someone is expected to perform at a high and effective level, why should one want to monitor or supervise that individual? 'People know that under some circumstances, being closely watched is linked to performance evaluation and attempts to compel distrusted persons to comply with the rules' (Enzle and Anderson 1993, 257). If surveillance and monitoring diminish intrinsic motivation and actual performance, because the individual is less motivated or less confident and more anxious, actual job performance may diminish. If so, the supervisor is faced with objectively worse performance, which seems to justify the need for close monitoring of the individual's efforts. In this way, if they create poor performance by diminishing motivation and effort and increasing stress and tension, surveillance and control can create exactly the behaviours they were supposed to prevent and produce even more efforts at surveillance and control to remedy the very poor performance results that were produced by surveillance and monitoring in the first place!

Furthermore, individuals often react negatively to attempts at control, particularly when such attempts have just been introduced and diminish the freedom and discretion those individuals formerly enjoyed. This response has been labelled 'psychological reactance' (Brehm 1966). Cialdini (1988, 232) has noted:

> As opportunities become less available, we lose freedoms; and we *hate* to lose the freedoms we already have. . . . [W]henever free choice is limited or threatened, the need to retain our freedoms makes us want them . . . significantly more than previously.

Constraints and controls can impel people to react against them. Not only is there the possibility of psychological reactance, but the constraints provide an external explanation for engaging or not engaging in a behaviour, thereby potentially negating intrinsic motivations that would otherwise govern that behaviour. For example, Wilson and Lassiter (1982) conducted an experiment in which subjects had the opportunity to cheat on a trivia quiz where the motivation to do so was minimal. They found that subjects exposed to a more severe threat against cheating actually cheated more than those exposed to a milder threat or than the control group which was exposed to no threat at all. They noted that 'broad applications of threats and restraints can be counterproductive because they may increase interest in the undesirable behaviours among the large number of people who had little desire to perform them in the first place' (818). Consider another example:

> Now and then Harriette Ternipsede stands up. . . . When she does, her supervisors at the Trans World Airlines reservation office . . . call across the rows of sales agents and tell her to sit down. Although standing up slows productivity, . . . she says, 'it's a way to show I'm a person.' (Kilborn 1990)

One wonders if, without the close monitoring and restrictions on her physical movement, it would be necessary, or even occur to her, to engage in behaviour to 'show she's a person.'

Again, a cycle of behaviour is created. When surveillance and control produce reactance and diminished motivation, managers confront even more behaviour and performance problems. The natural response is to apply even more close supervision, and the cycle continues. Imagine the response of the TWA reservation agent's supervisors—her defying their explicit instructions must surely cause them to believe that control is necessary and to wonder about ways of exerting more discipline in the workplace.

Loss and Risk Aversion

A final psychological process that can help explain managerial persistence in behaviours that are ineffective is loss and risk aversion. Research has demonstrated that a loss of a given magnitude has much more disutility than a comparable gain has utility—or, in other words, losses of a given amount are viewed much more adversely than gains of the same amount are viewed positively (Kahneman and Tversky 1984). Furthermore, most individuals are risk averse, which simply means that they need to be compensated for bearing risk. If we are both risk averse and loss averse, changes from present practices, regardless of their potential promise for performance improvement, may not appear to be attractive. The losses, the expenses, the risks are immediately evident and very real. The gains are in the future, if they come at all, and we may perceive them to be risky. This is why I have heard managers say that they would rather have the performance they know (and, by the way, have adjusted to) than the possibility of even superior performance in an uncertain future.

Thus, change appears to be risky and the risk of loss is overvalued; the behaviour one observes reflects the consequences of the managerial strategies one has already employed, so a reinforcing cycle of behaviour is established; exercising influence over another may itself be reinforcing and, in any event, it changes how one sees the other; the very act of managing commits individuals to the value of managerial action; and results that develop under an individual's control are, other things equal, more highly evaluated than when that individual has less control. All of these psychological processes would tend to perpetuate overly controlling management behaviour, regardless of its comparative effectiveness.

The Rewards for Managing

The previous explanations for failure to adopt high commitment work practices have addressed self- or other-perceptions that create self-reinforcing cycles of behaviour and in other ways build resistance to change. As such, these explanations also implicitly argue that, once in place, high-commitment work practices should be stable, since these self-reinforcing and committing aspects should serve to maintain them. This is certainly true, at least to some extent, but the evidence that innovations such as quality circles and employee-involvement efforts often do not persist suggests that more is going on (Drago 1988; Goodman 1980). Much of the fragility of high commitment work practices derives from resistance and problems emanating from the environment, topics taken up below. But one internal source of resistance and fragility comes from motivational issues confronting organizational members.

Consider two things. First, there is evidence that resistance and opposition to many high-commitment work practices emanates mostly from so-called middle managers, not from rank and file employees nor from the highest managerial levels (Klein 1984). Klein's research indicates that these individuals do not see any benefits for themselves in such changes. Second, consider the motivations or inducements in a first-line supervisory job. In many instances, there is little, if any, financial benefit. Some sales managers earn less than excellent sales people working on commission or incentive schemes. Many first-line supervisors in production environments earn less than those they supervise who have the opportunity for overtime earnings, a circumstance that applies also to office environments in which exempt employees, not eligible for overtime, may earn not much more than office workers who receive overtime or premium pay for working weekends or off-hours. Although some of these first-line or other mid-level managers may hope for promotion opportunities, the likelihood of obtaining significant promotion, particularly given the current trend toward reducing hierarchical levels, is small. If they do not get rich and have little potential for career advancement, what reward is available to low-level managers? One reward is likely to be exercising influence, control, or power over others. Particularly when other rewards are scarce, exercising power over others may be about the only thing managers get out of being in supervision, and there is, consequently, a large inducement to exercise this control and certainly to resist giving it up.

This line of argument helps to explain the following phenomenon: perfectly sensible faculty members become associate deans in business schools and suddenly undergo a transformation in which they become obsessed with minutiae and micro-managing internal processes, often then complaining that they have no time for longer run issues and strategic planning. Although information salience and time pressures may have something to do with this, my observation is that the activation of power motives is also important. In a position in which there is little extrinsic compensation and often even little colleague approbation, what is left to provide a reward for the often very demanding and thankless tasks? One reward is the exercise of power, and I have seen people, once in such roles, expand their interest in exercising power substantially. One might test this hypothesis empirically by measuring the power motives and behaviour of individuals both pre- and post-acceptance of some first-line administrative position. One would predict that the interest in power would increase subsequently, and moreover, one would predict that this increase would be particularly striking in those instances in which other rewards (such as financial remuneration) were absent.

Overcoming Psychological Barriers to Changing Managerial Behaviour

Understanding the psychological foundations of less effective management practices can at least suggest some avenues to explore to overcome these problems of change. The suggestions that follow obviously need empirical study, particularly in field settings, but on the surface they are plausible and consistent with other evidence.

To the extent that excess supervision and personal control arises from commitment processes, the commitment literature suggests several potential remedies. Perhaps the most straightforward is structuring managerial work to make close control almost impossible to effectuate. One example is Lincoln Electric, a company well known not only for its innovative incentive system but also for its strong culture, which includes encouraging employee suggestions, innovation on the job, and taking responsibility for quality. It is probably not by accident that Lincoln has very wide managerial spans of control. For instance, when Harry Handlin was the vice-president in charge of sales, he had 37 district sales managers as his direct reports. With a span of control of 37, close supervision is physically impossible. The movement to remove hierarchical layers, which automatically increases the average span of control, is thus quite useful in also mitigating the negative consequences of excessive control by making it simply more difficult to exercise that control.

Second, the commitment literature suggests that people are less committed to a behaviour to the extent that they perceive that behaviour as not under their control, not voluntarily chosen. One way of unbinding individuals from their commitments, therefore, is to provide them with external reasons for their behaviour. In the present instance, people can be told, for instance, (a) that their past, closely supervising, behaviour was consistent with what reasonable people would have done, but the information on what is good management practice has changed; (b) that they had no choice but to engage in a lot of surveillance given the technology or character of the work force, but because of changes in production methods and training of the work force, such circumstances have now changed; or (c) that the basis on which they were being evaluated and rewarded in the past encouraged their monitoring behaviour, but now they are going to be evaluated differently.

Part of what also makes commitment-effects potent is the salience of the supervisory activity. If one's efforts to monitor and control are foremost in one's mind, then of course one will be more committed to justifying or defending such behaviour and resistant to changing it. This suggests that making some other factor or condition more salient can reduce both commitment and perhaps the tendency to overvalue the work produced under closer surveillance. In the Stanford study described earlier, we used a 'team-like' induction in one condition, whereas in other conditions, we used more traditional hierarchical management language when giving the subjects their instructions about their monitoring duties. When subjects had the opportunity both to monitor intermediate work product and to provide direction, the tendency to overvalue the resulting output was diminished somewhat when they had been given the 'team' instructions. One interpretation of this as yet preliminary result is that the team instructions decreased the salience of their own controlling behaviour, thereby leading to somewhat less commitment to that behaviour.

The degradation of trust for another over whom one has exercised control seems to be associated particularly with using sanctions as opposed to rewards (Kruglanski 1970). This suggests that organizations emphasizing positive rewards as opposed to sanctions are likely to have a better chance of avoiding that problem. There is research suggesting that the demotivating effects of surveillance are related to the rationale for surveillance (Enzle and Anderson 1993)—surveillance introduced either under the guise of enforcing compliance with instructions (compliance) or to evaluate the subject's performance (contemporary performance evaluation) had more negative effects on intrinsic motivation than when the purpose was to see how people approached the activity (curiosity) or to monitor the equipment to ensure it was working properly (incidental surveillance). It would be useful to see whether different surveillance rationales also have different effects on those doing the monitoring and, specifically, whether surveillance conducted under an incidental, helping (ensuring adequate resources), coordinating with others in the organization, or curiosity rationale had a less negative effect on the monitor's perceptions of those being monitored. Such a result would suggest that the rationale provided to managers for their managing process can in turn affect how they come to view those they supervise.

Self-fulfilling expectation effects are somewhat more difficult to avoid, since there is evidence that the behaviour of others is affected by the actions of managers—so there is now an objective difference in the situation that is self-confirming. One possible intervention would be training in the psychological dynamics of this process to see if more awareness limits its potency, particularly on the behaviour of those in supervisory positions. Of course, changing expectations, as has been done in studies of the Pygmalion effect, is probably the most potent intervention. Studies have shown that raising performance expectations can actually increase performance (Eden 1984), and in a similar fashion, communicating trust and confidence is likely to elicit behaviour that justifies the trust and confidence. Expectations on the part of higher level managers, effectively communicated, that they believe their managers are themselves trusting individuals may influence managerial behaviour to become more trusting and less control-oriented.

Overcoming risk and loss aversion can be fostered by providing data indicating the substantial risks to the organization of maintaining the status quo. In this regard, benchmarking activities are quite useful. Obtaining external data to use as standards for productivity and efficiency can call into question the viability of merely continuing present management practices. Then, the risk or the loss is from staying the course rather than change, and the risk of change is correspondingly diminished.

Finally, one way of ameliorating the motivational incentives to exercise control is to provide other rewards for assuming managerial jobs and to provide continuing emphasis on the importance of the results or the goals the organization is seeking. It would be interesting to see to what extent management control was exercised more vigorously in those settings in which the exercise of control was a comparatively more important reward, and if the problem occurred less in situations in which supervisors enjoyed a greater salary differential or received other reinforcements for assuming that position. Recognition and appreciation for assuming the position might be important in this regard.

It is important first to understand the psychological dynamics that lead to unwarranted levels of supervision and monitoring by managers, and then to see what interventions can be employed to overcome these psychological processes. The literature on the effects of contingent reward on intrinsic motivation offers some hope, since there is evidence that with greater understanding of the psychological processes involved come interventions that mitigate the adverse effects of offering inducements on individuals' motivation and interest in the task.

Financial Control and Information Systems

Barriers to implementing high-commitment work systems also come from financial markets and the internal financial-control, budgeting, and information systems frequently in use inside organizations. In particular, the financial markets almost invariably reward the wrong behaviour, at least in the short run; internal budgeting processes often emphasize so-called 'denominator' management; and financial-reporting systems do not capture the value or effects of many management practices and often make virtues seem like vices and vice versa. I consider each of these problems and then some possible ways of overcoming them.

The Capital Markets

One of the quickest ways to get a short-term boost in one's stock price is to announce a large layoff—each layoff at IBM, Digital Equipment, Xerox, and Eastman Kodak (to name just a few) sparked a short-term jump in the stock price, and systematic studies provide evidence for our everyday experience that laying off workers increases shareholder value, at least in the short run (Cascio 1993). The logic appears to be inexorable. If a company lays off 1,000 employees (a mild, and barely newsworthy move in today's climate) who, on average, cost $100,000 per year in wages and benefits, the company saves $100,000,000—but it presumably saves this money every year (unless it goes out and immediately hires the same number back). Capitalized at even a modest 10 times earnings, this simple move increases the organization's value by $1 billion!

The problem is that, presumably, the 1,000 former employees were doing something in the past, and without them, those activities will go undone. Some of the foregone activities may occur in the area of quality improvement, some in the domain of customer service, some in new product or service development or innovation, and so forth. As a consequence, over the long term, the economic value (and productivity) of the enterprise is about as likely to diminish as to increase. As Greg Tucker, vice president in the San Francisco office of CSC Index Consulting, noted in an article by Barbara Noble entitled 'Questioning Productivity Beliefs' (*New York Times*, 10 July 1994, sec. F, p.21):

> Downsizing doesn't work because it usually doesn't change the nature of work. They just say do more and call it re-engineering to make it sound more responsible.

In the same article Noble reports on a study from the Center for Economic Studies of the U.S. Census Bureau which confirms the common sense wisdom that downsizing is often ineffective at increasing productivity:

> Examining Census Bureau data on 140,000 plants in operation from 1977 to 1987, the study found that 'successful upsizers'—companies that increase productivity and increase employment—accounted for almost as much improved productivity as 'successful downsizers,' those that raised productivity by lowering employment. (p. 21)

In fact, as Noble also reports, the data show that there were more companies increasing productivity while increasing employment (44,597) than those increasing productivity while reducing employment (36,238); moreover, there were some 19,289 companies with decreased employment whose productivity also went down, which means that a plant that decreased employment levels had roughly one chance in three of also experiencing diminished productivity.

These results are not surprising if one uses common sense. If merely laying off people—which anyone can do—could bring competitive advantage, everyone would do it, and it would no longer provide an economic edge. The things that provide sustainable competitive advantage must, by definition, be difficult to duplicate. Downsizing is not difficult to duplicate, and it is, in fact, often done. Cutting costs does not necessarily increase the quality or attractiveness of the organization's products or services, does not necessarily mean its employees work harder or smarter, or improve the quality of its strategy. The fact that downsizing does not always work is not surprising. What is surprising is the positive reaction of the capital markets. But in an era of increasing concern with a firm's stock price, the temptation to do something as a short-term palliative may be overwhelming.

Budgeting and Internal Control

It is typical in most organizations, profit and nonprofit, to have an annual budgeting cycle in which financial projections and forecasts for the coming period are made. In many organizations, managers are evaluated by whether or not they are able to outperform the operating plans that were created during this process. Particularly in large and geographically dispersed organizations, the budget process and internal financial controls enable senior management to ensure that line managers are performing effectively and to maintain adequate financial control over the organization so there are no unexpected financial reversals. Financial discipline is undoubtedly essential in organizations of all kinds and contributes importantly to effective management and oversight. But it is also true that the drive to meet short-term financial objectives, frequently assessed on a quarterly, monthly, or even weekly basis, can lead to actions that make it difficult to implement high-commitment work practices and that are sub-optimal in the long run.

The most obvious effect of internal financial controls is to put in place what is essentially a surveillance and monitoring system. It then becomes somewhat more difficult to promote a participative, egalitarian culture while implementing fairly rigorous financial controls. Another effect is to encourage 'making-the-numbers' behaviour at the expense of policies that might produce competitive advantage through the work force. For instance, if profit goals are not being met, there is a temptation to avoid filling positions (understaffing), to cut training, to try to hire less expensive (and therefore probably less experienced or competent) people, and to cut recruiting activity and costs. Although each of these cuts in expenses permits profit objectives to be met in the immediate period, each also has potentially deleterious long-term consequences.

Shrewd and effective organizations understand how to balance the real need for financial control and management oversight with the requirements for making long-term investments in competitive capability. For instance, Ray Waddoups, who was, when I met him, in charge of Motorola University West in Phoenix, related the following. I had asked him whether Motorola managers, in their need to make their numbers in a given quarter, ever succumbed to the pressure to postpone or eliminate training activities. Motorola, as many readers know, has maintained a substantial commitment to training over a long period as part of its fundamental business strategy. Ray responded that it was certainly true that a few managers did succumb to that temptation, but that if and when it was discovered, they would probably receive a call from the CEO telling them not to do it again. Motorola, after all, was interested in its development over a long period, not just next quarter.

Internal Financial Measures

The problem with relying on budgets and internal financial controls is that, with respect to managing the work force, they are often systematically misleading. As Deming (see Gabor 1990) and others have noted, financial management systems, with their emphasis on results, ignore the processes and capabilities that produce those results. As Meyer puts it:

> Many managers fail to realize that results measures like profits, market share, and cost, which may help them keep score on the performance of their businesses, do not help . . . any organization monitor the activities or capabilities that enable it to perform a given process. Nor do such measures tell team members what they must do to improve their performance. (1994, 97)

And, as already noted, investments in human assets and capabilities are tempting expense targets to cut when profit constraints tighten. There is no way of capitalizing such expenditures, nor do virtually any financial reporting systems differentiate between expenditures that do and do not build competency and skill in the organization.

The interesting paradox is that experienced managers understand the limitations of conventional, traditional management-accounting systems, and just as they do in the domain of manufacturing, they use their judgment to overcome these biases—but not always and not under all circumstances. The problem is that the numbers are present and visible and can, I believe, drive judgment out, under some circumstances. Such circumstances include pressure to meet immediate performance targets, requirements to justify managerial activities to others—which leads to a reliance on 'objective,' even if misleading, information—and the physical presence, in objective-appearing format, of the misleading information. In a series of studies about to get underway, Robert Cialdini, two doctoral students, and I are going to examine the effect of these and other conditions on the use of biased or misleading information, in an attempt to learn the conditions under which experts behave like novices because situational factors drive out judgment in favour of a reliance on inappropriate numbers. It is interesting that, while off-line, for instance, at a training session, executives almost invariably recognize the veracity of what I am saying and the problems they face, once back in the setting, the numbers dominate decision making again, almost regardless of their utility or helpfulness. Situational pressures and constraints do, indeed, drive out experience and judgment when the circumstances are right.

With misleading and inappropriate data, it is difficult for any manager to make sound strategic or operational decisions. The fact that few organizations collect process data, that few financial management systems are helpful in managing the work force for strategic advantage, and the fact that such financial or cost accounting data often dominates internal debate and discussion, makes the problem of adopting high-commitment work practices formidable. Such practices require information and measurements that support them, and those organizations that are known for their work force management often employ other measures—such as employee surveys—directly assessing the work force to supplement or moderate the use of traditional accounting indicators.

Surmounting Financial Pressures

In the face of these very real internal management-control practices and external capital-market effects, how are firms actually able to implement high-commitment work practices? With respect to the external capital markets, it is true that not all organizations are publicly traded. Levi Strauss, the apparel manufacturer, has implemented innovative gainsharing programs in many of its manufacturing facilities and is known as a pro-employee workplace. It went private in a leveraged buy-out a number of years ago. Peter Thigpen, one of its senior managers responsible for manufacturing at that time, told me that he thought many of the changes the company had made in its work practices, and for that matter other changes, would never have occurred had the company remained public. The leveraged buy-out movement has been interpreted by some, such as Michael Jensen, as being efficiency-producing because it provides greater incentives for management to act in shareholder interests. But it is also possible that the move toward more closely held companies, either by managers or employees more broadly, has efficiency effects because such ownership arrangements permit and, in the case of employee ownership, encourage the adoption of high-commitment work practices. In the case of Lincoln Electric, the very successful arc welding manufacturer, much has been made of the fact that because the stock is closely held by employees, the Lincoln family, and various trusts they have established, the firm can take a longer term view of its employment practices.

Even for firms publicly traded and widely held, management can make short-term stock price fluctuations either more or less salient. There are companies in which stock prices are posted every day—it is little wonder that in such places, as well as in organizations in which every discussion includes mention of the stock price, a short-term focus develops. One of the more effective ways to overcome this short-term focus on stock price is to have a vision or strategy, including implications for developing high-commitment work practices, as well as measures that assess how well the strategy is being implemented. This strategic focus, together with an emphasis on the development of skills and capabilities in the organization, provides an important counterweight to other external pressures.

The budgeting and financial-control problem is also at least somewhat solvable. Consider as an analogy how organizations deal with either research and development or capital investment. In both instances, there is a tendency for managers, in efforts to meet short-term budget objectives, to skimp on investment in capital or in research and development. In many organizations, capital expenditures, viewed as a long-term investment in organizational technology, are treated with a separate capital budget, and, similarly, many organizations have a separate decision process and even a separate department for research and development. It is recognized that these investments, if made appropriately, build competitive strength for the future and need to be considered in a process somewhat separate from the more immediate financial-control system. A similar thing could be done for investment in human resources and progressive work practices, if and when firms recognize that the work force, too, is an important source of competence and strategic advantage. Indeed, some companies do have distinct training and recruiting budgets, but unfortunately these are often the first things to be cut in times of financial difficulty. Nonetheless, separately budgeting for the development of a firm's organizational capabilities makes as much intuitive sense as budgeting for its capital investments and its expenditures to develop technological capability. Properly done, with the proper management support, it can help overcome the pressures to sacrifice high-commitment work practices for short-term financial pressures.

What would help immensely would be an innovation comparable to activity-based cost accounting in manufacturing (Cooper and Kaplan 1988) that would enable managers to measure the value of their expenditures on human resource practices and organization more accurately. Absent this, an intermediate step involves employing a straightforward diagnostic process that relates human resource policies and practices, and, for that matter, other management activities, to the underlying strategic objectives of the firm. The diagnostic process first requires the organization to specify its competitive strategy, what distinguishes it from its competitors and how it intends to succeed in its intended market. Given that strategy, managers then logically derive what skills, attitudes, competencies, and behaviours would have to be characteristic of the work force in order for the strategy as developed to be successfully implemented. Then, the organization can list what it is doing in various domains and ask, using logic, to what extent its activities are consistent or inconsistent with what it must develop to execute its strategy effectively. Often this analysis will illuminate policies and practices that are inconsistent with the necessary kind of organization and can also highlight activities that are basically wasted effort since they are not helping the organization accomplish important strategic goals. Table 2 illustrates how one organization used this form of analysis to find gaps in its training programs. The organization, a systems house doing work primarily for the Department of Defense, wanted to diversify and use its skills in commercial activities. The goal of business diversification was paramount, yet a review of the organization's training programs indicated that (a) business diversification was being served by none of them and (b) some of the programs were not meeting many of the organization's priorities.

Another useful analytical exercise is to assess the price premium, volume increase, or both, that the organization would obtain should it be able to implement its intended strategy successfully. This amount provides a standard against which it can evaluate the reasonableness of expending more resources to develop the organizational capability to implement its strategy. For instance, a San Francisco hotel operating in the luxury hotel segment began with the intention of differentiating itself by providing an exceptionally high level of personal service delivered through a staff of personal valets. But, probably because of other budget problems, the hotel paid its valets only $7.50 per hour, the same as a regular maid would get in other hotels, and kept the staffing quite lean so that the valets never were able to develop teams. Yet the hotel, because of its strategy, sought to get a 30 percent premium in its room rate, which came to more than $4 million per year. Obviously, skimping on staffing and wages for something this strategically important made neither operational nor economic sense: the hotel could have improved the quality and motivation of its staff through higher compensation and more effective work design and still had lots of money left over if these changes had resulted in it becoming the destination of choice

Table 2
Analysis of Congruence

Courses	Priorities						
	Shared understanding	Changing employee and manager role	Performance management	Business diversification	Specific skills	Compliance	Diversity
8-hour, all-employee course	x	x	x			x	x
Concurrent engineering	x	x	x		x		
Performance management		x	x			x	x
Leadership through facilitation	x	x			x		
Program management					x		
Systems engineering					x		
Compliance courses	x		x				x

for up-market clientele. Unfortunately, however, this particular hotel never solved its problems, and it was sold to an Asian chain.

The Normative Environment and Social Influence

Thus far, I have discussed factors inhibiting the adoption of high-commitment work practices that are primarily internal to the organization, either involving the psychology of management or the measurement and control systems in place. But the social environment plays a large role in either facilitating or inhibiting the adoption of high-commitment work practices, and thus also warrants attention as we seek to understand barriers to change.

Social Expectations

In early 1994, United Airlines completed a partial employee buyout in which employees gave up wages in return for majority equity in the company, thereby becoming one of the largest employee-owned firms in the United States. United Airlines had to overcome substantial employee skepticism, and the United saga reveals a lot of initial opposition on the part of banks and institutional investors, such as John Neff of the Vanguard mutual fund group. In newspaper articles detailing the institutional resistance, the phrase was repeated that shareholders were reluctant to trust their fortunes to a company in which, because of employee majority ownership, the shareholders' interests could not be enforced as automatically predominant. For instance, in an article entitled 'Can Unions Run United Airlines?' published in the *New York Times*, 9 December 1993, prior to the completion of the transaction, Adam Bryant noted that 'skeptical investors and analysts fear, as Samuel C. Buttrick, an airline analyst at Kidder, Peabody, said that "the interest of minority shareholders would get lost to job preservation issues"' (sec. C, p.1). Besides the obvious asymmetry—shareholders do not trust their welfare to employee judgments, but employees have to trust their welfare to shareholder interests—the discussion reveals a lot about social norms and expectations that obviously condition the adoption and diffusion of various work arrangements.

Or, as another example, consider the adoption, or rather lack thereof, of the producer or worker cooperative organizational form, particularly in the United States. While our economist friends might say that this simply reflects the lack of economic viability of this form (Williamson 1985; Jensen and Meckling 1976), much empirical research in Europe demonstrates that producer cooperatives have been founded at a greater rate in the recent past than traditional organizational forms, have no worse rates of survival, and have demonstrated positive productivity effects (e.g., Bradley, Estrin, and Taylor 1990; Estrin and Jones 1992; Estrin, Jones, and Svejnar 1987). The problem is that it is difficult to obtain bank financing for cooperative firms, because the form of organization is viewed as unconventional and therefore not totally socially acceptable (Levin 1984). Because bank financing is difficult to obtain and equity financing depends on the capital resources of the owner-workers, such firms are likely to remain small or to exist primarily in non-capital intensive industries, given the problems of raising capital. One of the most successful and largest cooperative systems, Mondragon in Spain, established its own bank early in its history. Because Spanish law gave cooperative banks the ability to offer depositors higher interest, the bank grew quickly and then served as a source of financing for the development of subsequent cooperatives in the Mondragon family (Johnson and Whyte 1982). This example illustrates both the role of legitimacy and the role of the state in providing ways to ensure legitimacy and overcome normative constraints affecting the form of workplace organization that develops.

Pressures for institutional isomorphism are strong—what DiMaggio and Powell (1983) have referred to as the 'iron cage.' In the early 1980s, Eastern Airlines entered into a unique (at that time) arrangement with its unions, led by Charles Bryan and the machinists. In return for a substantial equity stake in the company and four seats on the board of directors, Eastern got substantial wage concessions. However, the unions had the opportunity to earn back their wage concessions through productivity gains, and, most importantly, they had the right to review company books and records and involve themselves in the management process. In an interview on the program *Frontline*, Frank Borman, the CEO at the time, related to the interviewer how other executives, both in the airline industry and outside it, had accused him of 'caving in' and making unnecessary and unwarranted concessions. One wonders if the general disapproval by Borman's peers made him more ready to abandon a cooperative stance when economic difficulties reappeared in 1985.

It is hard to stand alone with little or no social support, and this finding applies as much to senior executives as it does to the subjects in conformity experiments in social psychology. Social influence is a powerful force (Cialdini 1988), and the evidence suggests that it will be difficult for senior executives to undertake high-commitment work practices to the extent that such practices are not generally socially sanctioned and when, in fact, making workplace reform brings not glory but rather disapproval from peers in other organizations.

Social Values and Theories of Behaviour

Social expectations and peer pressure are buttressed, in this instance, by social values that seemingly favour control and by implicit and explicit theories of behaviour that are strikingly inconsistent with building high-commitment workplaces. As for the social values in the United States favouring control, two facts help make the point. First, the United States has the highest rate of prison incarceration in the world, and a black male in the United States is five times as likely to be in jail as a black male in South Africa, which held second place in this statistic. Second, the United States spends a disproportionate amount of its health care budget—some estimates range as high as 25 percent (Woolhander and Himmelstein 1991)—on management and administration. This is money essentially spent overseeing and reviewing medical bills and medical practice, and this excessive expenditure on administration accounts for approximately one-half of the difference in medical costs between the United States and Canada.

This emphasis on control is consistent with theories of behaviour that dominate our management schools—namely economic theories that emphasize the view of workers as effort-averse shirkers, generally requiring incentives to work. My colleague James Baron has referred to this as a Newtonian view of human behaviour, after Sir Isaac Newton's first law of motion, which states that a body at rest will remain at rest unless acted upon by a net force. Talking about economic models of motivation, Baron noted:

> The image of the worker in these models is somewhat akin to Newton's first law of motion: employees remain in a state of rest unless compelled to change that state by a stronger force impressed upon them—namely, an optimal labor contract. Various incentive features of internal labor markets are claimed to provide forms of insurance to overcome workers' reluctance to work. (1988, 494)

Oliver Williamson's transaction-cost theory emphasizes the contracting difficulties required to overcome opportunism, which he defines as 'self-interest seeking with guile.' Williamson (1985, 47) argues that this 'includes, but is scarcely limited to, more blatant forms such as lying, stealing and cheating. Opportunism more often involves subtle forms of deceit.' In an age of decentralization and employee empowerment, Williamson's perspective emphasizes the efficiency of hierarchy: 'the least hierarchical models, in both contracting and decision-making respects . . . have the worst efficiency properties' (231). Agency theory emphasizes the conflict between principals and agents, and suggests how to devise efficient contracting or monitoring arrangements to ensure that effort-averse (lazy) workers do what is required of them (Jensen and Meckling 1976).

There is evidence that exposure to the self-interest model presented in economics alters the extent to which individuals behave in a self-interested fashion (Frank, Gilovich, and Regan 1993). People with economics training defect more often in prisoner's dilemma games, and economics faculty give less to charity than other faculty; in short, 'economists appear to behave less cooperatively than noneconomists along a variety of dimensions' (167).

Economic thinking and language undergirds virtually all business school curricula in North America. Perhaps that is why the companies that enjoyed the greatest stock market return over the 20-year period from 1972 to 1992—Southwest Airlines, Wal-Mart, Tyson Foods, Circuit City, and Plenum Publishing—have the following in common: none of them regularly recruits at the leading U. S. business schools. Nor, by the way, does Servicemaster, Nordstrom, Lincoln Electric, or many other organizations that have achieved outstanding levels of economic success through building high-performance and high-commitment workplaces.

But many of our leading companies are populated by people who have been trained in economics logic. Even if they long ago forgot the formal theory, the values of noncooperation and distrust imparted by those theories, and by language that emphasizes adversarial relations and conflict, may live on and influence subsequent behaviour.

Managing the Social Environment

An awareness of the potency of social influence and normative values can help organizations seeking to change to find ways to do so. Influence moves through social networks—whom one has contact with affects what and how one thinks about management issues. Firms that seek to build high-commitment work practices, therefore, can benefit mightily from closer associations with firms that already embody such practices; and they are harmed when they put directors on their boards and do business with firms that exhibit the opposite way of managing the work force. In this regard, the various quality awards such as the Malcolm Baldrige award in the United States and similar awards in other countries, such as Australia, help to diffuse high-commitment work practices. In most of these awards, leadership and building high-commitment work systems are important evaluative criteria. By holding up progressive companies for public emulation and by encouraging borrowing of best practices, these award programs help to diffuse effective ways of managing the employment relation.

There are other, even more interventionist roles government can play—and does, particularly in many industrialized countries other than the United States. The Scandinavian countries, for instance, are justly famous for their encouragement of quality of work life improvements more than twenty years ago, and many Northern European countries have laws mandating co-determination and protecting the rights of workers to form unions. Many countries have now adopted tax incentives to encourage greater employer-organized investments in training, and some countries have bureaus and agencies to actively facilitate the diffusion of more effective management practices across firms. The United States, captivated in part by its economics-driven ideology, believes for the most part in efficient markets and presumes that if there are more efficient work practices, then they will diffuse or firms that do not adopt them will be driven out of business. The role of government policy in promoting workplace reform is a broad and important topic and one that would take us far afield from the main points pursued here, but it is important to recognize that the social system in which firms exist is in part also one of their own creation (Pfeffer and Salancik 1978) and therefore a factor that they can actively do at least something about.

Conclusion

For some time now there has been an attempt to stimulate workplace reform by conducting the definitive study or set of studies that will demonstrate, once and for all, the superiority of high-commitment work practices. The Sloan Foundation has been particularly active in this effort, funding both a review of past attempts at reform as well as some industry studies—for instance, in the automobile, steel, textile, and financial-service industries—seeking to understand how human resource practices affect economic performance. Recently, the U.S. Department of Labor has begun the process of letting contracts to fund similar sorts of research. Without for a moment denying the tremendous importance of this research, particularly for learning more about what factors affect the diffusion of human resource practices, how the practices are related to each other, and what their various effects are, it seems that such efforts will be, at best, incomplete as efforts to promote fundamental workplace change. This is so for several reasons.

First, those inclined toward skepticism can always find ways to discredit the studies. In the real world, various human resource practices are seldom assigned randomly to entities in order for the effects to be evaluated. The fact that some organizations or plants have adopted some high-commitment work practices, while others have not, probably means that the organizations differ from each other in various ways. The factors that affect the adoption of workplace practices may themselves also affect the outcomes of those practices, and thus it is usually necessary to control for these differences to be sure the effects one observes are due to the practices themselves and not to some other, unobserved source. Few studies have done this, and in any event, fully controlling for the endogeneity of workplace policies and practices is virtually impossible.

Second, the presumed efficiency of markets means that if certain ways of managing the employment relation have not diffused, this is taken as prima facie evidence that such practices are not as effective as claimed. This is a difficult position to refute with evidence derived from field-based research. Such research, regardless of how carefully crafted and conducted, will, by its very nature, leave some things imperfectly measured or unmeasured and will always have problems of inference to general conclusions. Thus, we are unlikely to see the perfect, definitive study that will once and for all convince the skeptics.

Third, the course of workplace change is, like other administrative innovations, affected by political processes and self-interest, selective perception and recall, imperfect learning and imitation, and similar factors. Gary Johns (1993) has noted how few personnel practices that are well studied, such as selection methods, are actually implemented to any extent in organizations. The diffusion of any innovation, even ones with a more strictly technical component, often proceeds slowly. Diffusion problems are particularly likely to confront changes that strike at the very fabric of social values and at implicit theories of behaviour which are long and broadly held, which are reinforced through education and writing, and which, in the end, create the very behaviours that validate their accuracy, thereby making it quite difficult to break the cycle.

It is for all of these reasons that in this chapter I have articulated a complementary research agenda for understanding, and possibly enhancing, workplace reform—a perspective that seeks to find the sources of resistance to workplace change less in the absence of good technical data and more in a set of social-psychological, measurement-system, and external forces that make it difficult even for well-intentioned managers to make change. When I have presented material on ways of achieving competitive advantage through people, the questions asked are seldom about the validity of the findings or their evidentiary base. The kinds of practices listed in Table 1 are sensible on their face and already have good evidence to support them. Rather, the questions typically go to issues of implementation and change. And, much to my discouragement, I find that nodding heads during off-site training all too seldom translate into actual implementation of the ideas at the work site. Thus, it seems to behoove us to provide those in the field with not only a better and more sophisticated understanding of what to do but also a much more fine-grained understanding of the implementation problems they will face and some possible ways of overcoming those problems, at least partly.

Although this paper has covered quite a bit of ground in terms of the breadth of ideas about why workplace reform is so difficult to implement, it has nevertheless only begun to scratch the surface of what we need to think about to make change in the management of the employment relation a reality. We need to be both comprehensive—considering forces at various levels of analysis—systematic—collecting data that demonstrate the barriers and those things that can overcome them—and ambitious in our efforts to understand these important issues of implementation. I am increasingly struck by how many organizations, when they embark on changes in how they manage people, rediscover the wisdom of past ideas and experience. We sorely need to understand how to make that process of accepting fundamental ideas about how to manage people in organizations much easier to accomplish.

References

Aiello, John R. 1993. Computer-based work monitoring: Electronic surveillance and its effects. *Journal of Applied Social Psychology* 23:499-507.

Aiello, John R. and Carol M. Svec. 1993. Computer monitoring of work performance: Extending the social facilitation framework to electronic presence. *Journal of Applied Social Psychology* 23:537-48.

Arthur, Jeffrey B. 1994. Effects of human resource systems on manufacturing performance and turnover. *Academy of Management Journal* 37:670-87.

Baron, James N. 1988. The employment relation as a social relation. *Journal of the Japanese and International Economies* 2:492-525.

Bradley, Keith, Saul Estrin, and Simon Taylor. 1990. Employee ownership and company performance. *Industrial Relations* 29:385-402.

Brehm, Jack W. 1966. *A theory of psychological reactance.* New York: Academic Press.

Brown, Clair, Michael Reich, and David Stern. 1993. Becoming a high-performance work organization: The role of security, employee involvement, and training. *International Journal of Human Resource Management* 4:247-75.

Cascio, Wayne F. 1993. Downsizing: What do we know? What have we learned? *Academy of Management Executive* 7:95-104.

Chalykoff, John and Thomas Kochan. 1989. Computer-aided monitoring: Its influence on employee job satisfaction and turnover. *Personnel Psychology* 42:807-29.

Cialdini, Robert B. 1988. *Influence: Science and practice*. Glenview, IL: Scott, Foresman.

Cooper, Robin and Robert S. Kaplan. 1988. Measure costs right: Make the right decisions. *Harvard Business Review* 66 (September-October): 96-103.

Deci, E.L. 1972. Intrinsic motivation, extrinsic motivation, and inequity. *Journal of Personality and Social Psychology* 22:113-20.

———.1975. *Intrinsic motivation*. New York: Plenum Press.

DiMaggio, Paul J. and Walter W. Powell. 1983. The iron cage revisited: Institutional isomorphism and collective rationality in organizational fields. *American Sociological Review* 48:147-60.

Drago, Robert. 1988. Quality circle survival: An exploratory analysis. *Industrial Relations* 27:336-51.

Eden, Dov. 1984. Self-fulfilling prophecy as a management tool: Harnessing Pygmalion. *Academy of Management Review* 9:64-73.

Enzle, Michael E. and Sharon C. Anderson. 1993. Surveillant intentions and intrinsic motivation. *Journal of Personality and Social Psychology* 64:257-66.

Enzle, Michael E. and June M. Ross. 1978. Increasing and decreasing intrinsic interest with contingent rewards: A test of cognitive evaluation theory. *Journal of Experimental Psychology* 14:588-97.

Estrin, Saul and Derek Jones. 1992. The viability of employee-owned firms: Evidence from France. *Industrial and Labor Relations Review* 45:323-38.

Estrin, Saul, Derek C. Jones, and Jan Svejnar. 1987. The productivity effects of worker participation: Producer cooperatives in Western economies. *Journal of Comparative Economics* 11:40-61.

Fitz-enz, Jac. 1990. *Human value management*. San Francisco: Jossey-Bass.

Frank, Robert H., Thomas Gilovich, and Dennis T. Regan. 1993. Does studying economics inhibit cooperation? *Journal of Economic Perspectives* 7:159-71.

Gabor, Andrea. 1990. *The man who discovered quality*. New York: Times Books.

Gershenfeld, Walter J. 1987. Employee participation in firm decisions. In *Human resources and the performance of the firm*, edited by Morris M. Kleiner, Richard N. Block, Myron Roomkin, and Sidney W. Salsburg, pp.123-58. Madison, WI: Industrial Relations Research Association.

Goodman, Paul S. 1980. Realities of improving the quality of work life. *Labor Law Journal* 31:487-94.

Grant, Rebecca and Christopher Higgins. 1989. Monitoring service workers via computer: The effect on employees, productivity, and service. *National Productivity Review* 8:101-12.

Ichniowski, Casey, Kathryn Shaw, and Giovanna Prennushi. 1993. The effects of human resource management practices on productivity. Columbia University, Graduate School of Business. Duplicated.

Irving, R.H., C.A. Higgins, and F.R. Sagayeni. 1986. Computerized performance monitoring systems: Use and abuse. *Communications of the ACM* 29:794-801.

Jensen, Michael C., and William H. Meckling. 1976. Theory of the firm: Managerial behavior, agency costs, and ownership structure. *Journal of Financial Economics* 3:305-60.

Johns, Gary. 1993. Constraints on the adoption of psychology-based personnel practices: Lessons from organizational innovation. *Personnel Psychology* 46:569-92.

Johnson, Ana Gutierrez and William Foote Whyte.1982. The Mandragon system of worker production cooperatives. In *Workplace democracy and social change,* edited by Frank Lindenfeld and Joyce Rothschild-Whitt, pp.177-97. Boston: Porter Sargent.

Kahneman, Daniel and Amos Tversky. 1984. Choices, values, and frames. *American Psychologist* 39:341-50.

Kilborn, Peter T. 1990. Workers using computers find a supervisor inside. *New York Times,* 23 December, p.1.

Kipnis, David. 1972. Does power corrupt? *Journal of Personality and Social Psychology* 24:33-41.

Klein, Janice A. 1984. Why supervisors resist employee involvement. *Harvard Business Review* 62 (September-October):87-95.

Kravetz, Dennis J. 1988. *The human resources revolution: Implementing progressive management practices for bottom-line success.* San Francisco: Jossey-Bass.

Kruglanski, Arie W. 1970. Attributing trustworthiness in supervisor-worker relations. *Journal of Experimental Social Psychology* 6:214-32.

Lawler, Edward E. III, Susan A. Mohrman, and Gerald E. Ledford, Jr. 1992. *Employee involvement and total quality management.* San Francisco: Jossey-Bass.

Lepper, Mark R. and David Greene. 1975. Turning play into work: Effects of adult surveillance and extrinsic rewards on children's intrinsic motivation. *Journal of Personality and Social Psychology* 31:479-86.

Lepper, M.R., D. Greene, and R.E. Nisbett. 1975. Undermining children's intrinsic interest with extrinsic reward: A test of the 'overjustification' hypothesis. *Journal of Personality and Social Psychology* 28:129-37.

Levin, Henry M. 1984. Employment and productivity of producer cooperatives. In *Worker cooperatives in America,* edited by Robert Jackall and Henry M. Levin, pp. 16-31. Berkeley, CA: University of California Press.

Levine, David I. and Laura D'Andrea Tyson. 1990. Participation, productivity, and the firm's environment. In *Paying for productivity,* edited by Alan S. Blinder, pp.183-243. Washington, DC: Brookings Institute.

Lingle, John H., Timothy C. Brock, and Robert B. Cialdini. 1977. Surveillance instigates entrapment when violations are observed, when personal involvement is high, and when sanctions are severe. *Journal of Personality and Social Psychology* 35:419-29.

Livingston, J. Sterling. 1969. Pygmalion in management. *Harvard Business Review* 47 (July-August):81-9.

MacDuffie, John Paul. 1992. Beyond mass production: Organizational flexibility and manufacturing performance in the world auto industry. The Wharton School, University of Pennsylvania. Duplicated.

MacDuffie, John Paul and John F. Krafcik. 1992. Integrating technology and human resources for high-performance manufacturing: Evidence from the international auto industry. In *Transforming organizations,* edited by Thomas A. Kochan and Michael Useem, pp.209-25. New York: Oxford University Press.

Macy, Barry A. and Hiroaki Izumi. 1993. Organizational change, design,and work innovation: A meta-analysis of 131 North American field studies—1961-1991. In *Research in organizational change and development,* Vol. 7, pp.235-313. Greenwich, CT: JAI Press.

Meyer, Christopher. 1994. How the right measures help teams excel. *Harvard Business Review* 72 (May-June):95-103.
Osterman, Paul. 1994. How common is workplace transformation and who adopts it? *Industrial and Labor Relations Review* 47:173-88.
Pfeffer, Jeffrey. 1994. *Competitive advantage through people: Unleashing the power of the work force*. Boston: Harvard Business School Press.
Pfeffer, Jeffrey and Gerald R. Salancik. 1978. *The external control of organizations: A resource dependence perspective*. New York: Harper and Row.
Rogers, Katherine J., Michael J. Smith, and Pascale C. Sainfort. 1990. Electronic performance monitoring, job design, and psychological stress. In *Proceedings of the human factors society, 34th annual meeting*, pp.854-58.
Ross, Jerry and Barry M. Staw. 1993. Organizational escalation and exit: Lessons from the Shoreham nuclear power plant. *Academy of Management Journal* 36:701-32.
Salancik, Gerald R. 1977. Commitment and the control of organizational behavior and belief. In *New directions in organizational behavior*, edited by Barry M. Staw and Gerald R. Salancik, pp.1-54. Chicago: St. Clair Press.
Staw, Barry M. 1976. Knee-deep in the big muddy: A study of escalating commitment to a chosen course of action. *Organizational Behavior and Human Performance* 16:27-44.
Strickland, Lloyd H. 1958. Surveillance and trust. *Journal of Personality* 26:200-15.
Walton, Richard E. 1985. Toward a strategy of eliciting employee commitment based on policies of mutuality. In *HRM trends and challenges*, edited by Richard E. Walton and Paul R. Lawrence, pp.35-65. Boston: Harvard Business School Press.
Walton, Richard. 1987. *Innovating to compete*. San Francisco: Jossey-Bass.
Williamson, Oliver E. 1985. The *economic institutions of capitalism*. New York: Free Press.
Wilson, Timothy D. and G. Daniel Lassiter. 1982. Increasing intrinsic interest with superfluous external constraints. *Journal of Personality and Social Psychology* 42:811-19.
Womack, James P., Daniel T. Jones, and Daniel Roos. 1990. *The machine that changed the world*. New York: Rawson Associates.
Woolhandler, Steffie and David U. Himmelstein. 1991. The deteriorating administrative efficiency of the U.S. health care system. *New England Journal of Medicine* 324:1253-8.

3 Strategic Human Resource Management: An Idea Whose Time Has Come

Edward E. Lawler III

It seems logical that human resource management practices should be an important part of the strategy of any large corporation. The annual reports of most corporations argue that their human assets are their most important assets. For many organizations compensation is one of the largest, if not the largest, cost. In service organizations it often represents 70 to 80 percent of the total cost of doing business. When training costs and other human resource management costs are added to compensation costs, the human resource management function is often responsible for a large portion of an organization's total expenditures.

But the cost of human resources is not the only important consideration for business. Even when human resources account for very little of the cost of doing business, they account for a high percentage of the revenue of the business. In essence, without effective human resources, companies are likely to have little or no revenue, even the most automated production facilities require skilled, motivated employees in order to operate. There is evidence that senior managers are becoming more aware of human resource management issues and are assigning them more importance. One study, for example, found that in 86 percent of large companies, senior managers are now spending more time on human resource issues (Lawler, Cohen, and Chang 1993).

Role of Human Resources

Despite the compelling arguments that human resource management is a key strategic issue in most organizations, there is good reason to believe that historically human resource executives have not been and are not now strategic partners (Skinner 1981). Instead of being headed by strategic partners, the human resources function has been largely an administrative one headed by individuals whose roles are largely focused on cost control and administrative activities. Figure 1 summarizes this administrative model of the human resource function.

Figure 1
Model 1: Administrator

Aims	Free up the line to focus on the business Reduce wasted internal energy
Process	Establish policies, rules, and systems to create internal equity Functional orientation: put the basic in place Personnel administration Government regulation Labour relations
Planning	No formal consideration of HR (personnel) factors in the business planning process; post-hoc action-planning by HR (personnel) function

Source: Based on Evans (1994).

One recent study of large corporations and another study which focused on a cross-section of firms found that the major focus of most human resource functions was on controlling health care costs and on a host of other administrative issues (Lawler, Cohen, and Chang 1993; BNA 1994). Missing almost entirely from the list of issues were such key areas of organizational performance as improving productivity, increasing quality, and improving the ability of the organization to bring new products to market. Since it is likely that the organizations saw these areas as important, we must ask why they were not the most important ones for the human resources executives. Most likely, the executives in these firms simply felt that the human resource function could not have an impact on them.

The inability of the human resource management function to influence strategy and contribute to its implementation often starts at the top of the organization when the chief human resource executive is not part of the senior management team. Instead of reporting to the CEO, he or she often reports to an executive at the next level of the organization. This, in turn, often results in a pay level which is lower than that earned by heads of staff functions such as accounting, finance, and information systems. Because human resource management executives are not a part of the senior management team, they are not even present when many important strategy issues are considered.

There is some evidence that human resource management executives are playing a more major role in corporate strategy formulation and implementation (Mohrman and Lawler 1993). Their pay and their reporting relationships are rising. In corporations such as TRW, GE, and Motorola, they have already moved beyond their role as administrators. They are increasingly becoming involved in strategic analysis and change management. These positive developments for the field of human resource management raise a set of interesting questions about what the human resource management function should bring to the party. Clearly, it is one thing to be invited to the table; it is another to sit down at the table and contribute in major ways to the issues that are being discussed.

The literature on human resource management is dominated by articles and books which argue that the function should add value by acting primarily as a functional specialist. In this role, it is largely an implementor of strategy. It must be competent in such areas as training, compensation, selection, and so on. Here human resource managers can and should bring up-to-date technical and implementation knowledge, and their expertise should help the organization develop a competent, well-motivated work force that can execute a strategy. The human resource function should also be able to help the organization control its labour costs and be sure that they are comparable with or perhaps better than those of other organizations. In this scenario, the human resource function should focus on administration and benchmarking and on developing its technical knowledge of the various specialties within human resources management. Figure 2 summarizes this approach; it argues that the human resource function should be world-class in its technical specialties and should contribute to the organization's strategy and performance by offering outstanding support in its areas of knowledge. This represents a significant step beyond the traditional administrative role which is captured in Figure 1.

Organization and Competitive Advantage

There is a third strategic role which I believe the human resources function can play and which, potentially, can lead it to be a much more important and valuable strategic partner. It starts with the idea that the key to gaining competitive advantage in many businesses rests in the capabilities that the organization develops (Lawler 1992).

Figure 2
Model 2. Human Resource Management

Aims	Business orientation Services provided expressed as outputs or products Develop organizations human resources
Process	Build performance-management capabilities Development of managers: linking competencies to job requirements and career development Succession planning Enhancing organizational change capabilities Building an organization-wide HR network
Planning	Business plans 'inspected' by HR (and all other functions); inputs from HR may be inserted in the planning process

Source: Based on Evans (1994).

Organizational capabilities are those competencies that allow an organization to perform in strategically important ways. They differ from the core competencies that are often identified as competitive advantages for organizations in the business-strategy literature (Prahalad and Hamel 1990). Core competencies are the organization's technical capabilities: its knowledge of chemical processes, engineering and so forth. Organizational capabilities are organizational learnings about how to function effectively in ways that lead to superior products or services. These performance capabilities allow an organization to gain competitive advantage because it can organize and manage work better than its competitors. The advantage rests in the management systems an organization creates and in the knowledge and understanding of employees about how the organization works and how to get things done.

Organizations have rarely seen their organizational capabilities as a source of competitive advantage. Instead, they have looked to their technical knowledge, or core competencies, their financing, their access to markets, their control of natural resources, and a host of other factors. The problem with many of these historical sources of competitive advantage is that frequently they are hard to defend since they are available to a wide variety of organizations. As trade barriers have fallen, for example, market access has become easier to obtain. As the economy has become global, it has become hard for any organization to gain a competitive advantage by financing its operations in a superior way.

Indeed, in a number of respects, the last sustainable competitive advantage that is available to most organizations is the ability to organize and manage. There are a number of reasons why this advantage is potentially important and sustainable. Properly developed organizational capabilities can allow an organization to perform in ways that no other organization can and that are particularly pleasing and important to customers.

Many of the very things that make organizational capabilities a powerful competitive advantage also make it difficult for organizations to acquire them. Organizational capabilities rest in multiple systems and in multiple parts of an organization. As a result, it takes a considerable period of time to establish them. New systems have to be developed, integrated with other systems, and ultimately perfected to the point where they produce an organizational capability. Finally, strong leadership is usually needed to develop organizational capabilities. Since organizational capabilities cross functions and are often expensive to create, a single staff or line area cannot produce them. The entire senior leadership of the organization must agree that they are important and must directly and actively support their development.

Because organizational capabilities are often hard to develop, they are also often hard to duplicate. An organization cannot copy a capability simply by copying a pay-system practice or an information-system practice: over a long period of time, it must adopt a broad set of practices that often involve most of the important systems in an organization. Capabilities can be the key intellectual property of an organization. Because this key intellectual property is not held by one individual alone, and because it does not rest in one system, even if an important individual leaves, the organizational capability rarely disappears.

The list of capabilities that organizations can develop is long and continually growing. Organizational effectiveness often requires that organizations have world-class performance capabilities in several areas. Simply being good at quality, for example, often is not enough. This advantage may need to be combined with the ability to learn and respond quickly to changes in technology and the marketplace. The key for any organization is to develop a portfolio of world-class capabilities that fit its business strategy and offer the opportunity for long-term, sustainable competitive advantage. A few examples will help to better develop what is meant by an organizational capability.

Organizational Capabilities

One of the most obvious organizational capabilities is the ability to focus on quality. This has received extraordinary attention in the last decade because of the total quality management movement. As total quality management experts have correctly emphasized, developing a quality-focused organization is not a matter of having senior management give speeches on quality or of changing one function, one aspect of the organization. Rather, it is a matter of making many changes in a concerted and coordinated way so that senior management behaviour supports quality, reward systems support quality, training and development systems support quality, the information system supports quality, the design of work supports quality, and so on. It is only when all these systems are aligned that the organization is likely to have a world-class quality capability. Organizations such as Xerox and Motorola, which have done an excellent job of developing this capability, highlight this point quite well. They did not develop an organizational capability in quality quickly or easily: in both cases it took years of sustained and focused efforts at change. Now that they have this capability, however, it provides them with a powerful competitive advantage that is difficult for other organizations to duplicate.

Innovation is another corporate capability that has served companies such as 3M and Rubbermaid extremely well. These two companies have an extraordinary ability to create new products and to regularly get a high percentage of their sales from products introduced in the last few years. Their innovative capability is not the product of a simple change in a single system. In the case of 3M, for example, it represents a convergence of their budget system, their management and technical personnel policies, their reward system, and of course their capital expenditure program. All of these are targeted toward the development, support, and maintenance of a highly innovative organization that regularly brings new products to market.

Because 3M is exceptionally good at innovation, the company is often studied and benchmarked by others who wish to become more innovative. Interestingly enough, companies that benchmark 3M are rarely able to develop anything like 3M's innovative capability. The reason is obvious. At least in the short term, the amount of change and the interactions among the organizational systems that are required to produce an innovative capability make this capability extremely difficult to copy or duplicate. Thus, organizations that try to develop 3M's innovative capability often need to spend years and perhaps even decades changing their organization so that they can begin to perform as 3M performs.

I could go on to detail other organizational capabilities that can provide competitive advantage, but that would be beyond the scope of this paper. I will mention some, however, to give the reader a better idea of what they are. The ability to get products to market quickly, to focus on customers and customer needs, to operate in a global manner, to partner, to manage change, to learn, to grow predictably and regularly, and finally, to operate in an extremely low-cost manner, these are all examples of organizational capabilities that can potentially provide competitive advantage.

Role of the Human Resource Function

All the organizational capabilities discussed here require supportive human resource practices that are integrated with other key elements in an organization's design. A focus on organizational capabilities, therefore, creates the opportunity for the human resource function to be a major strategic player in the design and operation of organizations. In order to be successful, every strategy requires that an organization be able to function in particular ways and with particular organizational capabilities. This means that human resource executives can and should be involved in formulating strategy as well as in implementating it.

The human resource function is particularly well positioned to provide input about the current capabilities of the organization as well as about the possibilities for and obstacles to developing new capabilities. Because of this, the function should play a major role in determining what strategies are feasible and what the difficulties will be in implementing them. This is a particularly important point and bears repeating: the human resource function should be a strategic partner, not just in implementing strategy but also in developing it. All too often, human resource managers have been invited to join strategy discussions only after the strategy has been developed. The human resource function has then been asked to create systems that will make the strategy successful. Against this, I believe that the human resource function should be an important player in the strategy discussions themselves because of its unique ability to understand and influence the performance capabilities of the organization.

It is hard to deny that once a strategy has been selected, the human resource function needs to be involved in implementation: as has already been noted, this has often been its role and needs to continue to be part of its role. However, a strong case can be made that the human resource function needs to be involved in the implementation of strategy beyond just the traditional human resources' areas of pay, training, selection, management development, and the like. Its greatest opportunity to add value may well be through recognizing how the interrelationships among the different functions and areas of the organization lead to organizational capabilities.

Figure 3 presents the key elements of the model that is being suggested here. It argues that the human resource function should be involved in organizational design and work design, as well as in designing and interrelating information systems, budgeting processes, and all the other critical functions in the organization. In short, the human resource function should be a major player in creating organizational capabilities and, therefore, in creating an effective organization.

Figure 3
Model 3: Business Partner

Aims	Line management owns HR as a part of their role HR is an integral member of management teams Culture of the firm evolves to 'fit' with strategy and vision
Process	HR organized flexibility around the work to be done (programs and projects, outsourcing) Focus on the development of people and organizations (road maps, teams, organizational design) Leveraging competencies, managing learning linkages, building organizational work redesign capabilities Leadership development
Planning	An integral component of strategic and business planning by the management team

Source: Based on Evans (1994).

In many respects, the role that I have prescribed for the human resource function may be best described as an organizational-effectiveness function. Clearly, this role is very different from the traditional administrative role which human resources has had over the last decades. It is a role, however, which has the potential to position human resources as an important value-adding function and which clearly establishes it as a strategic partner with the line and other functions in the organization. The organizational-effectiveness function is also a logical evolution from the human resource function in the sense that it takes into account the interface between the areas human resources has historically had responsibility for and the other parts of the organization. It establishes clearly that the human resource management systems and practices of an organization need to be in alignment with the other parts of the organization and with the business strategy as a whole.

Too often, this alignment, or fit, is missing in the human resource management systems of organizations. All too frequently human resource managers search in a piecemeal way for the best way to pay people, the best way to develop them, the best way to select them, and so forth. The result has been a function that is dominated by subject experts who have a particular approach to sell. Too often, they do not understand the overall human resource function, much less the overall operations of the organization; as a result they cannot design human resource systems to fit an organization's strategy. This has often meant that many organizations have done essentially the same things in human resource management. Thus, the only way an organization can gain competitive advantage is through executing similar systems in a superior manner. The argument here is that competitive advantage can be gained not just from having different systems, but from having different interfaces between the practices in human resource management and the practices and systems that make up the rest of the organization.

Underlying my argument so far is the belief that organizations can best find competitive advantage through their ability to organize, not through having superior human resources. The implication of this for the human resource function is significant. Human resource executives have often argued that human resources are a source of competitive advantage, an understandable emphasis given their responsibility and desire to develop an important and respected human resource function. The problem with this approach, however, is that since human resources rarely provide a sustainable competitive advantage, other parts of the organization do not easily accept that it should be emphasized as a source of competitive advantage. More acceptable, more sustainable, and potentially more advantageous is an emphasis on the organization's ability to perform in particular ways: in short, its capabilities. Every part of an organization can understand that to win in the marketplace the organization must be able to perform better than its competitors.

The challenge for the human resource function is to determine what better performance is and then to become expert in the kind of organizational policies and practices that produce it. To do this, the human resource function has to be an expert in human resource management as well as in other areas that influence organizational performance. Once a human resource management function decides to focus on organizational capabilities, it needs to look at its own structure and operations to see if they match its new role.

Structure of the Human Resource Function

In order for it to be a strategic partner, the human resource function needs to be structured and staffed in a way that provides it with access to strategic discussions and decision making. Figure 4, which is based on a study that asked line and human resource managers what it should look like, helps define what is involved in human resources changing from a functional specialist to a business partner (Towers Perrin 1992). The change starts at the top of the organization and means that the head of the human resource function needs to be part of the senior management group. Also, in each business unit of the organization, there must be a human resource generalist who is part of the management team for that area. These senior generalists are the key individuals for creating a human resource function which is a strategic partner. They need to be knowledgeable

Figure 4
Key Changes

	Functional Specialist	Business Partner
Nature of HR and programs function	Responsive Operational Internal	Proactive Strategic Societal
Creation of HR strategy and policy	HR department has full responsibility	HR department and line management share responsibility
Organization of HR function	Employee advocate Functional structure Reporting to staff	Business partner Flexible structure Reporting to line
Profile of HR professionals	Career in HR Specialist Limited financial skills Current focus Monolingual National perspective	Rotation Generalist Financial expertise Focus on future Multilingual Global perspective

about the business as well as about the human resource function. This, of course, raises the whole issue of where they are to be found and what kind of career and training they should have.

Increasingly, organizations which are moving to a more strategic human resource model are filling senior human resource positions with line managers who do not have any experience in the human resource function. This is somewhat understandable since it is important to have someone in these positions who understands the business. However, it is far from ideal, since it is obviously also important that senior human resource managers have expertise in human resources. The ideal person for this role is one who has had experience within the function as well as in a line management position. In the future, it will be important for organizations to rotate individuals in and out of the human resource function so that they can develop managers with the kinds of skills it takes to be strategic partners. They also need to take advantage of the many business school-based programs that train managers in finance, marketing, production, and other key functions. Finally, human resource managers need to share jobs with managers in other functions and sit on key business task forces and teams in order to broaden their business knowledge.

Beyond the need for a senior human resource generalist in each business area, there are few, if any, givens for staffing and structuring the human resource organization. Administrative services such as payroll and benefits, which have traditionally been provided by a centralized human resource staff, can be provided in a number of other ways, depending on the organization's business strategy. An increasingly popular approach is to outsource these administrative services in order to control costs and develop a clear customer relationship with the providers of these services. The alternative is to create regional or national processing centres that duplicate the kind of service provided by an outsourcing organization. These centres can then be benchmarked against the quality and cost of service that can be received from an outsider and they can be staffed and organized in a way that gives them a clear customer focus. Customer satisfaction can be measured and small groups of service individuals can be grouped around particular groups of customers. This approach can be particularly appropriate for administering compensation and benefits, dealing with retirees, and managing employee relocations. For example, Corning has organized a centralized group that manages the delivery of pay and benefits. Within this area, small groups of administrative people are focused on particular groups of employees so that there is clear responsibility for service and customer relations.

External experts in human resource management bring advantages that are difficult to get from internal experts. First, they often have easier access to information about and experience with practices in other organizations. As a result, they can provide valuable insights into the best available practices. Second, they are much easier to eliminate when their expertise is not needed anymore. The need for particular kinds of expertise in human resource management expands and contracts over time, depending upon whether a system is being developed or is actually in operation. Thus, it is important that the human resource staff be flexible so that it can quickly change its mix of resources when a development process is over and administration is needed.

Regardless of whether the administrative services are delivered by an in-house service unit or contracted out, it may be desirable to have some human resource experts who are full-time employees of the organization. They are needed to monitor the technical quality of the work done by the internal and/or external service units and to be sure that the systems are designed to meet the strategy of the organization. Potentially, this kind of expertise can be provided by outside consultants, but there is a clear risk in relying too heavily on them. If an organization lacks internal expertise, it is not likely to be positioned to evaluate the quality of the consulting help that it gets or to manage and direct that help so that it supports the business strategy.

Process Organizing

In order for the human resource function to support an organizational-capabilities approach, it is critically important that experts in areas like compensation, selection, and training have the ability to relate their specialty to other systems. Often, in the traditional human resource department, the level of specialization is so high that there is little integration of the different activities. Training is not related to performance appraisal; pay systems and development are not related to selection criteria; and so forth. One way of forcing the integration of experts in areas like pay, selection, and training is to organize them around the key strategic processes in the human resource function. Directors of key processes can be appointed with a mandate to integrate the different human resource specialties which support the key processes. An alternative is to use a team-based model by creating process-teams which can be staffed by functional human resource experts in areas such as testing, selection, training, management development, and so on. With effective team building and clear mandates concerning their responsibilities and accountabilities, it is possible that these teams can integrate their specialties in a way that produces a more integrated operation of the key human resource management activities.

Depending upon how the organization is designed, somewhat different processes may be identified, but there are some that are likely to be common to most or all organizations. For example, the recruitment, staffing, and development of human resources is a key human resource process, as are the motivation and rewarding of individuals, teams, and organizational units. Managing and rewarding performance can take place at different levels of aggregation: at the individual, group or business-unit level.

There may be a focus on the human resource information system. With networked computers there is a potential for the human resource function to create a human resource information system (HRIS) that is more than just a record-keeping system. It can be an important support to human resource management, career development, and organizational design. An important human resource challenge here is linking the kind of data which go into an HRIS to the kind of organizational capabilities that the organization wants to develop. In addition, the HRIS needs to be able to adapt to change and distribute data in ways that are consistent with the organizational design and the strategy for making important staffing decisions.

Finally, organizational development represents a key process that should be a focus of the human resource function. There are elements of training and development in this process, but it also needs to focus on the measurement of employee attitudes, culture, and performance. It needs to be concerned with organizational arrangements and the fit between these and the overall strategy of the organization.

System Development

One final, critical point needs to be made. In Model 1 and Model 2 organizations (Figures 1 and 2), the human resource systems and practices are often developed by the human resource function or outside experts. They are also administered by specialists. As a result, the rest of the organization often has little ownership of them. When problems develop it is common for managers and others simply to say 'go see the human resource people, it is their system.' This creates two major problems. First, to succeed, many of the systems need strong support from the total organization. This is particularly true, for example, in such areas as performance appraisal and compensation. Second, it is extremely labour intensive and costly to have a large enough human resource staff available to answer the many questions that are referred to it when the line organization does not take responsibility for managing the systems.

The development of an organization-wide ownership over human resource systems begins with the development process. It is critical that the systems be developed by representative groups from all parts of the organization. One approach is to use a diagonal-slice task force that draws members from all levels of the organization and from multiple functions. The task force needs to be instructed and trained to communicate and link itself to the rest of the organization, and its work needs to be visible and well publicized. Proposals need to be checked with the rest of the organization and a sign-off on the final product obtained.

When a broad-based system-development process is used it increases the likelihood that the human resource systems will be owned by the organization and that people throughout the organization will have the information and expertise to operate it. It also has the obvious advantage of decreasing the need for human resource people to run the system, and it can decrease the expectation that the human resource department can and should make the systems operate effectively. The fact is that although the human resource function has technical expertise and can aid in the development of the systems, their successful operation often depends upon the rest of the organization and its willingness to implement and use the right practices.

Managing Dualities

It is important to stress that moving to a strategic partner role does not mean that human resource managers can completely forget about the activities that are part of the Model 1 and the Model 2 (Figures 1 and 2). They still need to be concerned about some of the custodial and staff-support activities, even if these have been outsourced. This creates a challenging set of dualities that every human resource manager must be aware of. They are presented in Figure 5. Model 1 calls for most of the human resource executive's time to be spent on the left-hand side of these dualities. Movement to Model 3 (Figure 3) and a business partnership approach requires human resource managers to spend the majority of their time on the right-hand side of this list. It does not mean completely abandoning the left-hand side, however.

There still are certain issues in which the human resource function needs to be a controller and to audit the behaviour of individuals throughout the organization. At times it is also appropriate for human resources to be the conscience of the organization and to be

Figure 5
Dualities in the Human Resources Role

Follower	—	Leader
Reactive	—	Proactive
Administrator	—	Strategist
Controller	—	Business Partner
Conscience	—	Business Person
Employee Advocate	—	Manager
Doer	—	Consultant

an advocate for employee well-being. It is still necessary for the human resource function to react to certain legal issues and to crises concerning employee well-being and organizational change. Finally, human resource managers still need to actually do some human resource administration. Only so much of it can be put in the hands of the line managers.

Careers In Human Resources

Model 3 has significant implications for the kind of career opportunities that are available in human resource management (Ulrich, Brockbank, and Yeung 1989). There still should be some opportunities within corporations for individuals who are specialists in particular areas of human resource management. These include specialists in information systems, compensation, and training: in short, the traditional human resource specialties. Most of the careers in these areas, however, may be in consulting firms and vendors rather than in traditional organizations.

Perhaps the most exciting career opportunities in organizations are those available to generalists in the human resource function who understand how to be business partners with the line organization. In order to develop the right skills, they must follow a different career track from the one that has traditionally been available to human resource managers. They need to hold jobs in the human resource function, in line management, and perhaps in other functions.

Summary and Conclusions

I have argued that the human resource function can and should be an important strategic partner, but that in order to accomplish this, we need to change its custodial, administrative role significantly. One alternative is for it to become a developer and manager of the human resources of an organization and to argue for human resources as the organization's most important competitive advantage. A second alternative is for human resource managers to become critical players in creating an effective organization. In this approach, the human resource function should be positioned to have particular expertise in the development, maintenance, and identification of organizational capabilities. As such, it should play a major role in choosing as well as implementing the organizational strategy. It should influence strategy by identifying the current capabilities of the organization and the requirements for developing new ones.

In the strategic-partner approach, perhaps the most important role of human resources is to design human resource management systems that interface effectively with the other systems to produce the desired organizational performance. More than any other function, human resources should be in a position to assess the performance capabilities of the organization and to understand how they can be enhanced and changed. In this approach, the services which it has traditionally offered in areas like benefit administration and training should be treated as services that can be delivered in multiple ways. They can, for example, be delivered by a central corporate staff group, delivered at the local level, or delivered by vendors, depending upon what is most effective.

In order to function as a business partner, the human resource function clearly needs to be staffed differently than it has been in the past. Individuals who are specialists in human resource management need to develop their understanding of business strategy and the other business functions. Similarly, line managers need to learn more about human resource management so that they can integrate human resource policies and practices into their strategic planning. Thus, line managers need to spend part of their careers in the human resource function, just as human resource managers need to spend part of their careers working in other parts of the organization.

Although there is an opportunity for human resource managers to become strategic partners, it is by no means certain that they will end up in the right kind of partnerships. They need to actively manage the formation of this partnership so that it goes beyond one of simply providing 'good human resources' to the organization. Clearly, this is a part of what they should do, but only a small part of how they can, potentially, add value and only one way in which they can make an organization more effective. There is a whole host of other things they can do to create human resource systems that develop key strategic organizational capabilities. In the long term, human resource functions can contribute the most and be the best strategic partners by focusing on organizational effectiveness and organizational capabilities rather than on the more limited objective of providing the right human resources talent.

References

Bureau of National Affairs (BNA). 1994. *SHRM-BNA Survey No. 59*. Washington, DC: Bureau of National Affairs.

Evans, P. 1994. Business strategy and human resource management: A four stage framework. Working paper, INSEAD, Fontainebleau.

Lawler, E.E. 1992. *The ultimate advantage: Creating the high involvement organization*. San Francisco: Jossey-Bass.

Lawler, E.E., S.G. Cohen, and L. Chang. 1993. Strategic human resource management. In *Building the competitive work force*, edited by P. Mirvis, pp.31-59. New York: Wiley.

Mohrman, A.M. and E.E. Lawler. 1993. Human resource management: Building a strategic partnership. In *Organizing for the future: The new logic for managing complex organizations*, edited by J.R. Galbraith, E.E. Lawler, and Associates. San Francisco: Jossey-Bass.

Prahalad, C.K. and G. Hamel. 1990. The core competence of the corporation. *Harvard Business Review* 68(3):79-93.

Skinner, W. 1981. Big hat, no cattle: Managing human resources. *Harvard Business Review* 59(5):106-14.

Towers Perrin. 1992. *Priorities for competitive advantage*. New York: Towers Perrin.

Ulrich, D., W. Brockbank, and A. Yeung. 1989. Human resource competencies in the 1990s. *Personnel Administrator* 34 (November):91-3.

Discussion

Ellen Glanz

I am the voice from the trenches here. I have spent the last ten years at Digital Equipment Corporation, trying to build an HR organization that embodies many of the strategies that Ed Lawler has been talking about. I am now consulting with diverse companies as a senior consultant at Conceptual Systems, Inc. to move in the same direction. So I would like to share some of my experience and thinking with you.

I will start with some wisdom from a Dilbert cartoon. The cartoon's caption says, 'Companies must learn to embrace change.' Dilbert's colleagues say, 'Uh-oh, it's another management fad. Will it pass quickly or will it linger like the stench of a dead woodchuck under the porch?' Then their manager says, 'I think we should do a change newsletter,' and everyone shouts 'Woodchuck!' The challenge here is to understand that we must make fundamental changes: these problems will not be solved by a flavour of the month or a disconnected new program. They require something more profound. The opposite danger is paralysis, which is satirized in a *New Yorker* cartoon showing a board meeting: 'Seasons Greetings looks OK to me,' says one board member, 'but let's run it by the legal department.'

If we do not transform the focus of our work and our methods of achieving success, we will not enable our organizations to make deep enough changes to compete successfully. The new business imperatives, whether they require increased speed, lowered cost, a capacity to work globally, or new kinds of customer service, quality, or innovation, require competitive advantage through people. While other sources of competitive advantage, such as technological, strategic marketing, and financial strength, can be copied or developed fairly easily, the capabilities and motivation of the work force and the alignment and flexibility of our organization cannot. So we need to develop this systemic capability through people and organization.

Interestingly, these same competitive pressures mean that only the value-added HR management roles which build this systemic capability will remain. We are seeing more and more companies assessing what they can outsource, automate, or reengineer. They are shifting resources to higher value work and then eliminating anything that is not really needed. They are outsourcing or using consultants for any services they no longer want as permanent overhead.

What does this mean for HR? In addition to the streamlined operational work that must continue, our strategic HR focus must be on two areas. The first area, as several speakers have discussed, is building employee capability and commitment. We must determine future business directions, figure out the competencies we will need to move in those directions, and then build, nurture and leverage these competencies in our work force. We also need to build a culture and work climate where employees are motivated to *use* their talents on behalf of the company. They need to feel good about their work, understand how it fits into the larger whole and feel good enough about the larger organization to commit their discretionary effort to make it succeed.

But that does not capture the whole strategy, because it does not ensure that individual resources are utilized effectively to achieve results. So the second focus must be on building the systemic processes that harness individual capabilities to make the necessary changes. The analogy from elementary geography is to countries that are rich in natural resources, but do not have the infrastructure to use them well. Similarly, in HR we need to build individual capability and commitment, but if the processes are not in place to utilize these resources well, we will not benefit from the capability and commitment that we have built. Instead, we will see wasted, redundant, and competing efforts. So HR, line managers and employees in partnership must focus on both sets of issues.

For HR the real challenge is to move on two fronts at the same time: the more traditional, operationally focused agenda and the newer strategically focused systemic agenda. Most companies are coming from the more operational or tactical part. That work does not go away: people still need to be paid, their benefits must still be administered, and all the rest. For this part of our agenda, we must find ways of doing those things cheaply, efficiently, quickly, and with the highest possible level of customer service. In this area, we must automate, outsource, reengineer, and eliminate as much as possible. We must reduce cost and effort here so that we can pursue the strategic HR agenda, which is tightly linked to achieving the business strategy.

In this second arena, we must develop 'outside-in' thinking; that is, we must orient ourselves to change so that HR solutions are derived from business imperatives, and not the other way around. We must focus on customer and stakeholder needs to determine HR priorities and approaches. Ed Lawler alluded to this when he said that he sees companies pursuing separate initiatives: the training department is doing this, the compensation area is doing that. The problem is that we all work from our own historical base: we do this work because it is what we have always done; it is what we know best. But it is not necessarily what is needed now and in the future. We must somehow find a way to turn this upside down, to determine the business strategy first (with HR input) and then to derive the 'vital few': the two or three integrated solutions that transcend the boundaries of any one traditional HR discipline that will really enable our companies to succeed. And yet, as Jeffery Pfeffer discussed, this strategy makes people uncomfortable, since it challenges their conception of their work and raises turf issues, problems of power politics, and so on. A manager is no longer 'a training person', but a person with multiple skills (including training) which can be brought to bear on any number of strategic issues.

This is a real change and one that we have been only partially successful in making. At Digital, we have found that some people are able to make these changes, while others experience great difficulty and pain. In some cases, it conflicts with their sense of their own identity and with their work motivation. For example, those who come into HR because they enjoy helping people may have a hard time with the stronger business focus. In addition to strong business skills, much of the new work requires excellent systems thinking and strategic and diagnostic skills. In partnership with the line manager and employees, the HR business partner must translate from the business issues to the HR approaches and then either provide or broker services. That requires an assessment of whether the work can be done in-house or whether it could better be done by outside sources. The HR partner must also perform an in-house consultative role to bring HR expertise, and then offer coaching, counselling, and consulting, so that the line organization can implement the different HR and management processes on behalf of their goals. In this work, flexibility, on-going learning, responsiveness, coaching skills, and the ability to partner across all kinds of organizations are critical.

The change for many of us is from doing this work ourselves to doing this work as consultants to the line. In many cases, we will be crafting tools, processes, and approaches which line managers and employees will then implement. But part of the problem is that many HR people feel that we are giving away our own expertise and our own power; and yet we may not be the best, or only, 'channel' to achieve the outcomes we want. We have often found at Digital that if we are the provider of the solution and we are in a surrogate management role, we are, in fact, set up to fail: it is not a role that we can perform appropriately. Employees want to hear from and be managed by their managers or their teams or whatever. And yet, we are very reluctant to give away what we see as our expertise, since we do not understand that there will always be other areas of valuable expertise that we need to provide. We are not going to run out of work.

Once again, we must focus on the key areas of HR investment; we must be much more focused. The leading-edge companies will identify the return on investment on any of the kinds of processes that we are advocating and make the trade-off decisions about the right solution for a particular problem. It could be a training solution, it could be a selection issue, it could be a rewards issue, or some combination of all these. Many companies are beginning to organize flexible pools of in-house consulting teams with expertise in one or more HR areas who can work with multiple businesses. These people may partner to design and implement corporate initiatives, as well as the initiatives of any business unit.

At Digital and with several other consulting clients, we have focused on redesigning our human resource processes and roles along the lines discussed above. As a result, we have created a very different kind of structure for the HR organization itself. This has been quite a massive change: the HR function has changed; the work itself has changed, as have the responsibilities of managers and employees. We have also developed a different funding process for HR work. We have created a partnership agreement process, which is both the contracting process with the line organization and the contracting process for the different parts of the HR organization.

There were also implications for HR capability planning and staffing. For example, within the HR organization we evolved three different kinds of roles. In one role, an HR-business partnership, people in the different parts of the organization provide counsel on business strategy, diagnose the HR needs of the organization, and provide or broker services. A second role is working in a 'shared service centre,' which may have two parts. One part is more focused on the HR operations. Here, it is important to determine what work needs to be done in many places, what work can be clustered in a few places, and what work can be done in one place for the whole company. The other part is comprised of distributed consulting centres with expertise in different kinds of HR practices and excellent consultation skills. These centres are distributed around the world and networked together, so they can learn from each other and share approaches..

A third role in the organization, being a part of a lean corporate staff, is focused on overall functional excellence and on driving a very few company-wide initiatives that may exist. In rethinking the role of a corporate staff, we realized that they could be sitting anywhere in the world, drawing resources for specific projects from the consulting centres, scanning for best practices internally and externally, and building that capability in the HR and line organization.

At Digital, we reconfigured HR work into four areas. First, there were the very few company-wide initiatives in which we said, 'If you are a part of Digital Equipment Corporation, you must follow this initiative because we want the entire corporation to focus on it.' Last year, performance management was our company-wide initiative. The second area involved what we called 'baseline work': the standard services that all Digital employees, regardless of what business they are in, would receive, based on local laws, customs, and competitive practices. We then developed a third category, 'menu work,' which involved additional items that a particular business could purchase from service centres, or centres of expertise. This enabled the business partners, in conjunction with their organizations, to customize HR services and programs to support their strategies and gave them more control over the funding of their HR investments. The fourth area was the HRM work that we talked about earlier.

In many companies, we have found that moving in these directions requires some very different competencies. In addition to knowledge of the business and HR functional expertise, we have now concentrated on what we call 'excellence factors' or 'success factors': factors that enable practitioners to apply their skills and knowledge to produce results. Often these 'success factors' concretize a company's vision or guiding principles by specifying skills and behaviours needed for future success. With several clients, we have developed a fairly generalizable set of competencies across the entire company. The business knowledge and the excellence factors are basically the same throughout the company because we are using them to 'pull' for new behaviour across the company. The only variation is the technical knowledge required for specific functions, such as marketing or finance or HR. And because of our need to move people into different kinds of roles in a very fluid way, we think it is important to have some common competencies.

What does this mean? For me personally, it means that the identification and development of competency has become a major part of my work. I am now partnering with numerous companies in a consulting capacity, through my work with Conceptual Systems. We focus on strategic development, which enables companies to translate their business strategies to the competencies and development processes that they need to achieve those strategies. I, like Ed Lawler, believe that in the future, we need to focus on competencies, not jobs. We need to emphasize the capabilities that are needed in a team or an organization and then determine how we are going to acquire them, develop them, apply them, and share them.

We also need to build processes to share and apply learning across organizations. It is not sufficient simply to build the individual's competence: the key is to leverage learning and innovation across different parts of the organization. Having worked with this at Digital, I know that it is very difficult to do. All the 'not-invented-here' disclaimers get in the way. Yet if we focus only on building competence and not on enabling its broad application and transfer, we will minimize the return on our investment. Clearly this has implications for our reward structures, for our career development processes, and for our communication, training, and performance-management processes.

A final implication I want to highlight is that there are no rigid boundaries and that we must be able to work across different kinds of cultures, be they geographic, cultural, corporate or organizational. It is clear that to achieve many of our goals, we will be using multiple sources inside and outside the corporation, through partnerships, alliances, and outsourcing from outside vendors and consultants. So competence in working across all kinds of cultures, dealing with ambiguity and diversity, and brokering and managing brokered services will be critical. We can use some of the practices that we have developed in valuing diversity work in a much broader way. It is most important to build and reward our skills in collaboration, partnering, and working in teams.

So this is the best of times and the worst of times in HRM. We have unprecedented visibility and opportunity; our work is finally being viewed as mission critical. But if we are to be more than marginal players, we must make major changes in both the focus and the methodologies we use to achieve our results. The challenge, I think, is for us to be clear on the new mission, to free up resources for the strategic agenda, build the competencies and commitment for the new work—and get moving.

I conclude with one last word from Dilbert on corporate life in the future. Dilbert is asked, 'So, what have you accomplished this year?' 'Well,' he says, 'I used my empowerment to create a new paradigm, and I teamed across functional boundaries to improve quality. I dare say I was customer-focused and market-driven. I proactively found excellence in the midst of chaos. I re-engineered my core processes and embraced change.' 'I give you Dilbert the perfect employee!' he exclaims. 'Was that sarcasm?' his manager asks. 'To be honest, I don't know either,' is the reply.

Louise Piché

I am here not to present research results or to represent a model of organizational transformation but as a typical HR executive. I have been in the same corporation, Canadian National (CN), for over nineteen years, all in HR except for a seven-month assignment in Operations. I will talk to you about my company's experiences with change and the effects on the human resource management function. But, before doing this, I first want to say that I was relieved when I saw Figure 5, Dualities in the Human Resource Role, in Lawler's presentation. Until then I was thinking, 'My God, I am really in trouble here! I should be moving a lot faster.' In acknowledging the dualities in the HRM role, Lawler identified the position in which I and, I suspect, many HR people find themselves.

Let me tell you about my company, CN, about the pace of change at CN, and about how we live with that change. CN was created in 1923; the first big change did not come, however, until the 1950s with the diesel engine. It took ten years to convert from steam to diesel and twenty years in all to get used to the diesel. In fact, our collective agreements still make some reference to earlier jobs, e.g. firemen, from the steam engine days. The next major change didn't occur until about 1970 when mainframe computers were introduced, followed in 1980 by the introduction of personal computers. These are examples of how quickly we move in the railways!

Through these years we were focussed on being a good railway; we were structured, organized, and dedicated to running a very efficient railway. Then, in 1987 everything changed—the market was deregulated and CN became customer-focussed. (And this is when, by the way, we became acutely aware of the duality of the HR role as outlined in Lawler's Figure 5.) Our next big shock came in 1992 with the arrival of a new CEO, an outsider who admitted knowing almost nothing about railways. This was particularly significant for our company in view of the fact that the previous CEO had been with CN for fifty-one years, had done all the jobs, and knew the corporation and its employees 'inside-out.' And finally, like many other corporations, there has been a significant change in the size of CN's work force, from 150,000 employees to about 22,000 by the end of 1995. This is noteworthy considering that CN now produces more than it has ever produced.

These changes are, as you know, some of the classic changes recognized in the literature as having the greatest influence on HR policies, i.e. changes in the marketplace and in management and culture. These events at CN—marketplace changes in 1987 and management and culture changes in 1992—have impacted on how we define ourselves and on what we think we should be doing as a company. We, including the HR people, now talk about business strategies and make strategic plans. These are positive results for HRM—we now play a more proactive, partnership role. However, the drive towards efficiency, productivity, and lower costs, which is part of our environment today, has created a sense of crisis in many organizations. For example, CN spent the first half of 1994 discussing a potential merger, then dealt with a purchase offer from Canadian Pacific for half of the corporation. And at the same time, the work force was being downsized by 10,000 people. This crisis environment creates barriers for the 'new' HRM. Under these conditions, there is pressure to continue the traditional, more reactive, HR functions, but more efficiently, of course. What we are experiencing then is exactly what Ed Lawler illustrated—a duality, and, in fact, a paradox in our role. On the one hand, we are expected to be a business partner, filling a leadership and proactive role, while on the other we are expected to be reactive, providing administrative and advocacy functions in times of downsizing and cost cutting.

In his paper, Lawler also discussed another HR development that is affecting many of us today—where line management fits into HRM. Although I wholeheartedly believe that it is the responsibility of line management to manage human resources, I do think that the necessary technical expertise has been underestimated. I have found over the years that we always believe we are good people managers: everybody knows how to manage people. We do not always know how to read a financial statement and will admit that. We do not always know how to develop a market plan and will admit that. But we are less willing to admit that managing people requires professional skills. HR people supply these skills; they must be the leaders. At CN we are now filling this role; we do performance management, we are involved in training, we lead.

If we define strategic human resource management as HRM that is a partner in the design and the implementation of business strategies, then, I would suggest, that cutting-edge HR will be found only in cutting-edge organizations. When HR people understand business better and are a part of that business, moving in tandem with the transformation of the organization, being a part of it, although at times difficult and uncomfortable, is an exciting position in which to be.

4 The Transformation of Work in the United States: What the Evidence Shows

Paul Osterman

The organization of work in America is up for grabs to an extent unknown since the Great Depression and the New Deal. An easy way to see this is to consider the range of anecdotes to which we are regularly exposed. At one extreme are stories about firms such as the Saturn Corporation or LTV Steel which have implemented far-reaching team-based power-sharing work systems. Yet we also learn that among the fast-growing companies in the nation—and by some measures the largest single employer, even surpassing General Motors, the parent of Saturn—is Manpower, Inc., the supplier of temporary workers.

This duality is often reflected within the same firms—companies such as Corning, Boeing, or Kodak—which on the one hand restructure and lay off large numbers of employees, while on the other hand seeking to implement work systems based on high levels of employee commitment. It is difficult to make sense of these seemingly opposite tendencies and to understand their implications for the management of human resources and for public policy.

In the next two sections I will describe in more detail the characteristics of restructuring (or the deconstruction of traditional forms of work organization), as well as initiatives by firms trying to implement new high-commitment systems. The second part of the paper will provide empirical data on these trends and will enable us to assess their relative power and likely direction. The final section will draw some lessons for human resource management and for public policy.

Restructuring

A wave of restructuring has swept over corporate America, brought on by three interrelated forces. First, increased competition, often international, has led firms to cut costs wherever possible. Second, the rise of activist stockholders has put companies under pressure to maximize returns, often short-run returns (Useem 1994). Third, new ideas about how best to organize business, ideas embodied in phrases like 'get close to the customer' or 'core competencies,' have pushed many functions within firms in the direction of decentralization and reduction.

The restructuring is having a pervasive impact in corporations. Senior management finds itself confronting newly aggressive boards of directors. Traditional organizational demarcations, for example, between design, engineering, and manufacturing, are breaking down. And, for employees and for human resource managers, traditional assumptions about the organization of work and careers are changing.

A useful way to think about these changes is to note that, taken together, they are undermining what might be termed the 'internal' system of work which, until recently, characterized virtually all large and many smaller American firms. The central principles of the 'internal' system were that employees would spend the better part of their careers working in one firm, that while blue-collar workers faced higher layoff risks than managers, these layoffs were typically followed by recall, and that promotions would be drawn from internal candidates.

The end of this system is well characterized by the head of the Power PC chip production at IBM, who said in the *New York Times*, 1 September 1994, 'I'm here for the duration, five years or so,' and by another executive who commented, 'The old cradle-to-grave psychological contract, "if I work hard the company will take care of me," is absolutely gone' (Reilly, Brett, and Stroh 1993, 169).

As these quotations imply, one element—and probably the crucial one—in the decline of the internal system is that the assumption of employment continuity is no longer valid. In the past recession 90 percent of layoffs were permanent, compared to an average of 40 percent in previous recessions. There is a long list of firms that permanently fired large numbers of employees despite the fact that they had traditionally had a long history of avoiding layoffs: IBM, DEC, Kodak, Proctor and Gamble, and many others.

Another element in the demise of the internal system is the growing willingness of employers to use workers who are not 'full' members of the organization. These so-called 'contingent' employees include persons on the payroll of temporary help agencies as well as members of internal temporary pools. Although to a certain extent the use of temporary employees is a new form of try-out or probationary employment (a fraction of the temps are eventually offered regular employment), more fundamentally it represents a new willingness by companies to sacrifice commitment and training for flexibility.

The deconstruction of the internal system raises important questions not only for practice but also for academic theory. Over many years, scholars from a variety of disciplines developed an elaborate rationale explaining why firms adopt the internal system. Their explanations included the firm's goal of obtaining a committed and socialized labour force, assuring predictable supplies of trained labour, and minimizing opportunities for employees to engage in opportunistic behaviour. However, with hindsight it is apparent that these researchers overlooked or minimized what many firms evidently view as a series of disadvantages inherent in the internal system. These include a high ratio of fixed to variable costs, a tendency to overstaff, the difficulty of obtaining 'new blood,' and the possibility that it may be cheaper to buy skills on the market than obtain them internally.

Clearly, if the central tendency is the substitution of market-mediated employment arrangements for the 'internal' system, this points to a very substantial change (for the worse) in the employment security of workers. It also requires researchers to change the way they think about work organization.

High-Performance Systems

While many firms are restructuring and introducing higher levels of employment insecurity, other firms, and sometimes even different parts of the same firm, are moving in what appears to be the opposite direction. They are implementing a version of so-called high-performance work systems.

Until a decade or so ago, the industrial relations system and work organization of the United States followed a traditional model: the workplace was organized around tight divisions of labour and narrowly designed, specialized jobs. Decision making was in the hands of supervisors who decided how the jobs were to be performed, how work was scheduled, and how workers were judged. Employee participation was limited, and clear, detailed rules, specified either in a personnel policy or in a collective bargaining contract, determined the criteria governing career progression from one job to another and the compensation associated with each individual job. Grievance procedures were the predominant voice mechanism for employees who believed their job rights had been violated by actions of the supervisor or by some other management decision. Finally, in the traditional model, employers were free to adjust employment levels as they wished, and hence, hire-fire was the rule.

This system is under attack because it is increasingly perceived as less productive than the alternatives. The central problem lies in the internal rigidities associated with the traditional model. Consider, for example, the situation at General Motors under the traditional system. Among the job titles were 'install front seats,' 'install rear seats,' 'install garnish moldings,' and 'install door-trim panels': a 'front-seat installer' would not install rear seats (Katz 1985). It is important to see that this system was not irrational. In a world in which employers hire and fire at will, rigid job classifications will emerge to provide at least some level of protection to the labour force. Hence the system made some sense given the constraints under which it was created.

Although not irrational in its own terms, the traditional system has increasingly been seen as failing to meet the needs of firms and employees. The sources of failure are several. The efforts by firms to improve quality and to better meet customer needs both have required a reorganization of production which puts more power in the hands of employees further down the organizational hierarchy. This tendency has been given further impetus by efforts to cut costs, which also lead to the elimination of bureaucratic layers and to greater responsibility at lower levels. In order to 'empower' these employees, it is necessary to ensure that their job definitions are flexible, that they have greater levels of discretion, that they often find themselves working in teams, and that they have higher levels of skill and training. All of these changes imply a transformation in the way work is organized.

In more specific terms, what do these reforms consist of? It is important to recognize that no single model is being adopted everywhere (see Appelbaum and Batt 1994 for a useful classification of alternative systems). In some settings, such as the General Motors Saturn plant, joint employee-manager activities extend from work teams on the shop floor to joint 'management' committees at every level of the plant and in every area, from product design to supplier relations. This, however, is only one model, and an unusual one at that. In other firms, where change is being driven by the quality movement, the transformation consists of a combination of work teams and off-line problem-solving groups.

A useful way of visualizing the new systems is to break them down into their component parts and examine the options for each component. As we work our way through these elements it should become clear that the central principle is increased employee power and responsibility. However, the extent to which this occurs is not uniform across all employers who introduce elements of the new systems.

The Organization of Work

At the core of the new systems are changes in how employees do their jobs. Perhaps the most typical innovation is the introduction of work teams. In many instances these teams are led by a management employee, but that person's role has changed to one of 'coach' or 'facilitator.' In other instances the teams are self-directed. In either case, the central idea is that the employees take responsibility for a group of tasks, that there is a sense of responsibility for the team's product, that the workers are broadly skilled, and that there is an element of job rotation.

In many cases the teams themselves can decide how best to do their jobs, but this is not always true. For example, at the General Motors-Toyota joint venture, NUMMI, each task is rigidly prescribed. However, employees do have considerable power to make suggestions for altering the prescriptions. This brings us to the second point.

Involvement in Off-Line Activities

In many 'transformed' firms, employees are involved in other tasks besides direct work activities. The most common examples are problem-solving groups which often consist of a cross-section of employees and hence, to some extent obviate traditional managerial-nonmanagerial distinctions. These groups address problems such as production techniques, quality issues, and health and safety. In their most extreme form, these groups can take up topics which in the past have been seen as clearly 'managerial,' for example, outsourcing and supplier policy.

The Link To Broader Objectives

Organizations frequently implement the innovations described above as part of broader efforts to transform themselves. These efforts include a flattening of the organizational hierarchies and a renewed emphasis on quality and customer satisfaction. Both objectives are consistent with empowering workers.

The Link to Other Human Resources Policies

Organizations that implement these changes in work organization typically also transform other aspects of their human resources systems. The two most frequent changes are the increased use of performance-based compensation and increased levels of training. The importance of increased training is straightforward: to the extent that employees have more responsibilities and to the extent that they exercise greater discretion, they need to be prepared.

Performance-based compensation shifts risk from the employer to the workers, and in this sense, can be interpreted as a degradation of employment conditions. On the other hand, it also gives workers and teams which have new powers the opportunity to reap rewards from their efforts.

There is greater variation in other human resources policies. Some employers have linked work reorganization with higher levels of employment security: examples include Saturn, NUMMI, and Xerox. However, these appear to be in the minority. Firms also vary in their approach to unions. In some settings the new work systems are implemented in cooperation with unions, but in others, the new systems are either part of a policy to avoid unionization or they are implemented unilaterally without the cooperation of the existing union. Again, a difficult question is whether in the long run the more conflictual strategies are viable.

I have now described the two broad strategies, seemingly quite distinct, which are currently being implemented in American enterprises. I will now turn to the empirical evidence of the extent of each strategy.

Empirical Evidence

Restructuring and Downsizing

The extent of restructuring and downsizing among large firms is apparent in Table 1, which is based on a survey of 406 large employers conducted by the Harris organization for the Conference Board.

It is apparent that the restructuring trend is quite widespread and that firms have used several strategies. Furthermore, as Table 2 shows, the trend is likely to continue, in part because, as demonstrated in Table 3, senior management is relatively satisfied with the results of this downsizing.

One of the trends most often associated with deconstructing the employment relationship is the use of temporary or contingent employees. In some cases these are workers on the payroll of a firm supplying temporary help, but in other instances employers establish their own in-house temporary-worker pools. In both instances employers use these workers as a source of flexible labour but do not provide them with the same (or any) degree of security and benefits offered to regular workers.

Anecdotal evidence suggests that the use of these employees is growing, and the popular press often contains estimates of very high rates of use of so-called 'contingent' labour. The problem with many of these estimates is that they include part-time workers, a group which is distinct from temporary workers and a group whose status, demarcated by hours, does not necessarily imply anything about the firm's strategy for work organization.

Estimates of the number of workers employed by agencies supply-

Table 1
Extent of Restructuring within the Past Five Years (percentage of employers)

Shut down some operations	64.3
Sold any business units	51.0
Imposed hiring freeze	57.1
Substantial layoffs	47.3
Combined operating units	62.3
Offered early retirement incentives	40.4
Significantly reduced managerial staff	38.4

Source: Harris/Conference Board Survey (1991).

Table 2
Manager's Expectations for Job Elimination in the Next Few Years (percentage)

A lot of jobs	4.7
Some jobs	62.6
No jobs	28.3
Not sure	4.4

Source: Harris/Conference Board Survey (1991).

Table 3
Management's Satisfaction with Results of Downsizing (percentage)

Very satisfied	49.6
Somewhat satisfied	41.3
Minimal satisfaction	4.0
Not satisfied	0.9
Not sure	4.3

Source: Harris/Conference Board Survey (1991).

ing temporary help suggest that the use of contingent labour is much lower than the estimates in the press suggest. Seavey and Kazis (1994, 12) quote industry reports that only 1.6 percent of the U.S. labour force works for such firms. The National Survey of Establishments found that 5.2 percent of employees in establishments in the survey were on the payroll of firms supplying temporary help. The survey also asked about in-house pools of temporary workers and found that an additional 5.2 percent of workers were part of these. These numbers, while not trivial, are nonetheless well below the estimates in the popular press. The survey also asked whether establishments expected increased use of these employees over the next five years and 8 percent of establishments gave a positive response with respect to temporary employees from in-house pools, while 15.5 percent of establishments gave a positive response with respect to employees from temporary-help firms.

Recent research using both the Current Population Survey and the Panel Survey on Income Dynamics shows that expected probability of remaining with the same employer has fallen, but again, the drop is not as dramatic as might be expected given the public rhetoric (Rose 1995; Diebold, Neumark, and Polsky 1994).

In short, it is apparent that restructuring is quite widespread, particularly in the form of layoffs. This restructuring has also led to changes in the employment relationship of those who remain; however, it appears that, here too, the popular press has somewhat exaggerated the extent of change. We know, for example, that the amount of training offered by firms has increased in recent years (Knoke and Kalleberg 1994; Osterman 1995), and this is not consistent with extensive destruction of internal labour markets. However, the nature of those internal labour markets has changed in other ways, and it is to this that we now turn.

The Implementation of High-Performance Work Organization

How much work reorganization is occurring in America and what are the characteristics of the employers who are undertaking these activities? Until recently there has been relatively little information available to answer these questions, but now several surveys have probed these issues. I begin with the National Survey of Establishments (see Osterman 1994), which asked about a series of practices (all with respect to the 'core' job family, the largest group of non-supervisory workers directly involved in the production of the good or service; these could be either blue- or white-collar workers). In analyzing that survey I will focus on the four practices most often seen as central to transformed organizations: self-directed work teams, job rotation, employee problem-solving groups (or quality circles), and total quality management (TQM).

Respondents were asked whether any of the four practices were employed in their establishments, and if so, what percentage of core employees were involved (the percentage involved is termed the penetration rate). The precise definitions given for each practice are shown in Appendix A.[1]

Table 4 shows the distribution of each practice for two levels of penetration: if the practice is used at all and if at least 50 percent of core employees are involved.

It is clear that if we simply asked whether or not a given practice is used among any fraction of core employees, then we would conclude that the elements of flexible work are quite widespread. For example, over half of the establishments use teams and 33.5 percent of the establishments employ TQM.

The story is different, however, when we examine penetration. If we look at the intermediate category of fifty percent or more employees involved, the rates fall sharply: by roughly fifteen percentage points for each practice. Even so, the distribution of self-directed work teams is surprisingly widespread, so there is clearly some discontinuity between the prevalence of this practice and the others.

The manufacturing/blue-collar patterns are similar in that there is a substantial diffusion of the practices at any usage level, and there is a drop-off at the fifty percent threshold of participation. Self-directed teams appear less widespread in manufacturing than elsewhere in the economy,[2] but the other practices are more common in manufacturing.

These data lead to the natural question of whether the practices form groups from which identifiable patterns emerge and whether the patterns might be thought of as the new systems discussed in the literature. Table 5 shows how the practices cluster together when a fifty percent penetration threshold is set (no conclusions are changed when other thresholds are imposed). It appears that there is no predominant cluster of practices, since there is some representation for each of the possible combinations, and in most of the cases, the distribution of clusters seems rather even.

Another source of information on the distribution of new work systems is the Harris Survey, which was limited to Conference Board members and hence to the largest firms. This survey asked how much effort and resources the respondents' firms had put into four practices: work

1 The survey did not directly observe the actual work practices. There may be a tendency of respondents to exaggerate, in the direction of socially acceptable responses, their actual practices. However considerable care was taken to work with the most knowledgeable available respondent. Furthermore, as the statistical results below demonstrate, the responses are not simply noise; they are correlated in sensible ways with explanatory variables. Nonetheless, as is true in all surveys of this kind, the point estimates of the practices should be treated with caution.

2 Jan Klein (1991) suggests that this may be because self-managed work teams place strains on the inventory management system in manufacturing.

Table 4
Distribution of High-Performance Work Practices

	All establishments	Manufacturing
Percentage at any level of penetration		
Teams	54.5	50.1
Rotation	43.4	55.6
TQM	33.5	44.9
QC	40.8	45.6
Nothing	21.8	16.0
Percentage with at least fifty percent of employees involved		
Teams	40.5	32.3
Rotation	26.6	37.4
TQM	24.5	32.1
QC	27.4	29.7
Nothing	36.0	33.2

Source: National Survey of Establishments.

Table 5
Clustering of Work Practices
(percentage with at least fifty percent of employees involved)

	Entire sample	Manufacturing/blue collar
Nothing	36.0	33.2
All	4.8	5.0
Teams only	14.4	5.5
Rotation only	7.0	11.7
QC only	3.1	2.4
TQM only	2.6	4.5
Team/Rotation	4.8	4.6
Team/QC	4.3	3.3
Team/TQM	4.6	4.2
Rotation/QC	3.0	3.3
Rotation/TQM	1.5	4.5
TQM/QC	4.4	4.9
Team/TQM/QC	3.6	4.2
Team/Rotation/TQM	1.2	1.6
Team/Rotation/QC	2.3	3.4
Rotation/TQM/QC	1.4	2.9

Source: National Survey of Establishments.

redesign, employee involvement, total quality management, and the introduction of advanced technologies. The results are shown in Table 6.

Consistent with the National Survey of Establishments, it is apparent that an important fraction of firms have devoted their resources to various forms of work reorganization (however, a caution is that the survey does not define the term 'significant,' and there is no effort to measure the fraction of employees involved). Two other notable findings are that, in their efforts to become more competitive, firms value technology over work reform and that about thirty-seven percent of firms have made significant investments in two or more work practices. This is consistent with the pattern in the National Survey of Establishments.

Table 6
Harris Survey

Amount of Effort/Resources

	Work redesign	Employee involvement	Total quality management	Advanced computer tech
Significant	44.0%	38.6%	37.4%	72.9%
Some	46.5	43.6	33.2	24.8
Not Much	9.1	16.7	26.6	1.9
Not Sure	.2	.9	2.7	.2

Which Received the Most Effort/Resources

Work redesign	Employee involvement	Total quality management	Advanced computer tech	Not sure
10.2%	6.1	14.8	65.4	3.3

Number of Work Practices Which Received Significant Effort/Resources (work redesign, employee involvement, TQM)

0	1	2	3
36.0%	25.6	18.4	19.2

Source: Harris Survey.

Sustainability of Workplace Innovations

So far we have stressed the forces that are leading some American companies to move toward mutual-gains workplace practices. But what is to keep these innovations from becoming just another element in the long list of fads that have come and gone in American industry? This is a real concern since the few historical or longitudinal studies available to date show that there is a relatively high attrition rate for workplace innovations. For example, consider the evidence from employee representation plans established after World War I by companies attempting, in part, to ward off union organizing. These plans spread quite rapidly between 1916 and the mid-1920s, during the height of the 'red scare' (the fear that the Bolshevik revolution in Russia might spread to the U.S. via trade union organizing efforts). At their peak, these programs covered just under ten percent of the work force, mainly in the largest manufacturing, communications, and financial service firms in the country. But over the course of the 1920s, their growth gradually tapered off as manufacturing employment declined, the recession of 1921-1923 took its toll on plans in smaller firms, and the threat of union organizing declined. The Great Depression dealt another blow to these efforts, and then these 'company unions' were outlawed in 1935 by the *National Labor Relations Act*, in 1935 which served as the final nail in the coffin of the employee-representation or 'American Plan' movement. Perhaps more than any other historical example, the employee representation movement of 1916-1932 serves as an historical parallel to the current wave of workplace innovations.

In 1980, Paul Goodman looked back at more recent major cases of workplace innovation sponsored in the 1970s by the National Commission on Productivity and Quality of Work and found none of them had survived (Goodman 1980). Other studies report a high attrition rate for quality circles started in the early 1980s (Lawler and Mohrman 1987; Drago 1988). A recent longitudinal study in Canada confirms this as well: Gordon Betcherman and Anil Verma found that one-third of the employee-participation programs and pay-for-skill programs reported to be in place in establishments surveyed in 1986 were no longer present in 1992 (Betcherman and Verma 1993). Thus, there is no guarantee that, once started, these initiatives will be sustained. The question therefore becomes, what influences their staying power? I will discuss the role of two key sets of forces that are critical for sustaining innovations and that can be controlled by decision makers within individual enterprises: reinforcing personnel practices and employee and/or union participation in the innovation process.

The argument is that in order for a company to sustain workplace innovations it must embed them in supporting human resources practices. That is, the entire human resource system must be congruent with and support innovations in work practices. Without this support the work practices cannot survive. Three clusters of personnel practices seem to be of special importance: employment security, training, and compensation.

A word of caution is in order: because I lack longitudinal data, I cannot follow the course of workplace innovations and determine in which settings they are sustained and in which they are abandoned. But I can ask whether the human resources practices which theory suggests are important for reinforcing workplace innovations, namely, commitment to employment security, investment in training and development, and some form of contingent compensation system, are present in those firms that have sustained workplace innovations for an extended period of time. This is a second-best strategy, but it provides suggestive evidence of the factors that influence sustainability.

As we have already seen, the National Survey of Establishments shows that a substantial proportion of American firms have two or more innovative work practices in place at the fifty percent penetration rate or better. The idea of sustainability, however, implies that these practices have been in place for some time. Specifically, we define an establishment as having sustained innovation if the practice has been in place for five or more years. Table 7 shows the percentage of establishments having zero through five practices (at the fifty percent level of penetration) which have been in place for five or more years.

It is apparent that the percentage of establishments that meet the sustainability criterion falls well below the percentage of those that have the practice in place. Sixty-three percent of the sample have no innovative practices which meet this criterion, twenty-four percent have one, and only ten percent have two practices that cover at least fifty percent of their core workers and that have been in place for at least five years. This divergence does not necessarily imply that most innovations fail to last: some of the difference is simply due to the fact that the spread of these policies is fairly new and some have not had the chance to meet the five-year test. Nonetheless, it is striking that the distribution of long-lasting innovations is so limited.

For each of the human resource practices, I tested for a statistically significant relationship between the presence of that practice in an organization and the presence of sustained innovations (defined as having two or more practices at the fifty percent level of penetration for five or more years). These tests controlled for other important factors.[3] The percentage of the establishments that have each of the human resources practices in place is shown in Table 8 and the practices with asterisks next to them were statistically significant predictors of sustainability.

3 An establishment was defined as having sustained the mutual-gains system if two of the four work innovations had been in place with fifty percent of the core work force involved for five years or more. To test the relationship between a particular human resource practice and whether the mutual-gains system was sustained, a regression was estimated in which the dependent variable was the human resource practice in question and the independent variables included a dummy variable which took on the value of one if the establishment had sustained the mutual-gains system and zero otherwise, as well as controls for industry and occupation.

Table 7
Distribution of Sustained Practices

Number of practices	Percentage of establishments
0	63.0
1	23.8
2	9.9
3	2.1
4	1.0
5	0.0

Source: National Survey of Establishments.
Note: A practice is 'sustained' if it involves at least 50 percent of core employees and has been in place for five years or more.

Table 8
Supporting HR Practices and their Role in Sustainability

Percent of establishments that	
Have pay for skill	30.4**
Have gainsharing	13.7**
Have profit sharing/bonus	44.7**
Pay a wage premium	36.5
Assign an important role to the HR department in strategic decisions	54.1**
Have an explicit or implicit employment security policy	39.8
Percent of core employees who receive formal off-the-job training	32.0
Percent of core employees who receive cross-training	43.5**

**Statistically significant at the .01 level.

Employment Security

As already noted, employment security poses a dilemma for both workers and employers. While it is a well-accepted fact that workers are reluctant to help improve competitiveness if they think they will work themselves out of a job, as a result few if any individual firms are able to make a credible, iron-clad guarantee of life-time job security, especially in markets that change rapidly or in industries where demand is no longer growing as rapidly as in earlier phases of their life cycle. Moreover, improving productivity will reduce the number of workers required unless the productivity gains increase demand for the firm's products or are recycled into new job-producing investments within the firm.

What role then does employment security play in innovation? Several examples may help illustrate the complexities involved here and reinforce the conclusion that employment security may be more important in sustaining support for innovations already begun than it is in the initial stages of their adoption and implementation.

Consider the now familiar case of Xerox and its decision whether or not to contract out the assembly of wiring harnesses for its copiers. About a year after starting its employee-involvement process, Xerox announced a significant downsizing and employee severance program that reduced its blue-collar work force by nearly 15 percent. As part of its efforts to reduce manufacturing costs, it also began looking for opportunities to purchase work more cheaply from outside vendors, and its engineers and finance staff targeted the assembly of wiring harnesses for outsourcing. Management estimated that it could save more than three million dollars by contracting out this work and thereby reducing its work force by approximately 300 people. But employees and the local union were already upset by the general work force reductions, and this decision was even more upsetting because there was an active employee-involvement program underway in the wiring harness area. The employees and the local union made it clear to management that if they went ahead and outsourced this work the employee-involvement effort was doomed. As a result the company and union leaders agreed to let a cross-functional task force of workers, supervisors, engineers, and accountants study this operation to see if enough changes could be made to reduce the costs of doing this work in-house and make it competitive with outside vendors. The task force produced recommendations for reorganizing work, supervision, accounting systems, plant layout, work scheduling, and staffing that exceeded the $3 million target. Subsequently, the company and union agreed to follow a similar procedure in all future contracting-out situations and, in return, negotiated a no-layoff pledge for the next three years.

Management, on the other hand, would never have agreed to a no-layoff pledge without some expectation that they had already reduced their overall numbers to an appropriate level, given projections of future product demand, and that they had the flexibility either to contract out high-cost operations or to improve the productivity of those operations with the help of the employees and the union.

The Xerox case illustrates that employment security, productivity, and workplace innovations are highly interdependent. But given the complex bargains, trade-offs, dynamics, and lagged effects involved, it is not surprising that cross-sectional surveys will not necessarily reveal a positive correlation between employment security and workplace innovation. Indeed, this is exactly what the establishment survey did not show. Although, again, over half of the firms indicated that they followed policies to minimize or avoid layoffs, those reporting these efforts had no higher rates of innovation or more sustained innovation over the five years examined than did firms that did not indicate a commitment to avoid or minimize layoffs. This suggests that if employment security is critical to workplace innovation, either it must come from someplace other than the policies of individual firms, or individual firms will need to manage their resources in a significantly different way.

Training

Training and development is also believed to be important to sustaining workplace innovations. New work systems entail higher levels of employee skill, and hence, in order to sustain new systems, the employer must be willing to invest in the skills of the labour force. High levels of investment in training do not come naturally to American employers, in part for the reasons just noted—the firm's investments in training are lost when employees leave the organization, either voluntarily or involuntarily. In the Survey of Establishments, one of our two training variables was indeed significantly related to sustainability (Table 8).

Compensation and Reward Systems

As is often noted, compensation and reward systems can either reinforce or deter support for workplace innovations. These practices are relevant both to the rank-and-file employees at the workplace and to the supervisors and middle managers who support innovation. Case study evidence suggests that many firms that have moved toward more flexible work organization have also introduced comparable changes in compensation practices. This is on the theory that when employees are given more power to determine outcomes, they should also have a financial stake in the success of the enterprise. Indeed, Levine and Tyson's review of the evidence on employee participation leads them to conclude that employee participation and contingent compensation, taken together, produce stronger positive payoffs than each can achieve individually (Levine and Tyson 1990). This survey asked about three different contingent pay practices in the Survey of Establishments: pay for skills, group incentives or gainsharing plans, and profit-sharing or bonus plans. All pay practices proved to be significantly related to sustained innovation.

Unions and Employee Voice

One of the more controversial issues in U.S. circles is the question of the effect of unions on organizational innovation. Thus, it may come as a surprise to some observers that, congruent with other surveys completed in recent years, the National Survey of Establishments did not find a significant negative or positive relationship between unionization and the initial adoption of workplace innovations. However, case study evidence does provide many examples of situations where, if it had not been for the support and insistence of union leaders, the initial management commitment to innovation would have given way in the face of financial or other obstacles. Similarly, we have observed cases where innovations have been held hostage to broader labour-management conflicts or have slowed down because of internal union political conflicts or leadership challenges. Thus, while there is no universal 'union effect' on innovation, the quality of the union-management relationship is crucial.

The Role of Human Resources within the Firm

As Table 8 shows, when human resources is an important player in strategic decisions, workplace innovations are more likely to be sustained. Table 9 demonstrates that establishments in which the human resources function is more important are more likely to have in place two or more innovative practices at or above the fifty percent level of penetration. In other research using the National Survey of Establishments, I also find that the level of training is higher in establishments where the human resources function is powerful (Osterman 1995).

Table 9
Importance of HR Considerations for Innovative Work Practices (percentage of establishments)

	Innovative practices at fifty percent level of penetration	
	Less than two	Two or more
Not important	6.6	5.3
	11.9	4.1
	29.2	32.0
	42.9	34.1
Extremely important	9.1	24.0

Source: Calculations by the author using data from the National Survey of Establishments.

The Harris Survey asked a number of additional questions about the role of the human resources function in firms. It is apparent from Table 10 that in recent years, human resources has been regarded as more important by senior executives. Indeed, Table 11 suggests that middle management is a greater obstacle than senior management to establishing an important place for human resources in a firm's strategy.

Table 10
Management Time and Energy Devoted to HR Issues over the Past Five Years (percentage of establishments)

Increased significantly	51.2
Increased somewhat	35.4
Stayed the same	10.8
Decreased	.9
Not sure	1.4

Source: Harris Survey/Conference Board (1991) and National Survey of Establishments.

Table 11
Importance of Obstacles to Changes in Human Resource Policies (percentage of establishments)

	Major barrier	Minor barrier	Not a barrier
Getting top management attention	14.2	33.0	51.9
Lack of support from middle management	15.7	52.7	30.3
Opposition from employees or union	10.3	37.1	50.4
Focus on short-term goals	28.0	40.3	30.3
Cost of change	32.2	49.7	16.7
Need to address immediate crises	29.0	43.8	26.1
Corporate culture lacks HR focus	19.4	36.2	43.1

Source: Harris Survey/Conference Board (1991).

Conclusion

This paper began by describing the apparent paradox of companies whose restructuring undermines their commitment to their employees at a time when they are introducing new systems of work organization seemingly requiring higher levels of commitment. The two obvious questions are, which trend is the stronger, and are the two strategies compatible or incompatible over the long run?

With respect to the second question, the reality is that we do not have strong evidence. As a matter of logic one might expect that employees will eventually withhold commitment if faced with an employer who is bent on restructuring. However, to date, many firms have managed to follow both paths with substantial gains in productivity. It is possible that the level of fear is so high that employees are prepared to accept considerable uncertainty and still cooperate with work reform. The academic literature on the impact of layoffs on survivors is not very extensive, but what there is does not suggest that a major revolt is likely (Brockner et al. 1992; Reilly, Brett, and Stroh 1993). Nonetheless, this remains a major open question and the traditional view that commitment is not attainable in an environment of extensive insecurity may yet turn out to be true.

With respect to the relative power of the trends themselves, one approach is to understand the barriers which limit the diffusion of high-performance work systems. A 'consensus list' might include:

- Small and midsize firms may lack the resources, knowledge, and managerial time to implement substantial changes. In addition, smaller enterprises operate on the margin and cannot afford to take the risks associated with broad transformations in how they do business.
- Financial markets limit the willingness of many enterprises to invest substantially in human resource development. This is because these investments are harder to measure than more tangible items such as plant, equipment, and research and development. Hence, they are undervalued by financial analysts even though, as we have seen, their payoff may be substantial.
- A related point is that the governance structure of American firms gives complete weight to the interests of stockholders (the financial markets) and none to the interests of other stakeholders (e.g., employees). This is in contrast to the governance systems in other nations, such as Germany and Japan, which provide mechanisms for valuing employee and other stakeholder interests. Stakeholders such as employees may favour work reform and provide a constituency for it which could help offset contrary pressures from the stock market.
- Even companies whose leadership wishes to undertake substantial work reform may face internal obstacles. These may include middle- and lower-level managers, who may be threatened by employee empowerment, as well as unions who are unwilling to move away from traditional adversarial relationships.

Some of these obstacles can be overcome with creative public policy. For example, the problems facing small firms can be addressed by assistance programs which provide training grants and technical assistance. Examples of effective programs along these lines are the Prairie State 2000 program in Illinois or some of the small manufacturing assistance centres (so-called NIST Centers) supported by the federal Department of Commerce. Typically these programs help assess the business plan of a small firm and provide assistance in introducing new production processes or technology and in establishing programs to meet quality standards. These efforts often involve retraining employees.

The internal political problems facing firms are not insurmountable, particularly if the perceived gains are large enough. This is a lesson which can be learned from examples such as Xerox, or even Saturn. However, broader changes in the governance structure are more problematic. The prospects for substantial labour law reform are uncertain and the chances for establishing stakeholder governance structures are even more murky.

An assessment of work reform over the past few years does suggest that considerable progress has been made. We have no true longitudinal data, but the two waves of the Government Accounting Office surveys, those for 1987 and 1990, show substantial growth in activity. In addition, the National Survey of Establishments finds that there is much more activity than was previously thought, and this conclusion is generally supported by the other surveys reviewed here.

The conclusion is that we are in a period of flux and uncertainty. Shifts in work organization are underway in many settings, but we cannot be sure about the extent of diffusion. Certainly, however, the impulse to reorganize employment is more deeply embedded and more likely to have a long-term impact than at any other time since the Second World War.

References

Applebaum, Eileen and Rose Batt. 1994. *The new American workplace: Transforming work systems in the United States*. Ithaca, NY: ILR Press.

Betcherman, Gordon and Anil Verma. 1993. Follow-up to the new technology survey. Paper presented to the Canadian Industrial Relations Research Association, June.

Brockner, Joel, Steven Grover, Thomas F. Reed, and Rocki Lee Dewitt. 1992. Layoffs, job insecurity, and survivors' work effort. *Academy of Management Journal* 35:413–25.

Diebold, Francis X., David Neumark, and Daniel Polsky. 1994. Job stability in the United States. Department of Economics, University of Pennsylvania. Mimeographed.

Drago, Robert. 1988. Quality circles: An exploratory analysis. *Industrial Relations* 27(fall):33-51.
Goodman, Paul S. 1980. Quality of work life projects in the 1980s. In *Proceedings of the 1980 spring meeting of the Industrial Relations Research Association*. Philadelphia, PA: IRRA.
Katz, Harry. 1985. *Shifting gears: Changing labor relations in the U.S. auto industry*. Cambridge, MA: MIT Press.
Klein, Jan. 1991. A reexamination of autonomy in light of new manufacturing practices. *Human Relations* 44(1):21-38.
Knoke, David and Arne Kalleberg. 1994. Job training in U.S. organizations. *American Sociological Review* 59:537-46.
Kochan, Thomas and Paul Osterman. 1994. *The mutual gains enterprise*. Cambridge, MA: Harvard Business School Press.
Lawler, Edward and Susan Mohrman. 1987. Quality circles after the honeymoon. *Organizational Dynamics* 15(spring):42-54.
Lawler, Edward, Susan Mohrman, and Gerald Ledford. *Employee involvement and total quality management: Practices and results in Fortune 1000 companies*. San Francisco: Jossey-Bass.
Levine, David and Laura D'Andrea Tyson. 1990. Participation, productivity, and the firm's performance. In *Paying for productivity*, edited by Alan Blinder. Washington, DC: The Brookings Institution.
Osterman, Paul. 1994. How common is workplace transformation and how can we explain who does it? *Industrial and Labor Relations Review* 47:173–88.
———. 1995. Skill, training, and work organization in American establishments. *Industrial Relations* 34:125–46.
Reilly, Anne H., Jeanne M. Brett, and Linda K. Stroh. 1993. The impact of corporate turbulence on managers' attitudes. *Strategic Management Journal* 14:167–79.
Rose, Stephen. 1995. *The decline of employment stability in the 1980s*. Washington, DC: National Commission on Employment Policy.
Seavey, Dorie and Richard Kazis. 1994. *Skills assessment, job placement, and training: What can be learned from the temporary help/staffing industry?* Boston, MA: Jobs For The Future.
Useem, Michael. 1994. The two faces of corporate restructuring. Department of Sociology, University of Pennsylvania, Philadelphia, PA.

Appendix A

The following are the definitions which the interviewers used in the National Survey of Establishments when the respondent requested clarification.

Self-Directed Work Teams: Employees supervise their own work; workers make their own decisions about pace and flow and occasionally about the best way to get work done.

Job Rotation. Self-explanatory example: In some banking firms you spend six months in the real estate division, six months in pension plans, and so on, simply rotating jobs.

Problem-Solving Groups/Quality Circles: Quality programs where employees are involved in problem solving.

Total Quality Management: A quality-control approach that emphasizes the importance of communications, feedback, and teamwork.

Discussion

Eileen Appelbaum

I think most of you are aware that Canadian data are much better than U.S. data, and that we in the United States do not have a regular ongoing survey of workplace practices we can rely on to observe what is actually happening in firms. Over the last ten years there have been quite a few surveys of workplace change, but they have been of large companies, members of particular organizations, or subscribers to publications like *Industry Week*, and not generally representative samples. We are very grateful to Paul Osterman for the huge job that he has done in putting together a representative sample that gives us reliable information on how these practices are diffusing. Since I do not have any specific criticisms of what he has done or of his sample, I will elaborate on the two alternatives that he has laid out, the two approaches to work restructuring that companies are taking in the United States.

At this conference, we have discussed what it takes for individual companies to succeed, but there is also a question of whether nations can succeed—whether U.S. companies will put in place the kinds of practices that are going to allow us as a country to achieve rising wages and a reasonable standard of living. As Paul Osterman has said, wages in the United States have been stagnant or falling. At the fiftieth percentile, they have been falling steadily, and now they are falling even for college graduates. So the question is whether U.S. companies can pay American wages and still be competitive in world markets. This is a question facing all industrialized economies; it is part of what has led us to the conclusion—broadly shared at this conference, I think—that we have reached the limits of mass production as a method of organizing work and as a method of organizing companies, and that changes are going to be necessary. I will not belabour the point, but it does mean we need to think about what will replace mass production.

If we give up mass production as a way of organizing work and as a method of organizing production and distribution of goods, the gains achieved by moving down the learning curve are also given up. These gains come simply from learning how to produce standardized goods more efficiently—the reductions in cost come with increases in cumulative volume and are achieved fairly easily in a mass production system. Organizations today have to replace moving down the learning curve with new kinds of learning; this is one of the very important issues they face. How will they do this? Where will they locate the new learning activities? There is no single answer for every industry and every company. Organizations must identify what the gains are going to be, what efficiencies can be achieved, and then think about the changes that need to be made.

My study of the apparel industry and Paul Adler's study of the auto industry have very different results in terms of what gains these industries can accomplish, where to locate team work, where to locate participation, and where to locate learning activities in order to achieve the particular cost-reduction economies available in these two very different industries. A 'one-size-fits-all' kind of organizational framework is obviously not appropriate. Rather, organizations will have to determine what particular kind of work organization will enable them to achieve the efficiency and quality gains they want.

It is important to use broad measures of performance and to avoid using only labour productivity; it is, in fact, possible for companies to reduce costs without raising output per worker. While productivity is not the problem in the apparel industry, nor are high wages, it turns out that, nevertheless, work organization is the solution. One of the gains from the new team production in apparel is the possibility of guaranteeing virtually perfect quality to Walmart and other retailers. That is not to say that no mistakes are ever made, but that the teams of workers identify and correct the mistakes themselves, so no mistake ever leaves the plant. Companies like Walmart will pay a small premium for perfect quality and for continuous replenishment if apparel manufacturers can respond quickly to new orders. In other words, Walmart can order on Monday and have delivery on Friday in the new system, and retailers are willing to pay a premium for that. The system has become more efficient, but there is no increase in labour productivity. To whom does the premium belong? How should it be shared between the workers and the manufacturer? If we limited the discussion to labour productivity, we would have to say that labour can share in the gains only if its productivity goes up. We need, therefore, to identify a broader range of performance gains and consider how these various kinds of gains might be shared.

In any event, this is the context in which organizational change is taking place: there is no alternative; companies within the industrialized countries will have to change. The fact that organizations have to change does not mean that they will change or that they will change in the right direction. Great Britain is our best example of a country whose industries, on the whole, failed to adapt to change.

The British brought us the industrial revolution, but they did not master mass production. And not every industrialized economy will master the kinds of organizational forms that will follow mass production. Because of the British example, we cannot simply say, as some economists would have us do, that if it works, it will be adopted. Although there are clear measures showing that the performance of the U.S. mass production system was superior, it did not diffuse widely in Great Britain.

In the 1980s, there was a fairly clear distinction in the U.S. between companies following a slash-and-burn policy to reduce costs and those following a high-performance policy to reduce costs. Companies were generally taking one path or the other. As a result, we did see the diffusion of high-performance work systems accelerate in the United States in the 1980s. The various surveys from that decade indicate that an increasing number of companies were adopting innovative practices. And Paul Osterman's numbers, while we would all like to see even more progress, are somewhat reassuring. In the 1990s however, and especially in the last two years, we have seen in the United States an increasing number of companies that are trying to pursue both downsizing and high-performance/high-commitment strategies at the same time. I do not think this can succeed; the types of organizational change discussed at this meeting are threatened by downsizing. Jeffrey Pfeffer was right to emphasize the extent to which downsizing is Wall Street driven. I look at this as the Wall Street fad of the 1990s. In the 1980s we were told that all those well-managed companies with a cushion of liquidity were 'cash cows' not maximizing shareholder equity and that they needed to be leveraged as much as possible. Now, many of those companies, certainly in the industries with which I am familiar, are in trouble. In retailing, which is the main recipient of the production of the apparel industry, the famous names are either gone or in bankruptcy, and a lot of the gains in apparel manufacturing which have not been shared with workers are not held by the manufacturing companies either. Instead, they are being captured by retailers and dissipated in paying off old debts. That is what Wall Street brought us in the 1980s; in the 1990s they are bringing us downsizing.

The Wall Street idea that downsizing improves productivity or efficiency has been internalized by many companies. Compensation for a company's top three to five executives has changed in the last ten years. Their pay is much more closely tied to stock options than it was just a decade ago. This has led to a split in perception between managers in the executive offices and managers in plants and offices whose job it is to focus on customers and to deliver quality products and services. Since executive pay is tied to stock-price performance, executives have an incentive to please Wall Street. Stock prices usually rise on the announcement of downsizing. Production and service managers, on the other hand, have an incentive to invest in workplace restructuring and worker training in order to meet quality, scheduling, and service goals.

Many downsizings do not actually improve productivity, and often, do not even reduce the number of workers at the work site, although they do reduce the number on the payroll. This has some implications for Paul Osterman's comments about the number of contingent workers and how this number is measured. I will give you two examples. I like Jeffrey Pfeffer's remark last night about 'managing by denominator.' This is what companies like Kodak have done. Kodak moved its internal data processing activities: they moved the workers onto the payroll of another company (EDS), and they moved the computers into the asset base of EDS. They now have the same workers sitting at the same desks doing exactly the same jobs, so there is no global improvement in efficiency. But overnight, this gave Kodak an increase in return on assets and an increase in return per employee; Wall Street rewarded this. Apparently, the Wall Street analysts could not understand that nothing real had happened.

Companies may announce downsizing just for the announcement effect—to produce a one-time increase in the stock price. The downsizing may never actually be carried out. On a MacNeil/Lehrer News Hour on downsizing, Morty Bahr of the Communication Workers of America remarked, 'If AT&T had carried out all of the downsizing that it has announced, there would be no employees left today at AT&T.' It is certainly true that AT&T has cut 20,000 positions in the last few of years, 9,000 of them union positions, but the cutbacks fall far short of the announcements.

There are a number of myths associated with downsizing. A recent study using the Census of Manufacturers showed that about half of the productivity gains in manufacturing in the United States have come from companies that upsized, so downsizing is not always correct; it is clearly not true that every company has to downsize. The study also made clear that there are many unsuccessful downsizers, a point that is also admitted by consultants. Surveys done by consulting companies show that less than a third of the companies that downsized achieved their productivity goals, less than half raised their profit, and less then half improved market share. Thus, more than half of the companies are not achieving their goals through downsizing, which suggests that firms should take a much more careful approach to downsizing as a tool for improving efficiency.

The organizational change to high-performance work systems is under great threat from downsizing. Organizations also face internal problems as they move from traditional to high-performance organizational structures. I agree with Ed Lawler that organizational transformation is difficult: it is costly, it takes time, and there is a tendency to cut corners. This is certainly true in the apparel industry. When we went into the field, we discovered that there are traditional organizations, there are the new high-performance ones everybody is writing about, and then, because the innovative practices are so expensive to implement, there are compromise innovations.

The compromises are intended to produce the gains of team work without initially investing all the money required to change to teams. Managers in plants with compromise innovations would answer all of Paul Osterman's survey questions in the affirmative. Yes, we have work teams; yes, we have job rotation. But while the plants have trained the workers on many jobs, and while they have asked them to rotate, when we went onto the shop floor, we found that not very many people are rotating. There is an obvious difference between firm policies and practices. These are companies sincerely trying to improve quality and delivery times, but they are trying it with a low-cost innovation. We found that you cannot produce performance gains in the apparel industry with this sort of hybrid work organization. Since these plants do not really have teams with autonomy and control over the work process, they put a lot of emphasis on team building. They provided workers with formal training in team building, conflict resolution, problem solving and quality improvement. In the end, we found that in this hybrid case the training did increase organizational commitment. But since the plants did not also restructure the work so that it could be done better and more efficiently, training for teamwork did not lead to performance gains.

Finally, in addition to the high costs associated with self-managed teams, the other important problem we observed is compensation. I think Jeffrey Pfeffer put his finger on it in observing that the key compensation issue is equity. Pay setting is not so much a question of incentives as of equity. It is unclear in many situations, even when there is goodwill between employees and/or unions on one side and the company on the other, how to deliver a compensation package that is fair to workers and fair to the company. How should performance gains unrelated to productivity, like those in the Walmart example, be distributed? The workers see that they are producing substantial gains for the company, but the company usually responds with a small quality bonus that workers hardly notice. In our study, the workers in the most transformed plants were dissatisfied with the fairness of their pay, and that contributed to the low levels of organizational commitment in these plants. The plants are improving performance, but you have to wonder how long this can last. Workers in the restructured plants report their jobs are more creative, more challenging, and make better use of skills, but they are also more stressful. Workers went into the new team-based production systems with the idea that the change would be good for the company and good for them. They see the payoff to the company, but their wages have not increased. That is what workers report, and in our cross-section regression analysis, we can confirm that their wages are not higher, compared to other workers in traditional work systems.

Thus, there are problems to overcome in getting to high-performance work systems, and there are tremendous pressures on companies to downsize. As a result, the optimism I felt about workplace restructuring in reviewing developments in the 1980s has turned into concern about the future of workplace reform in the 1990s.

Randall Schuler

There are many important developments in high-performance work practices and workplace innovations, which have been documented well by Jeffrey Pfeffer, Ed Lawler, and Paul Osterman. There is evidence now that not only are these innovative work practices spreading—though perhaps, as Jeffrey Pfeffer pointed out, not as rapidly as we might expect—but also that, in fact, the organizations in which they do exist seem to be more productive. They seem to have higher growth in earnings per share, for example, better health and safety records in some cases, fewer defect rates, and lower scrap rates. These fairly hard indicators suggest that some changes in workplace practices are working well. Indeed, anyone looking at all these results would conclude that this is great stuff. We all know that HRM is important, and we are now seeing the fruits.

We might conclude from this that all we have to do is select these best practices, or these high-performance workplace practices and implement them in the workplace to achieve success. But as we all know from experience and from well researched evidence, this non-contingent approach to workplace practice might be too ambitious and premature at this time.

There are cases (see the work of Peter Cappelli at the Wharton Human Research Centre) of organizations, some using high performance workplace practices, others not, being equally effective. This can be illustrated using the example of Federal Express and UPS, two package companies. UPS has thousands of industrial engineers and relatively unempowered workers who are fairly happy and pleased with the organization. Federal Express, by contrast, has a highly empowered work force involved in workplace design, does a lot of feedback surveys, and has skill-based pay. We might conclude from this that Federal Express follows the high-performance workplace practices, while UPS does not. Would we then, in fact, deny the success of UPS and encourage UPS, and other organizations like UPS, to move to the Federal Express model? Should we feel comfortable saying that there is a whole set of human resource practices that can be applied in this non-contingent way? The complexity, of course, increases when we look at UPS in more detail. In his paper, Jeffrey Pfeffer identified a number of workplace practices that he would regard as high-performance. One of these is gainsharing and stock ownership: UPS has this as well. Then how, in fact, do we understand UPS? It seems to be low in some high-performance workplace practices, but high in others. Examples like this make it more difficult to get really excited about offering non-contingent solutions to organizations.

Thus, we see these 'high-performance workplace practices' which appear to be working and spreading and which are somewhat non-contingent, but we also see organizations in the same industries that are doing things quite differently; we know that some do not always follow these 'high-performance practices'.

Today we are seeing both contingent and non-contingent human resource practices. When we need to think about a contingent strategy, we have to think about the reasons why we are going to select certain types of practices. Lee Dyer has a model which asks what are the strategies of the business? what are the productivity levels that are needed? what are the other constraints on the business that have human resource implications? and then, what are the human resource practices that are needed? We have a very contingent framework based on the needs of the business, and we have a non-contingent framework called 'high-performance workplace practices.' This is one important contrast in HRM today.

The other important development that I can see in the presentations at this conference is a tendency to use the terms 'policies' and 'practices' and 'procedures' as if they were all the same. However, we are clearly seeing important differences between workplace practices—what occurs on the shop floor—and human resource policies and human resource philosophies. The L.L. Bean corporation is a good example, I think, of the importance of keeping both practices and policies in place. We might think of high-performance workplace practices and policies. We might also think about packages of practices and policies. Here, not only are we thinking about packages in a horizontal linkage of HR but also in a vertical linkage of HR. So, not only do we have practices at the shop level that we can see as a package, we also have policies at a higher level and above that, even, philosophies about managing people that we can see as a package. The L.L. Bean example is a good illustration of the importance of consistency in the vertical package. A number of years ago in the late 1980s, when L.L. Bean did total quality, the first brush was to do more statistical process control, more training and development of the skills of the people, in order to reduce the return rate by ensuring that the correct packages and products were shipped out. Everyone's knowledge and skills improved, as a result, and the employees were better at spotting defects. But L.L. Bean found, in fact, that they were not getting any payback from all their skills training! The defect rates stayed about the same until they realized that, in fact, the HR philosophy of the organization was blocking progress. The group had the skills, but they did not feel that it was their prerogative to exercise those skills, because the L.L. Bean corporation had always been somewhat paternalistic; top management told the people what to do. So the HR philosophy was blocking the HR practices. The employees had the skills, but they were waiting for direction! Now they do have the vertical package of HR activities in place along with the horizontal. This reminds us again, that we need to move HR activities together, whether or not they are in a high-performance system.

Overall, I am excited about the trends today. I feel a little uncomfortable, however, about claiming that we have a set of non-contingent HR practices that organizations might adopt in a wholesale manner. I feel even more uncomfortable given the warnings we have heard here that, if HR professionals do not make good progress in learning all the necessary business skills, they are either going to be replaced by non-HR professionals, or some other group will do their job. If we propagate the notion of non-contingent, high-performance practices too soon, too prematurely, we might be providing an HR elixir for non-HR professionals. They might believe that to solve their problems all they have to do is select high-performance practices. This approach is non-diagnostic. But a diagnostic approach is more appropriate for the problems of human resource management that we face today. Different conditions warrant different HR practices. We have a lot of research over the past fifty years demonstrating that there are many contingent factors in HR management: technology, organizational size, structure, strategy, union status, top management goals and values, and national culture. We have a lot of research, and you have a lot of personal evidence, in fact, that these are major, contingent constraints on the implementation and success of human resource practices. We all need to have a diagnostic framework in place and identify the practices that make sense in a particular environment, the practices that are going to work. So in a way, Jeffrey, I am glad that there is some resistance to change, because we would not want the movement to go too far forward without having these caveats in place.

5 Workplace Transformation in Canada: Policies and Practices

Gordon Betcherman

Business competition, technological change, and a host of other forces are changing the way human resources are managed and even the nature of the employment relationship itself. As researchers have studied these issues, a consensus has built up around three points. First, the traditional workplace models that emerged in the first half of this century no longer meet the needs of employers or workers. Second, the new workplace must move toward a set of participation- and incentive-based principles most frequently referred to as 'high-commitment' or 'high-performance' work systems. Third, there has been some diffusion of the new models, but the transition from the traditional systems is slow and far from universal.

These observations and the evidence which underlies them have been based almost exclusively on the American experience.[1] Until now, there has been very little comparable research in Canada, in large part because of a lack of data on human resource practices in this country. In the absence of direct evidence, two very different assumptions can be made about the state of affairs in the Canadian workplace. On the one hand, one can assume—as is so often the case—that the U.S. experience, perhaps slightly moderated, must apply here as well. On the other hand, it could be argued that in this case there are grounds to expect dissimilar trends in the two countries. The most obvious ground is the far greater reach and power of unions in Canada, which, one might reasonably argue, must have implications for human resource management.

In this paper, I am going to draw on new Canadian data to describe workplace trends in this country. The research is based on a number of studies that were undertaken for the Human Resource

1 For a few examples of a large literature, see Lawler, Mohrman, and Ledford (1992); Osterman (1994); and Appelbaum and Batt (1994).

Management Project, a recently completed national study carried out under the auspices of the Industrial Relations Centre at Queen's University.[2] In particular, I am going to offer an analysis based on the 1993 Human Resource Practices Survey (HRPS), which collected detailed information on the human resource strategies, policies, and practices of 714 establishments in four major economic sectors. To the extent that this survey sample is broadly representative, these data allow for a more complete assessment of workplace trends in this country than has been possible until now.

The next section provides the context for this paper by briefly describing the traditional workplace models and the challenges to those models that have emerged over the past fifteen years. Following this, I review the HRPS evidence on current workplace practices in Canadian industry. After documenting the trends, I go on to consider the relationship between human resource management practices and firm performance. In the final section, I take stock of the overall picture based on the survey results and then discuss issues surrounding the future diffusion of new workplace models in Canada.

The Challenge to the Traditional Models

My starting point is the traditional workplace models that emerged in the first few decades of this century. As described by Osterman (1988), there were two dominant variants—the 'industrial' and the 'salaried' models, which applied to blue-collar and white-collar work systems, respectively. Although Osterman's typology is based on the American experience, the evolution of these models generally applied to Canada as well.

Without going into too much detail, we can say that the industrial model typically (although not exclusively) has been found in unionized settings. Key features include tight job definitions and work rules, seniority-based labour deployment, wages attached to jobs (rather than people or performance), and no formal job security. The salaried model has usually been applied in nonunion professional, technical, and administrative work settings. Unlike the blue-collar system, it has been based on broad and fluid job definitions, assignment and compensation based on merit, and a commitment to job security.

It is important to underline that each of these systems was fairly effective in balancing the interests of employers and employees from

2 For a synthesis of the project's findings, see Betcherman, McMullen, Leckie, and Caron (1994).

the 1940s through the 1970s. For the most part, of course, these were prosperous decades of strong productivity and wage growth. While the economic success obviously cannot be attributed exclusively to the prevailing workplace practices, the traditional models fit well with the environment in which they had been designed to operate.

The deteriorating economic performance in the second half of the 1970s and into the 1980s brought new challenges to the established systems, first in the United States and then in Canada. The clearest indicator of these economic problems was the productivity slowdown. As Figure 1 shows, the three and four percent annual growth rates achieved in Canada during the 1960s and 1970s decreased substantially beginning in the 1970s. Since 1980, annual productivity growth has been only about one percent.

Figure 1
The Productivity Slowdown; Change in Real Output per Person-Hour, 10-Year Averages, Canada, 1950s to 1990-92

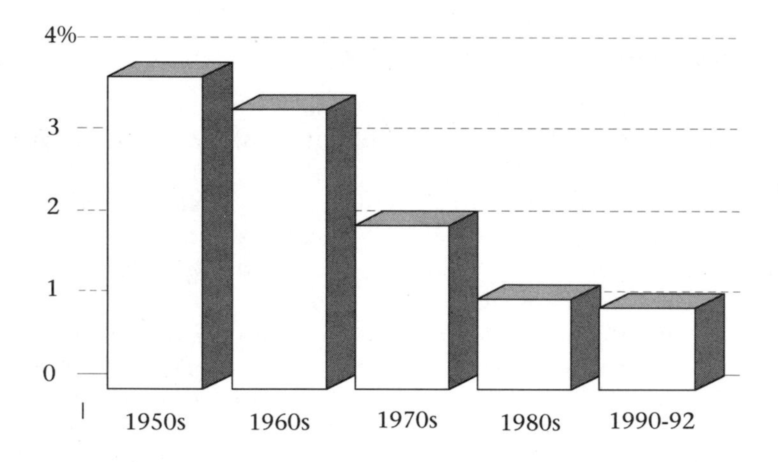

Source: Based on data from Statistics Canada.

At the same time that this slowdown set in, product markets began changing dramatically. Deregulation and globalization were intensifying competition in virtually every sector. This combination of more difficult productivity gains and greater competition forced most businesses to rethink all aspects of their operations, from those at the most strategic level to day-to-day activities. Human resource management and labour relations were not immune to this scrutiny.

It was employers, then, who initiated the challenges to the traditional workplace systems, beginning with the industrial model and the inefficiencies and inflexibilities that had built up over the decades. In the United States, many employers reacted by attempting to move away from their unions and collective bargaining obligations (Kochan, Katz, and McKersie 1986). In Canada, where the labour movement is stronger and business antipathy to unions perhaps weaker, employers have been less likely to pursue this strategy (Kumar 1993). In both countries, the challenge to the salaried model has come more recently. In many respects, this system has the operational flexibility that employers are looking for. However, as business pressures continued to mount through the 1980s and into the 1990s, many companies started to weaken and then back off from the job-security pledge that had been at the centre of the model itself.

Two additional points about the pressures on the traditional models deserve mention. First, while economic factors have been most prominent, the pressures on the traditional systems have not been solely economic. Technological change has also played an important part. Around 1980, computer technologies began diffusing through most industries in Canada and elsewhere. To provide a sense of the spread of these technologies and the extent of their penetration into the Canadian workplace, Figure 2 summarizes results from the Working With Technology Survey, which collected data from a sample of establishments in 1985 and again in 1991. As this figure shows, the proportion of employees working directly with computer technologies more than doubled over that period. With this diffusion, which has touched virtually every company and every activity, skill requirements, hierarchical structures, and information flows have all been affected. In turn, this has affected how human resources can and should be managed. The rigidities of the industrial model, in particular, have proven to be incompatible with high-technology flexible production.

Second, while the pressures on the traditional models were initiated largely by employers, workers and their unions have more recently posed challenges as well. In part, this has been due to the recognition that these systems were no longer 'delivering the goods,' in the form of gains in earnings and job security, that they once delivered. For example, after twenty-five years of increases, wage growth essentially stopped in both Canada and the United States in the mid-1970s. In Canada, as Figure 3 indicates, real wages were stagnant after this period, and in fact, they were higher in 1976 than in 1993.

Pressures on the traditional models also grew because the work force itself had changed dramatically. The traditional systems were designed for a primarily male, largely high school educated labour

Figure 2
Working with Technology
(Percentage of Employees Working Directly with CBT, Establishment Mean)

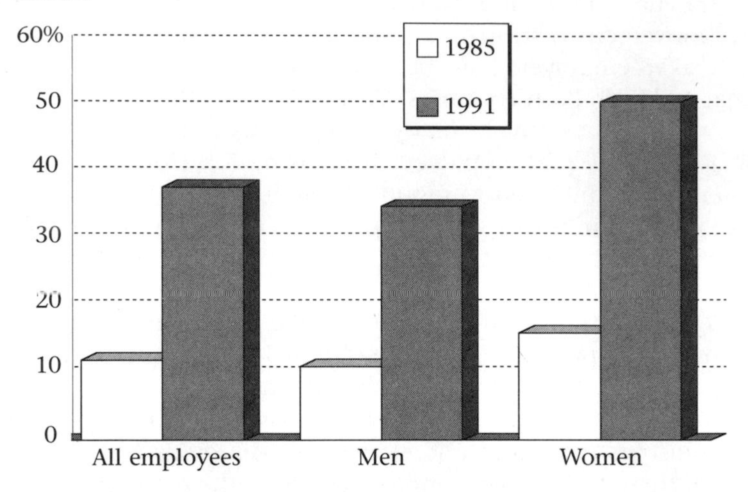

Source: Working with Technology Survey.

Figure 3
Hourly Wages and Salaries, Canada, 1967-91

1989 dollars per hour

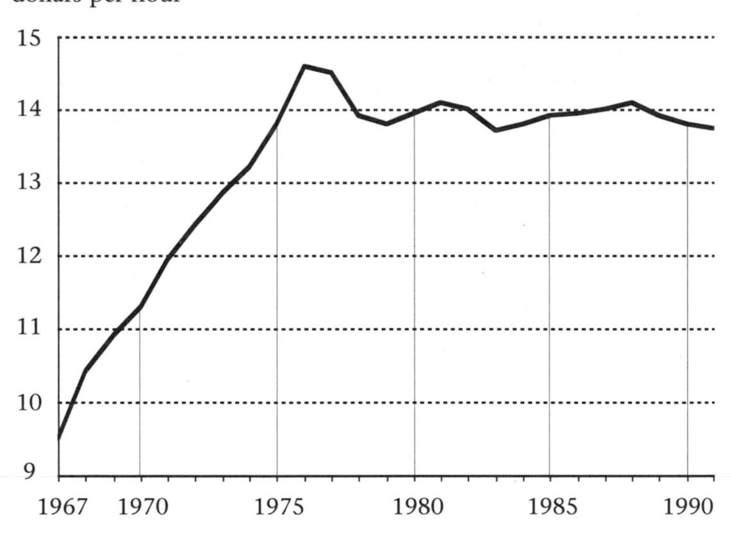

Source: Estimates by the authors, based on data from Statistics Canada.

force which bears little resemblance in terms of composition, expectations, and attitudes to today's heterogeneous and largely well-educated labour force. An illustration of the poor fit is the fact that clearly relevant issues like balancing work and family responsibilities and employee involvement in decision making were effectively outside the old models.

Responding to the Challenges

A major objective of our research was to learn how Canadian businesses were responding to this changing environment. Using data gathered through the Human Resource Practices Survey, much of the analysis reported in this section focuses on employer strategies and practices. Before describing our data base and results, I begin with a brief discussion of how Canadian unions are responding to issues surrounding workplace reorganization.

Union Strategic Responses to Workplace Pressures[3]

While the real impact of organized labour in the United States is now limited to a few industries, unions in Canada continue to be a factor in most industries outside of the private service sector.[4] Accordingly, even though the debate over workplace reorganization has been led by management, Canadian unions have a potentially important part to play.

When Canadian business started thinking about workplace reorganization in the 1980s, unions faced a difficult dilemma. To begin with, unions were not prepared for the ensuing debate, which involved issues traditionally outside their jurisdiction and expertise. Without the immediate resources to develop their own positions on workplace reorganization, unions really had only two choices. One was to accept management initiatives passively, despite the fact that, in many cases, the initiatives ran counter to the equity-orientation of the union and longstanding protections for the membership. The alternative was simply to oppose them and risk the charge that unions were outmoded institutions clinging through self-interest to an unsustainable status quo.

Neither strategy has proven to be viable. If management is interested in reorganizing the workplace, it is typically prepared to act

3 This discussion is based on Kumar (1995).

4 The union density rate in Canada is over 35 percent, approximately double the U.S. rate. It is true, however, that unions in the private sector are facing difficult times in Canada as well, although they remain much stronger than their American counterparts. For a discussion, see Kumar (1993).

alone. And, if the union is not actively involved, there is no means for safeguarding the members' interests. As a consequence, in recent years some of the larger Canadian unions, including the Canadian Auto Workers, the United Steelworkers, and the Communications, Energy, and Paperworkers have started to develop much more active agendas on workplace change.

While these agendas accept the need for change, they aim to shape the reorganization to reflect the interests of labour. Different unions have different strategies; however, there appear to be many common elements, including equal partnership in conceptualizing and implementing workplace change, an insistence on negotiated change through collective bargaining, meaningful labour input into improving productivity and quality, a share of any dividend going to workers, and a definition of workplace reorganization that incorporates 'good' (that is safe, healthy, and skill-deepening) job designs.

The union agendas demonstrate that at least part of the labour movement has moved forward in developing a strategic response to the changing environment. However, research undertaken as part of the Human Resource Management Project indicates that labour's influence on workplace restructuring remains limited. For example, Downie and Coates (1994) concluded from their case studies of major unionized corporations that genuine workplace partnerships were rare. And less than 10 percent of Atlantic Provinces' companies surveyed by Wagar (1994) reported that their union was involved in strategic management decision making. While these results probably reflect a continued strategic shortfall on the part of many unions, they also suggest that many employers still see issues associated with workplace reorganization as management's prerogative and therefore have little interest in sharing control.

The Human Resource Practices Survey

The principal data source for the following discussion of employer strategies and HR approaches is the Human Resource Practices Survey (HRPS). The HRPS was carried out in 1993 through telephone interviews followed by self-administered questionnaires. It gathered data from responding establishments on their organizational environment (e.g., market conditions and technological change), business strategy, on various performance measures, and on practices in a number of human resource areas.[5]

The HRPS sample includes 714 establishments drawn from across the country in four broad sectors: wood products, fabricated metal

5 For more details on the HRPS, see Betcherman et al. (1994).

products, electrical and electronic products, and a range of business services. These sectors were chosen for their diversity representing, respectively, a natural resources industry, a traditional manufacturing industry, a higher value-added, export-oriented manufacturing industry, and a 'dynamic' service industry. While the sectors included reflect a large part of the Canadian industrial structure, they do not cover the public, quasi-public, or traditional service sectors (e.g., retail and wholesale trade and consumer services). Like most surveys of its type, the HRPS also underrepresents small establishments. These sample characteristics must be kept in mind when evaluating the generalizability of the survey results.

I should make one additional comment about the survey. 'Extensive' evidence from surveys such as the HRPS needs to be interpreted carefully. Self-reported data on strategic and human resource issues, for example, may not always reflect what would be observed through more intensive observation. An important aspect of the project's overall research design, then, was to interpret the data from the HRPS (and the other surveys undertaken as part of the research) in the light of the more qualitative interviews and case studies that were also carried out. The main themes emerging from the 'harder' survey evidence, as reported below, were broadly consistent with the analysis of project researchers using other methodologies.

Strategic Responses of Canadian Businesses

An important step in understanding how Canadian firms are managing human resources in response to the new environment and, in particular, to the intensified competition is to appreciate overall trends in business strategy. 'Business strategy' refers to the choices firms make to position themselves in the marketplace, that is, how they try to achieve competitive advantage.

Companies can consider a range of options in devising an overall business strategy. On the one hand, they can choose to compete on the basis of costs; this can include minimizing labour costs or other operating costs. Alternatively, they can follow what Porter (1990) has labelled a 'differentiation' strategy, which involves competing through product development and quality, service, and specialization. This approach will typically involve an emphasis on innovation through technological and organizational change.

Earlier research has shown that business-strategy choices are often a significant determinant of the firm's approach to human resource management (Arthur 1992). For example, a cost-minimization strategy is unlikely to create incentives to invest in human resources. Rather, when this type of strategy is in place, we expect Taylorist job designs and workplace practices that exploit economies of scale. Differentiation strategies, on the other hand, are more likely to lead to high-investment human resource practices.

Establishments participating in the Human Resource Practices Survey were asked about the principal elements in their business strategies. On the basis of these responses, we were able to identify three basic strategic orientations: cost-minimization, innovation, and an emphasis on human resources. The most common was the cost-minimization strategy, describing about 60 percent of the respondents. The innovation strategy followed with an incidence rate of just over 50 percent, and the human resource-based strategy was the least frequent, characterizing less than 45 percent of the respondents.[6]

Human Resource Practices

As noted, the HRPS collected detailed data on a range of human resource practices in the responding establishments. Practices covered in the survey included the organization of the human resource function, job design policies, staffing, training, compensation, employee participation programs, flexible scheduling, and family care policies.

Rather than focus on these individual practices, we have found it more useful to consider HRM systems—complete sets of practices within establishments. This approach is based on the notion that for economic, psychological, and technical reasons, companies are likely to adopt complementary policies in different functional areas. And, in fact, where researchers have looked for distinct HRM patterns using an establishment-level database like the HRPS, they have tended to find them (e.g., Ichniowski 1990; Ichniowski, Shaw, and Prennushi 1993).

Distinct patterns of human resource practices were also evident with the HRPS data. We found, for example, a highly significant degree of association between the absence or presence of different practices within individual firms. In order to identify the dominant types of HRM systems in the sample, a statistical technique called 'cluster analysis'[7] was applied to the survey data for nine different types of human resource practices in the functional areas listed above. Three distinct HRM systems were identified among the HRPS respondents.

6 The incidence rates do not add up to 100 percent because some respondents fit the criteria for more than one category. For more details, see Betcherman et al. (1994) and Leckie (1994).

7 Cluster analysis assigns establishments to clusters so that the variation within these groups is minimized while the variation between them is maximized. For more details, see Leckie (1994).

The first system, which we call traditional, includes firms placing very little, if any, strategic priority on human resources. These establishments have HRM strategies based on a low degree of commitment between workers and employer and low levels of investment in the work force. Organizations in this cluster are likely to have conventional (i.e., Taylorist) job designs, limited employee participation in the operation, 'straight' compensation systems (i.e., systems without incentive-based features), little or no training, no flexible scheduling arrangements, and little integration of human resource issues in overall business planning. Firms fitting into the traditional model do not see human resources as a decisive competitive factor and, as a consequence, do not make investments to enhance work force skills and commitment. In contrast, organizations in the other two clusters view human resources as a key to competitiveness, and this is reflected in their HRM strategies. These firms clearly are doing more than just keeping their labour costs lower then their competitors. To some degree, they are moving toward 'high-performance' work systems. However, while establishments in each of these groups have implemented strategies designed to develop and tap the capabilities of their employees, the two models differ in the specific practices that are emphasized.

The participation-based model describes firms emphasizing job design, the work process, team work, employee involvement, and information sharing. The focus of these organizations is on the quality of work and intrinsic rewards to motivate employees. Establishments fitting into this system typically have some form of employee participation (through programs such as labour-management committees, employee involvement, problem-solving groups, and the like). They also strive to enhance job design (e.g., with some combination of job enrichment or rotation or teams) and to invest a considerable effort in training.

In contrast, the compensation-based model emphasizes extrinsic rewards to create productivity incentives. Firms fitting into this model typically report sophisticated compensation systems, including above-market wages, extensive benefits, and variable, or incentive, pay schemes. They also tend to be characterized by strong career ladders, with promotion from within and an emphasis on training.

Figure 4 shows how the HRPS establishments fit into these three HRM groups. As Panel A indicates, the traditional model is the most prevalent, describing slightly more than one-half the respondents (53 percent). The remainder are relatively evenly split between the participation- and compensation-based systems. The incidence of these systems varies according to different organizational characteristics. I

Figure 4
Distribution of Establishments into HRM Clusters, with and without Weighting, 1993

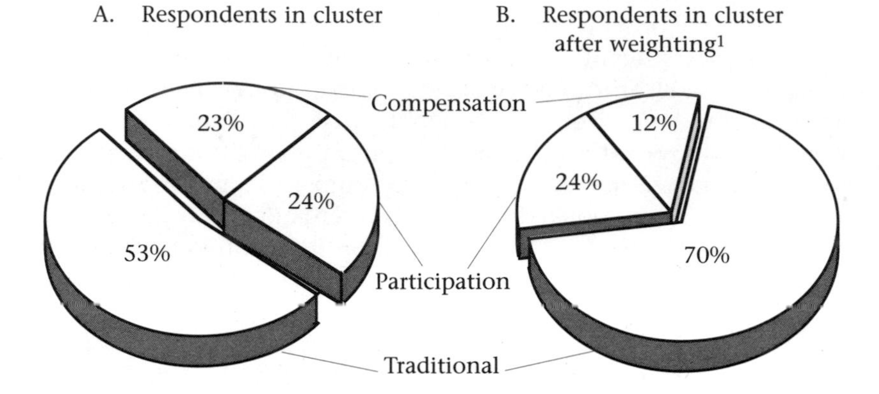

Source: Estimates by the authors, based on data from the Human Resource Practices Survey.
1 The sample results were weighted using Statistics Canada establishment-count data on establishment size (number of employees) in each of the four sectors that were surveyed for the HRPS.

have already mentioned that the establishment's overall business strategy is a significant determinant of its HRM approach. For example, from a list of eight possible elements in a business strategy, firms falling into the traditional model were most likely to cite reducing costs as part of their strategy, while those in the two 'high-performance' clusters—the participation- and compensation-based groups—were most likely to cite increasing employee skill levels.[8]

There was also a correlation between HRM practices and the firm's environment: establishments in the traditional group tended to see their environment as less turbulent than did those in the other clusters. The industrial sector of the firm appears to matter as well: the two 'old-economy' sectors (wood and fabricated metal products) were overrepresented in the traditional group, while the incidence of the participation- and compensation-based models was highest in the electrical and electronic products and business services sectors.

8 The elements included reducing labour costs, reducing other operating costs, increasing employee skill levels, developing new products and markets, introducing new technology, reorganizing the work process, enhancing labour-management cooperation, and undertaking research and development. Respondents were asked to check off all of the elements that were part of their business strategy.

Probably the most important correlate is establishment size. The survey revealed that the probability of fitting into the traditional cluster decreased for larger firms. For example, 70 percent of the respondents with fewer than 50 employees followed the traditional model, but the corresponding figure for those with 250 employees or more was only 18 percent. Because of this strong influence of size and because our sample underrepresents small establishments, it is evident that the distribution of HRM systems shown in Panel A of Figure 4 understates the true incidence of the traditional model. Accordingly, we reestimated the distribution after weighting the HRPS sample so that it reflected the establishment size patterns of the four sectors in the real economy.[9] As expected, the traditional system is even stronger after this adjustment: it has an incidence rate of 70 percent, while the participation- and compensation-based models account for just 18 and 12 percent, respectively (Figure 4, Panel B).

HRM Systems and Firm Performance

Do the so-called 'high-performance' systems indeed generate positive outcomes for the firms that adopt them? Given its real-world implications, this question ranks among the most important for researchers studying human resource management. Unfortunately, it is not an easy question to answer. Few researchers have access to data bases that have the range of information required to fully profile the HRM practices and the performance of an adequate sample of firms. And even when data are available, it is difficult to isolate the impacts of human resource practices from the myriad of other forces that can potentially affect firm performance.

Nonetheless, we now have a limited research base consisting mainly of studies carried out by Americans using American data. The earlier studies focused in particular on the impact of individual practices on performance. On balance, this research has yielded mixed results, since some practices have weak or nonexistent performance effects, while others—especially variable pay and employee-participation plans—appear to have stronger effects.[10] But some recent work, also American, suggests that the impacts of HRM are clearer and stronger when systems, rather than individual practices, are considered. A growing number of these studies conclude that firms with 'high-performance' human resource systems do receive positive payoffs (e.g., Macy, Bliese, and Norton 1991; MacDuffie and Krafcik

9 For more details, see Leckie (1994.)

10 For a review of this literature, see Weber (1994).

1992; Ichniowski, Shaw, and Prennushi 1993).

The HRPS data offer some support for this conclusion.[11] We find that establishments with high-performance HRM systems—in our case, the compensation- and participation-based models—were more likely to report improved performance trends than respondents with traditional systems (Table 1). Econometric analysis undertaken to isolate the effects of HRM from other potentially influential variables confirmed this finding for a number of the 'labour' performance indicators and one 'efficiency' indicator. The estimated performance advantage was particularly evident for firms fitting into the participation-based model. With other firm characteristics held constant, establish-

Table 1
Proportion of Establishments Reporting Improvements in Performance Outcomes, by HRM Cluster, 1988-93

Performance outcome	HRM cluster Traditional	Compensation	Participation	All
		(Percent)		
A Labour outcomes1				
Quits***	42.0	54.0	55.0	48.0
Layoffs	13.0	14.0	19.0	15.0
Accidents	37.0	39.0	46.0	39.0
Grievances	33.0	38.0	40.0	35.0
B Efficiency outcomes				
Labour productivity	79.0	88.0	85.0	82.0
Unit costs**	35.0	49.0	49.0	41.0
Customer complaints1	67.0	68.0	72.0	69.0
Product/service quality	95.0	94.0	94.0	95.0
C Financial outcomes				
Sales	63.0	61.0	66.0	63.0
Market share	66.0	72.0	71.0	68.0
Profits	47.0	46.0	52.0	48.0

Source: Estimates by the authors, based on data from the Human Resource Practices Survey.
1 Improvements are signified by decreases.
**Differences among the groups is significant at the .05 levels.
***Differences among the groups is significant at the .01 levels.

11 The empirical analysis is reported in Betcherman et al. (1994) and in Leckie and Betcherman (1994).

ments with these HRM systems were about 10 percent more likely to report improved performance in the areas of quits, layoffs, and accidents and 20 percent more likely to report improved unit costs than their counterparts with traditional HRM systems.

Neither the descriptive analysis nor the model estimates identified any significant differences in financial performance across the three HRM clusters. This is an important result because from a business perspective, impacts on financial outcomes such as sales, market share, and profits are probably of greatest interest. The fact that we found no statistically significant effects on these outcomes could mean one of two things. It is possible that there is no discernible financial payoff from high-performance workplace practices. Or, alternatively, it may be that payoffs do exist but that these could not be captured with our data and methodology. Certainly, the farther performance measures are removed from the office or shop floor, the more difficult it is to control for the range of factors that could be exerting an influence. Since we are not able to sort this out definitively, the latter explanation—that a performance effect exists but was not identified—seems plausible, because one would naturally expect that the positive impacts of the high-performance models on labour and efficiency outcomes would eventually translate into financial gains as well.

Ultimately, using survey data to analyze the links between firm performance and HRM systems creates a potentially major problem, because a company's human resource practices as set out in reply to a questionnaire may not accurately reflect what is really happening in the workplace. For example, establishments reporting practices such as employee participation, training, or variable pay programs may not necessarily have instituted these throughout the organization, nor may they have a strong commitment to them. We have found that a substantial number of firms experiment with high-performance practices, but they are never more than 'frills.' Longitudinal data from the Working With Technology Survey indicate that about one in three firms reporting employee participation and variable-pay programs in the mid-1980s had dropped them by the early 1990s (Betcherman, Leckie, and Verma 1994).

An interesting finding from this database is that the sustainability of high-performance practices is unrelated to observable factors such as union status or firm size. This suggests that the critical variables in successful workplace innovation are intangibles like commitment and trust. Indeed, Wagar (1994) found that variables capturing the degree of social responsibility and sharing of decision making and information were more powerful determinants of performance among the firms he surveyed than any concrete programs or practices.

Diffusing Workplace Change in Canada

I began this paper by identifying three points of consensus that seem to have emerged from American research on human resource management trends: (1) that there are major environmental pressures on longstanding HRM models; (2) that the 'high-performance' work systems based on participation and incentives seem best suited to the new environment; and (3) that some diffusion of the new models is taking place, but the transformation is far from universal.

The new evidence presented in this paper indicates that these observations largely apply to Canada as well.[12] A number of forces, especially more intense competition and rapid technological change, have clearly created pressure for change. To the extent that the HRPS data are representative of the Canadian business sector, however, they indicate that traditional HRM models based on low commitment and low investment are still the norm. This is particularly true of small firms and of 'old-economy' industries.

Only a minority of firms seem to be moving away from these traditional approaches and toward proactive strategies based on some combination of employee participation, compensation incentives, high-quality job designs, and investment in skills. In fact, in the sectors surveyed, we estimate that just 30 percent of firms are pursuing some type of high-performance workplace model. Moreover, as the data on the sustainability of practices indicate, some of these establishments undoubtedly have only a partial commitment to the high-performance approach.

The persistence of traditional HRM practices appears to have a number of unfavourable consequences. In this paper, I have addressed one—the implications for firm performance. Although the links between HRM strategies and performance outcomes, particularly financial outcomes, are difficult to establish definitively, our research has reinforced the growing body of evidence that on a number of dimensions, firms with traditional HRM systems do not perform as well as firms that make a sustained and coordinated effort to elicit employee participation, invest in training, and use compensation to reward performance.

I have not considered here the implications for workers of the con-

12 It is difficult to compare precisely the extent of workplace change in Canada and the U.S. based on survey data in the two countries. Sample characteristics and survey instruments are never exactly the same. However, my qualitative assessment is that the degree of change, while roughly comparable, is probably slightly greater in the U.S. One reason for drawing this conclusion is the higher incidence of small firms in Canada; as our research (and others) has concluded, these firms are less likely to have moved toward high-performance HRM systems than medium and especially large organizations.

tinued dominance of the traditional HRM model. However, as elaborated in Betcherman et al. (1994), it does contribute to the high degree of employment insecurity in the labour market. Traditional HRM systems offer no job security and little in the way of employment security—that is, they do not provide the experience or skills development necessary to improve the general employability of most workers. The low commitment intrinsic to these systems is an important part of the reason for the high turnover and short tenure in so much employment in Canada (and in the United States).

Not surprisingly, when a large percentage of jobs are 'nonstandard' (i.e., part-time or short-term jobs doing contract work), the investment in workplace training will inevitably be minimal and limited, typically, to a core of employees who already have high levels of skills. The result is that, in an era when human resource development is widely seen as critically important, the overall level of investment in Canadian industry may well be inadequate. Moreover, training in many companies is probably exacerbating rather than reducing the polarization that we see in the labour market.

While our research underlines the shortcomings of traditional HRM, it is a mistake to assume that high-performance workplace systems provide a magical solution. This has been demonstrated by the succession of 'alphabet' programs that have had their day and then disappeared. There is no single approach that fits all situations. The particular features of a successful HRM approach will depend on the characteristics of the firm, its history and culture, and its environment.

Nonetheless, while the specifics may vary, the following general elements appear to be important for meeting the needs of both management and labour: (1) a flexible work organization; (2) a commitment to training; (3) employee participation; (4) the sharing of information, privilege, risk, and rewards; (5) a work process designed to improve health and reduce stress; and (6) family friendly policies.

The first four are relatively standard features of high-performance models. The last two are less commonly considered. However, our research indicates that many organizations implementing high-performance practices like employee involvement and incentive-based pay turn out to be stressful organizations because people are being given a lot more responsibilities, but often without the resources or the support to handle them. One critical aspect of that support involves balancing work and family responsibilities. Most companies report a range of employment problems because of difficulties employees are experiencing in this area; however, only a small minority are actively addressing this issue through assistance with day-care, flexible scheduling, and other practices.

A number of barriers need to be overcome if high-performance practices are to be more widely diffused. Businesses, employees, and unions need access to more information on workplace reorganization, including how it can be implemented and successfully sustained. Governments, too, need a much clearer understanding of workplace issues and, in particular, of the ways in which public policies can provide better support for high-investment, high-commitment strategies.

In many respects, current institutions and policies actually act as disincentives for high-performance HRM. For example, the unemployment insurance system allows employers to rely on layoffs as an adjustment mechanism without any extra costs for the additional unemployment created. Collective bargaining has sustained a tradition of reserved management rights and separable employer and employee interests, rather than one of workplace partnership. Employment standards and benefit regulations have created cost advantages for nonstandard work. While governments cannot legislate flexibility, partnership, a learning culture, or employee involvement in the workplace, they can examine how their policies influence decisions made by employers and employees. And as major employers in their own right, governments can play a direct role in the diffusion of high-performance work practices.

Ultimately, workplace change is a social process and, as such, it is a difficult process. It is not surprising that the majority of companies are trying to succeed in the new competitive environment by cutting costs or trying to stay ahead in the technology race. In many respects, these strategies are less complicated than strategies genuinely based on competing through a flexible, involved, and well-trained work force. Moving toward a high-performance workplace system inevitably involves substantial trade-offs for all parties. Accepting these trade-offs, however, will promote the innovation, productivity, and quality that a high-cost country like Canada must have to compete and to maintain its standard of living in the current economic environment.

References

Applebaum, Eileen and Rose Batt. 1994. *The new American workplace: Transforming work systems in the United States*. Ithaca, NY: ILR Press.

Arthur, Jeffrey B. 1992. The link between business strategy and industrial relations systems in American steel minimills. *Industrial and Labor Relations Review* 45:488-506.

Betcherman, Gordon, Norm Leckie, and Anil Verma. 1994. HRM innovations in Canada: Evidence from establishment surveys. Working Paper Series, Queen's Papers in Industrial Relations 1994-3, School of Industrial

Relations, Queen's University, Kingston, ON.
Betcherman, Gordon, Kathryn McMullen, Norm Leckie, and Christina Caron. 1994. *The Canadian workplace in transition*. Kingston, ON: IRC Press, Industrial Relations Centre, Queen's University.
Downie, Bryan and Mary Lou Coates. 1994. *Traditional and new approaches to human resource management*. Kingston, ON: IRC Press, Industrial Relations Centre, Queen's University.
Ichniowski, C. 1990. Human resource management systems and the performance of U.S. manufacturing business. Working paper No. 3449, National Bureau of Economic Research, Cambridge, MA.
Ichniowski, Casey, Kathryn Shaw, and Giovanna Prennushi. 1993. The effects of human resource management practices on productivity. Columbia University, Graduate School of Business. Draft manuscript.
Kochan, Thomas A., Harry C. Katz, and Robert B. McKersie. 1986. *The transformation of American industrial relations*. New York: Basic Books.
Kumar, Pradeep. 1993. *From uniformity to divergence: Industrial relations in Canada and the United States*. Kingston, ON: IRC Press, Industrial Relations Centre, Queen's University.
———. 1995. *Unions and workplace change in Canada*. Kingston, ON: IRC Press, Industrial Relations Centre, Queen's University.
Lawler, Edward E. III, Susan A. Mohrman, and Gerald E. Ledford, Jr. 1992. *Employee involvement and total quality management*. San Francisco: Jossey-Bass.
Leckie, N. 1994. *The choice of human resource practices: Patterns, determinants, and outcomes*. Kingston, ON: IRC Press, Industrial Relations Centre, Queen's University.
Leckie, N. and G. Betcherman. 1994. The impacts of HRM practices on establishment performance. *Canadian Business Economics* 2(4):36-45.
MacDuffie, John Paul and John F. Krafcik. 1992. Integrating technology and human resources for high-performance manufacturing: Evidence from the international auto industry. In *Transforming organizations*, edited by Thomas A. Kochan and Michael Useem, pp.209-25. New York: Oxford University Press.
Macy, B.A., P.D. Bliese, and J.J. Norton. 1991. Organizational change and work innovation: A meta-analysis of 131 North American field experiments, 1961-1990. Paper presented at the meeting of the National Academy of Management, Miami.
McMullen, K., N. Leckie, and C. Caron. 1993. *Innovation at work: The working with technology survey, 1980-91*. Kingston, ON: IRC Press, Industrial Relations Centre, Queen's University.
Osterman, Paul. 1988. Em*ployment futures: Reorganization, dislocation, and public policy*. New York: Oxford University Press.
———. 1994. How common is workplace transformation and who adopts it? *Industrial and Labor Relations Review* 47:173-88.
Porter, M. 1990. *The competitive advantage of nations*. New York: The Free Press.
Wagar, T.H. 1994. *Human resource management practices and organizational performance: Evidence from Atlantic Canada*. Kingston, ON: IRC Press, Industrial Relations Centre, Queen's University.
Weber, C.L. 1994. *Effects of personnel and human resource management practices on firm performance: A review of the literature*. Kingston, ON: IRC Press, Industrial Relations Centre, Queen's University.

Discussion

Prem Benimadhu

I would like to compliment Gordon Betcherman, first of all, for a very interesting study of human resource management. We at the Conference Board are presently completing some research in the same field. We have been talking to about fifteen CEOs from across Canada, and we have interviewed and surveyed a number of vice presidents of human resources, mostly from large Canadian corporations. For the first time, we have also talked about the human resource function with line managers, who, I think, are important members of the equation. I came here well prepared to provide you with the results of our study, but I discovered that what I was going to say has already been eloquently covered by Ed Lawler, Louise Piché, and others at this conference. So, with the permission of the chair, I have discarded my original presentation, and I have decided to talk to you about my perceptions of developments in the Canadian private sector, while touching very briefly on the results of our survey.

As most of you know, the Conference Board runs about ten councils of human resource and industrial relations executives, along with work and family councils, at our compensation research centre, giving us constant access to about 450 senior vice presidents and directors of human resources. These councils give us a good picture of developments in these organizations.

From our survey of about 110 large organizations in Canada, I have concluded that the human resource function has transcended the purely technical side of HR and has been able to forge a close relationship with the CEOs in order to lead change in Canadian organizations. Of course these are the HR executives who know the business well, but I am perturbed when I read sometimes, for example, that the human resource executive is not as important as the vice president of finance or the vice president of marketing, or that the HR function is not as sexy as accounting. My experience shows this is wrong: most of the CEOs that I have been talking to during the last two months have indicated that when they seek change in the organization, they go to the human resource function. The vice president of marketing would not know what it is all about; the vice president of accounting or finance would talk about cost-cutting. So the CEO goes to the vice president of HR. The role of the CEO is critical here: every case in Canada in which HR has played an important role in creating a high-performance organization has been inspired by the CEO. The strategy works well when there is good chemistry between the CEO and the vice president of HR: then there is wonderful leadership for HR. I have also found that the HR executive today is very very different from the HR executive of ten years ago. We now have people who have been through marketing, have been through accounting, who know the business, and who speak the language of business. Three of these people who are in our councils have become CEOs in Canada. This is really a first, I think, for HR executives.

I did another study in this area four or five years ago. Some vice presidents told me that people in HR complained when they were not invited to the strategy table, but that not being invited had absolutely nothing to do with the function and everything to do with the value people could bring to the table. Today HR people are bringing and adding considerable value to the discussion at the strategic level, and they are participating actively.

There are four or five points I would like to make about HR today. First, the HR function is not the Cinderella of management functions, occasionally treated as a key element but usually relegated to a minor position. On the contrary, in the larger organizations we work with at the Conference Board, the HR function has moved to centre stage, is seriously courted by the CEOs, and required to make a significant business contribution to the organization.

Second, we heard last night, and again this morning, that HR now has a business-oriented approach. Quite a few people are moving away from being good functional professionals to being partners for profit, and there are some companies in Canada in which the HR function is in fact becoming a business unit. Of course this has its own drawbacks, which we may wish to talk about later on, but it is clear that the strategic orientation is very much a part of HR today.

So far we have not mentioned the problem of quantifying the returns from HR expenditures, and of course there are very heavy expenditures on HR matters, including training and development. There is lot of pressure for people in the HR department to quantify the contribution they are making. I am not talking about a precise quantification of the contribution of a particular policy or practice, but only about some degree of quantification of the returns.

We also talked this morning about HR becoming a partner with line management. All of the HR executives that I studied, for example, now report to CEOs: this is indicative of the importance of the function, although I am sure that in small and medium-sized organizations HR is still reporting to the vice president of finance. In 1987, when I did our study, 86 percent of organizations indicated that their vice president of HR reported to the CEOs. Five years before that the figure was 76 percent, and today it is even higher than in 1984, which clearly indicates that this function is becoming more important.

I do have some concerns about these changes, however, because when HR is being driven into the business partner role with the CEO and the other vice presidents, there is a danger that HR will not be recognized by the employees in its traditional role as a referee, as the conscience of the organization. In the past HR was there to protect the employees against excessive demands from management. This is precisely the point that was made at one of our roundtables about a month ago by Keith Willard, the President and CEO of Zeneca in the United States.

While we are finding here in Canada that a lot of HR activities are being undertaken more and more by line people, I am concerned that there is tremendous resistance among line managers to assuming that responsibility. They still feel that it is not their responsibility, that it should be done by the HR crowd. This problem will have to be addressed, and one of the things we talk about is that if the changing HR function is to continue to be effective, there must be a major change in the organization itself, and a major change in the perception of HR by other people within the organization.

I now turn to consider what has been happening more generally in Canada during the last decade. Some major developments in the business environment have led management in Canada to take actions that have, in fact, resulted, explicitly or implicitly, in the shattering of the employment contract. We have all heard about these developments. Gordon Betcherman talked about the major impact of competition on what we do in organizations and on how we manage people. You will remember of course, that former President Reagan, in one of his rare moments of lucidity, said that there is nowhere to hide from competition, and he was right. We have talked about the elimination of trade barriers under the FTA, NAFTA, and the GATT. We regularly mention rapid changes in technology. These factors are very important, but there are two others that are rarely mentioned but which are, in fact, having a serious and indirect impact on the workplace today.

The first one is a subtle shift in the world economic order. You will recall that in the 1970s Edward Heath, the British Prime Minister, and Willy Brandt, the Chancellor of West Germany, joined together to raise awareness of the fact that the wealth of the world was concentrated in the northern hemisphere and that poverty was widespread in the southern hemisphere. They were saying that for the sake of global peace we needed a redistribution of wealth. Well, that redistribution has taken place and it is still taking place, but not from the efforts of the largest of the industrialized countries—not at all—but rather because of these burgeoning economies of the south, the economies of Singapore, Malaysia, Indonesia, India, and my own country, Mauritius. During the last two decades, they have been able to combine state of the art technology with a relatively inexpensive but, very highly trained labour force to produce extremely competitive goods and services of high quality. They have been able to do this because there is a vision in those countries, which was clearly evident in Manilla last year when I attended a meeting of the Asian countries. The prime ministers, the civil servants, the labour leaders, people in the universities, high schools, and primary schools, were all talking about their vision of 2020. What will the Asian countries look like then? What sort of education should children now entering primary school receive so that by the year 2020 they will be ready to assume the mission that will be assigned to their countries? As a result of this kind of commitment, we see in those countries that, despite the severe recession in North America, in the U.K., in France, in Italy, and in Germany, GDP has been growing at 7, 8, 10, or 12 percent every year for the last decade and will continue to do so.

Here in Canada, the tremendous turmoil in the market is also contributing to a new employment order in our workplace. The turmoil that we see in the 1980s and 1990s is in sharp contrast to what happened after the Second World War. At that time, firm steps to protect home industries and to build a very stable framework for economic growth were seen by many people in Europe and in North America to be highly desirable. The United Nations Monetary and Financial Conference at Bretton Woods agreed on measures to stabilize exchange rates, and it established bodies to oversee economic development. All over Europe, during the 1950s, 1960s, and 1970s, cartels were defining the structure of industries and the nature of products and their prices. There was always full agreement among competitors. It was a stable, predictable environment, because all of the players, the ten industrialized countries, would agree what should happen. Of course, occasionally there were some external shocks, like the oil price shock of 1973, which could rudely knock over those agreements, but generally they held.

Because of the stability in the economic environment, management developed in a very special way. Management could ensure job security, employment security, increases to base: all this was no problem. Everybody gave five or ten percent increases. The hierarchy was there to prevent uncomfortable individuals from taking initiatives, and that hierarchy could survive, because agility and responsiveness to the customer were not very relevant to business people at the time. This is not so today. That is the second change that is having a major impact on organizations.

We have talked about developments in technology that have made tremendous changes in competitiveness, and as trade barriers disappear, the organizational environment is in turmoil. When the most productive competitor in the world can reach out and seize your customers without warning, relying on outdated, albeit comfortable, management principles will bring no protection at all. So we need to change, and that is what Gordon Betcherman was talking about. The traditional method of managing people is gone: we have to look at new strategies. All the people that we talk to in the Canadian private sector recognize that to continue a business-as-usual approach, whether in human resource management or in labour relations, would be suicidal. The old ways that worked in the past no longer have any raison d'être today. This has had a significant impact on HRM in all the industrialized countries, including Japan, where many people are talking about employment security, where the whole concept of employment security in Japan was, in fact, shattered last year when Nissan announced a plant closure in Japan. The whole concept of high wages was also shattered last year when Volkswagon negotiated a twenty percent reduction in pay with a proportionate reduction in working time. When companies like Mercedes-Benz and BMW decide to start manufacturing in Malaysia, these are important things that we have to consider.

The awareness of these two developments has forced the social partners, both labour and management, to take certain actions in the workplace that have seriously jeopardized the employment relationship. If I may be allowed to use an overworked expression: there has been a 'paradigm shift' in the workplace. But it is a paradoxical shift, because it entails the destruction of the old way of gaining commitment from employees. The old way to ensure loyalty was to ensure employment security and to provide a continued emphasis on the base salary. Destroying all that and adopting a new value system has led us here in Canada into a period of renegotiation of the contract between employees and employers.

What has been the impact in Canada over the last few decades? We have gone through a period of downsizing: some would call it 'right-sizing,' or 'resizing' or 'capsizing.' This right-sizing has been unparalleled in the history of Canada since the Depression. All of us know Canadian companies that have been reducing their work force to stay afloat: three thousand this month, two thousand two months later, another one thousand next year. I know of organizations where jobs used to be guaranteed, not only for those who held the jobs but also for their sons and daughters. But now, in those industries where deregulation is changing the whole structure of those organizations, even the father's job is gone, and we are seeing people committing suicide because they cannot cope with that kind of a change. This will continue. Vice presidents of HR that I talk to who have engineered two, three, or four downsizings are telling me that they hope this is the last one, but they are quite sure that there will be more. It is hard for the companies, because perceptive companies realize that by downsizing they lose valuable employees.

Another important development I now see in Canada is a strong emphasis on variable compensation. Many companies are shying away from increases to base salary, so variable compensation will become extremely important. Contingent pay is now far more widespread in the United States then it is here. That is also a big change. In a survey that we conducted last month, we found that 75 percent of organizations across Canada have some form of variable pay, and it is interesting to note that while variable pay used to be the exclusive domain of CEOs, vice presidents and, senior management, it is now spreading throughout the organization. Clerical people are not receiving an increase in their base; they are receiving variable compensation. If we look at the longest period of sustained economic growth in Canada, the period from about 1983 to about 1988, after the recession of 1980-82, we find that while GDP was growing at 6, 7, or 8 percent, Canadians did not receive a real salary increase or a real wage increase during that period. Unionized people know that.

I have already mentioned that security is gone, but I am not talking only about job security or employment security. The security of small things, like having a stable incentive program in an organization is also gone. Now one executive told me that in the 1950s and 1960s, he used to tell everyone that this program, this bonus scheme will be in place for the next two or three years. Today he spends an equal amount of time convincing everybody that this incentive plan, this bonus scheme may not be in place in two months. Some organizations are cutting all benefit costs, for example, in order to survive. That sort of security is gone. And so is job security, as we have seen. No one will negotiate employment security today.

The final important development is that in organizations today, the CEO is promoting a vision disconnected from the HR policies and practices that are required to support the organization. The CEO talks about total quality management and team-based behaviour, and yet performance management is focused on a reward system that pays for individual contributions. We see inconsistencies like this. To summarize, then, my basic message is that the stable workplace is gone, and many organizations are trying quite seriously to find the next glue that will once more unite employers and employees. As some of you may know, the Centre for Creative Leadership has done a lot of work in this area with David Noer. He has recently published *Healing the Wounds* (San Francisco: Jossey-Bass, 1993), which outlines an exciting strategy for motivating employees who have lost trust, who have lost everything they believed in in the past.

Ken Delaney

Because I come from a union, I am going to give you a union perspective on current approaches to workplace change. In order to do that, I will briefly put the issue in a macroeconomic context, and I will then say something about high-wage, high value-added, or high-performance strategies versus low-wage strategies and about the threats and opportunities this presents for unions. Finally, I will talk briefly about some of the experiences of the union, particularly at Algoma Steel.

As I look at the clock, I see that I have only fifteen or twenty minutes to get all this done. I guess this is proof that, if given the opportunity, workers will in fact self-manage and set production targets that truly challenge their abilities.

First of all, let me try to put some of this into a 'macro' context. We are faced with very serious problems that have a tremendous impact on the way I do my job and the way all my colleagues do their jobs. Everybody knows about the serious unemployment problem we are confronting. Several other speakers have talked about such things as the increasing reliance on contingent workers and we all know there are tremendous pressures on traditional collective bargaining systems. I would like to identify two of these pressures: one is globalization and the increased mobility of capital; the other is technological change. Despite Gordon Betcherman's optimistic view showing the trendlines of Canadian unionization, the rate of unionization has in fact dropped to about 20 percent or probably a little lower in the private sector. We in the labour movement are having serious problems. I am concerned that productivity growth is increasing while wages have stagnated: since the late 1970s, productivity has been increasing by roughly 1 percent per year, so wages are not keeping pace with improvements in productivity. This raises the question already raised earlier: Who is benefiting from the increases? I am certain that it is not my members.

The second thing I want to talk about in a macro context is globalization and capital mobility. Notwithstanding Prem Benimadu's argument that the shift of investment to the south is necessary for world peace, I think that many workers in those countries, particularly in South America, are not, in fact, receiving much benefit from this increase in capital investment. In the mining sector this is a real problem for us. About 25 percent of our members are in mining, and right now South American countries are offering very lucrative deals to persuade Canadian mining companies to come down. It is true that there are some very attractive ore bodies there that mining companies have been afraid to explore in the past. It is ironic that since the 1970s when Chilian President Salvador Allende nationalized a copper company, everybody has been nervous about investing in Chile. Obviously those days are past, since governments now scramble to offer lucrative subsidies encouraging mining exploration and development. When you consider also the low wages and the trade union repression in those countries, you can see that globalization is a serious problem.

If we are to constrain that kind of low wage competition and focus once again on trying to raise consumption, we will need new forms of international institutions capable of tackling this problem, because we cannot regulate and respond to an international economic problem on a nation-by-nation basis. Whether for trade agreements, or international collective bargaining, or something else, at some point we will need to develop the appropriate international institutions. At the moment, however, it is very difficult to imagine what those institutions might be. Consequently, here we are in Canada, faced with severe price competition and trying to find a way to respond to it.

Firms typically have responded in one of two ways: with a low-wage strategy or with a high-wage, high-performance strategy. In my opinion, most employers in Canada are pursuing the low-wage strategy, and unions have to do more to push them the other way. Obviously, we would prefer firms to focus on a high value-added, high-wage, high-performance strategy, since by definition, high value-added strategies leave more room to negotiate high wages. Obviously, as trade unionists, we have a tremendous stake in this sort of fundamental business decision about how firms are going to compete. High performance work systems can foster improved training, greater autonomy in the workplace, and the like, and they have the potential for increasing the quality of work. These are just a few reasons why unions should be interested in business strategies.

In 1991, my union published a document called *Empowering Workers in the Global Economy*, in which we put forward a strategy to achieve a high-wage, high value-added economy. We included labour law reform and new capital strategies such as the development of alternative sources of capital which could be used to encourage investment in high-wage enterprises. The study also discussed the need for new training and work-design systems. This document continues to be quite controversial in the labour movement.

Traditionally unions have responded to globalization and severe price competition in one of two ways. One strategy is the 'reject and deny approach' claiming that all our problems stem from the corporate agenda. (By the way I do not believe that there is a corporate agenda, and, in fact, I would prefer that there was one, because at least I would know who to talk to about trying to solve some of these other problems.) The other strategy is what I call 'acceptance will come,' which is the passive response of the helpless or hopeless: You are right I must just accept lower wages, and whatever else you want in the workplace, to maintain and hold on to my job. But what we have tried to do is to focus on a third alternative, which I call the 'good-jobs strategy': we try to improve the workplace and determine if there is a connection between good jobs and what firms typically refer to as a high-performance systems.

To pursue this third alternative, we had to do some research, and so several years ago we embarked on a project funded by the Ontario Government called TARP—Technology Adjustment Research Project—in which we did a number of case studies that examined what was happening in the workplace and the potential for improving the quality of work. We also received some assistance from Labour Canada. (I mention this because I think there are some bureaucrats here, and I want them to understand that we might need some more money in the future.)

One of the surveys which was done by Gordon Betcherman, found that in several ways, high-performance systems give workers the opportunity to improve the quality of work and move forward to the good-jobs agenda. For example, there is an opportunity to increase the skill content of jobs, to enhance existing skill levels as well as to provide meaningful training. And perhaps there is a greater opportunity for autonomy and increased discretionary authority in the workplace, and for workers to have some control over the design of the workplace so they can begin to deal with problems of ergonomics, stress in the workplace and so on. This would permit them to socialize with other workers; it would reduce the psychological demands of the workplace and improve the quality of work. Perhaps these goals could be met by implementing high-performance systems. But unfortunately, our research also shows that workers can be threatened by the introduction of high-performance work systems.

In more than 60 percent of the workplaces we looked at our informants told us that something was happening: somebody was asking them to participate in the development of an ambiguous vision statement, or there was some form of job rotation in the workplace, and so on. As a result our study identified several threats to the union and to the quality of work. First of all, many attempts to introduce new systems focused on a commonality of thought between workers and management but downplayed the areas of conflict which will always exist as long as corporations can make money by lowering wages. Second, we found that in many cases there was little increase in discretionary authority for the workers, so negotiated changes in work rules and increased flexibility simply meant that supervisors, but not necessarily workers, were able to make more decisions. We also had some concerns about pay-for-knowledge systems, because they might be introduced in a way that undermines the principles of pay equity. Not everybody, particularly not single women with children, has access to the same kind of training.

Finally, there is the issue of the intensification of work. In many cases high-performance work systems simply increased the pace of work, and job enlargement simply increased the number of boring, repetitive tasks: people were not necessarily working smarter at all. Also, significantly, when efficiencies were gained from the introduction of participation systems and the like, there was often no debate as to who should keep the benefits. When we are interested in participating in new systems, and when we tell our members it is in their interest to participate, we need a method to determine who benefits from the increased efficiencies. Why would a worker divulge a secret from the shopfloor about how to do something more efficiently? Why in the world would that worker provide that information if there was no sense that the gains would be shared?

We see a combination of threats and opportunities from these high-performance systems, so we advocate a bargained approach which recognizes that there are different agendas in the workplace. We want to create better jobs, but we need to be able to talk about this separately, to work on our agenda, and to negotiate solutions which include a sharing of the efficiencies.

The examples from my union that have probably received the most publicity are Stelco, Lake Erie Works and Algoma Steel. In the interest of time, I will focus primarily on Algoma Steel.[1] Algoma Steel has been very successful in the sense that it has become quite profitable and I am the first to concede that a major reason for that has been the decline in the Canadian dollar relative to the U.S. and the boom in the auto industry. It is arguable that without those two things we would be in a lot of trouble [at Algoma] in Sault Sainte Marie. The fact remains, however, that the worker buy out has succeeded and we have had a lot of successes on the shop floor. We have introduced self-directed work teams, improved productivity and improved quality of work.

There are a number of observations that I want to make about our experience at Algoma Steel. First of all, technology really does seem to matter: I do not know why, but it does appear to be easier to introduce self-directed work teams on the finishing side of the operations than it is on the hot side—in the early stages of the process. Second, there has been a tremendous resistance to workplace change within some groups at the bargaining-unit level and, more notably, at the supervisory level. There is a history of differences, particularly between supervisors and workers. Supervisors were never laid off, but workers were frequently, because of the cyclical nature of the steel industry. Supervisors have a much better pension plan, and a number of class distinctions still continue to be a source of frustration today.

Third, we encountered structural problems when setting up self-directed work teams and trying to advance our agenda of improving the quality of work within the context of our existing political structure. And we have had what I refer to as 'lean production problems.' With the drive to improve efficiency, we have occasionally found ourselves unable to train the people because we did not have the slack in the production system to free people up and allow them to receive the training for which we had funding. There have also been the predictable agenda issues. Quite candidly, I think that in many cases we have focused too much on the activities and not enough on improving the quality of work. But I am sure that if one of my counterparts from Algoma were here, he or she would say that the opposite is true. This raises an important HR issue: if you want unions to cooperate in redesigning the workplace, it is important to recognize the immediacy of the good-jobs agenda. Workplace change must be about making jobs better for people and not only about improving productivity.

Before I close, I would also like to respond to the speakers' com-

[1] The restructuring of Algoma Steel involved an employee buyout.

ments about changes in the composition of the work force such as the increased participation by women and the ethnic diversity resulting from immigration patterns. These are issues which must be addressed in the workplace as well. We have merged with some other unions, the Retail Workers Union, for example, so we have experienced some tremendous internal cultural changes. We have also had to decide how to respond to those changes and how we are going to address the issues confronting female workers and ethnic minorities. Interestingly, we found that when we developed a course called 'women of steel,' our goal was not to help women work their way up the ranks, become local union presidents, get on staff, and so forth. That was not what people wanted. What they did want was to be better able to have their concerns addressed in the traditional collective bargaining process, to become a political force within the union and to put the issues that are important to them on the collective bargaining table. And that is what we have tried to do. So the second point I would like to emphasize is that the accommodation of these concerns is going to be an HR issue, because unions are deciding how to protect and advance the agenda of women and ethnic minority workers.

Finally, I want to talk for a moment about the trend towards smaller workplaces and nontraditional work. This trend poses a real challenge for traditional collective bargaining systems. In my opinion the Wagner Act model on which our own labour legislation is based is badly in need of reform because it simply does not apply to many sectors: we are currently negotiating agreements for security guards, and the traditional model of collective bargaining simply does not work effectively for this industry. We need alternative systems, such as collective bargaining on a sectoral basis. We need new approaches to bring forward a strong voice for working people and to bring workers an effective, independent voice in the workplace. I hope those new forms of collective bargaining are on the horizon; at least, we will be pushing for them to be on the horizon.

I want to close by saying that while many of the changes in the workplace are being driven by increased competitive pressures from globalization, technological change, severe price competition, and so forth, important issues will still remain even if we can come to grips with these problems. Our experiment in codetermination at Algoma, our efforts to improve the quality of work and our efforts to accommodate the new demographics of the work force as well as the new systems of collective bargaining are examples of issues that will remain and will have to be addressed.

6 Is There a New HRM? Contemporary Evidence and Future Directions

Lee Dyer and Thomas A. Kochan

Is there a new human resource management? Yo. That is, yes and no. A new perspective—strategic human resource management—emerged during the 1980s to take its place, alongside the more traditional operational and programmatic perspectives, as a major influence on the field. This perspective has rapidly progressed in terms of theory and research (if not practice). But it continues to take many shapes and forms and even with its various permutations, is far from universally embraced by scholars or practitioners.

What follows is a brief look at the strategic perspective of the field. It begins with a summary of some common themes. This is followed by an illustrative review of extant theory, distinguishing, in particular, between the two dominant theoretical streams which have thus far emerged: (1) the multiple-model theorists (MMTs), who are given to building typologies of human resource strategies and describing or prescribing the conditions under which the various types work or should work best, and (2) the dominant-model theorists (DMTs), who are rather less preoccupied with contingencies and rather more concerned with the details and promulgation of their preferred models or strategies within and across firms.

Next comes a look at the diffusion of these two views in actual practice. The evidence is sparse, but their diffusion appears to be rather limited thus far. This naturally gives rise to a discussion of the factors which seem to encourage and, especially, discourage diffusion. Particular attention is paid to the adoption of the so-called strategic business partner role by human resource executives, managers, and professionals, and to the adequacy of this role as a catalyst for the diffusion of the strategic perspective across the U.S. and Canadian economies. Finally, suggestions are made regarding future theoretical and empirical work which might help keep the strategic perspective moving ahead.

Common Themes

What is the strategic perspective all about? A reading of the rhetoric brings to mind the parable of the blind men and the elephant. Everyone, it seems, has a somewhat different slant on the matter. Nonetheless, there are some common themes which, when taken together, help sharpen the general concepts.

A View from the Top

Because strategies involve decisions about key goals, major policies, and resource allocations, they tend to be formulated, or at least blessed, at the top of organizations. Accordingly, a strategic perspective starts with a broad organizational, and even extra-organizational, view. This, in turn, adds another dimension to the traditional programmatic and individual-level perspectives of human resource scholars and to the managerial and operational perspective of most human resource practitioners (Tichy, Fombrun, and Devanna 1982; Kochan, Katz, and McKersie 1986).

A Goals Orientation

Correspondingly, human resource strategies focus on goals as well as activities, and particularly on broad organizational goals, usually expressed in terms of competitiveness or competitive advantage or more specific sources of competitiveness or competitive advantage such as low labour costs, improved productivity, high quality products or services, reduced cycle-times, a high degree of flexibility, or enhanced organizational innovativeness. Such a focus lends organizational salience to traditional concerns with human resource outcomes such as individual or group-level performance, behaviours, or attitudes. (More recently, some commentators, for example, Kochan (1994), Kochan and Dyer (1993), Kochan and Osterman (1994), have urged an even broader perspective, adding to the integrative goal of enhancing competitiveness a corresponding distributive goal of improving the living standards of employees; but more on this point later.)

The Centrality of People

A further shared perspective is the belief that in today's world a major means—some would say the only viable means, especially for American and Canadian firms in an increasingly competitive global environment—of attaining sustained organizational competitiveness or competitive advantage is through a quantum improvement in the management of human resources (Dyer 1993; Jones and Wright 1992; Lawler 1992; Ulrich and Lake 1990; Walker 1992; Wright and McMahan 1992). As Pfeffer (1994, 6) notes: 'Traditional sources of success—product and process technology, protected or regulated markets, access to financial resources, and economies of scale—can still provide competitive leverage, but to a lesser degree now than in the past, leaving organizational culture and capabilities, derived from how people are managed, as comparatively more vital.'

A Holistic View

Human resource strategies are usually defined in terms of a set of integrated, mutually reinforcing, and synergistic goals and activities. This is known as internal fit. There are, as will be seen later, variations in what are seen as the critical components of these models. Nonetheless, the general view is that competitiveness or competitive advantage (and, for that matter, enhanced outcomes for employees) are, at best, only moderately affected by altering any single human resource activity (e.g., a pay program). Rather, strategists believe 'that these practices reach full potential when they are combined in a comprehensive system' (Kochan and Osterman 1994, 59). To support this view, proponents cite evidence from the auto (MacDuffie and Krafcik 1992) and steel (Ichniowski, Shaw, and Prennushi 1993) industries, as well as case studies of such diverse companies as Lincoln Electric and Xerox (Cutcher-Gershenfeld 1991) and a recent meta-analysis of organizational change efforts (Macy and Izumi 1993). Dissenters, however, suggest that there is some reason to believe that too much internal fit may stifle organizational flexibility (for a review, see Milliman, Von Glinow, and Nathan 1991).

A Contingency View

Human resource strategists are all, more or less, contingency theorists; that is, they subscribe to the view that organizational effectiveness (but not necessarily a higher standard of living) is enhanced when human resource strategies are consistent or 'in sync' with the organizational environments in which they are embedded. This is referred to as external fit. Once again, evidence from the auto industry (MacDuffie and Krafcik 1992), various case studies, and the aforementioned meta-analysis (Macy and Izumi 1993) can be cited to support the relevance and power of external fit. It should be noted, though, that there is less than general agreement on the critical (as opposed to the merely interesting) features of the organizational environment, on the relative importance of external fit (vis-à-vis internal fit), and on the applicability of equifinality (which is, basically, the opposite of determinism: that is, the notion that for any given set of environmental circumstances, there are always variations—although not an infinite number of variations—of viable human resource strategies).

The Role of Human Resource Organizations

Consistent with the preceding notions is the view that, while human resource strategy is (or at least should be) the province of top executives and key line managers, there is also a critical role to be played by human resource executives, managers, and professionals. Occupants of this role, popularly referred to as strategic business partners, are said to work closely with business strategists to analyze relevant features of the organizational environment in search of critical human resource issues and, in turn, to formulate appropriate human resource strategies to deal with these issues (Walker 1992). Again, though, not all agree with the adequacy of this role definition (Kochan and Dyer 1993; Kochan and Osterman 1994). And there is a real question concerning the extent to which the role (even narrowly defined) has become institutionalized in U.S. (Towers-Perrin/IBM 1992) and Canadian (Downie and Coates 1993) businesses.

Theoretical Perspectives

A simplified model of the strategic perspective, derived from the preceding material, is shown in Figure 1. It is meant to reinforce the importance of internal and external fit. Theorists (and researchers) approach this model in several different ways. Some attempt to bring clarity to one or both of the major components—human resource strategy and organizational environment. Others seek to clarify relationships between the two components. The latter, in turn, fall into two camps: those who start with the organizational environment and work inward, referred to here as multiple model theorists (MMTs), and those who start with a human resource strategy and work out, the dominant model theorists (DMTs). What follows is an illustrative and reasonably comprehensive (but certainly not exhaustive) review of this work.

Figure 1
The Strategic Perspective

Clarifying Constructs: Human Resource Strategy

A common approach to delineating human resource strategies is the development of typologies. Four of many possible examples are shown in Figure 2.

Two of the four examples come from the human resource strategy literature: Walton's (1985) well-known and widely cited Control and Commitment dichotomy and Dyer and Holder's (1988) break-out of Inducement, Investment, and Involvement strategies. The other two are from the literature on internal labour markets. Begin's (1991), which is the most thoroughly explicated of those cited, consists of four basic configurations (which he calls employment policy systems, or EPSs)—Simple, Machine, Professional, and Adhocratic—plus a fifth—Divisionalized—a composite of the others. Dunlop's (1994) typology consists of eight types: Small Enterprises, Participants in Worker Pools, Owner-Operators, Civil Service, Multitier Internal Labour Markets (ILM's), Short-Tier Internal Labour Markets, Clerical-Oriented Organizations, and Technical and Professional Amalgams. To facilitate comprehension without getting bogged down in excruciating detail, Figure 3 provides brief illustrations of one configuration taken from each of the four typologies.

Figure 2
Sample Typologies of Human Resource Strategies

Walton (1985)	Dyer and Holder (1988)	Begin (1991)	Dunlop (1994)
Control		Machine	
Commitment	Involvement	Adhocratic	
	Inducement		
	Investment		
		Simple	Small enterprises
		Professional	Technical and professional
		Divisionalized	
			Worker pools
			Owner-operators
			Civil service
			Multitier ILMs
			Short-tier ILMs
			Clerical-oriented

Figure 3
Sample Configurations from Four Sample Typologies

Walton (1985) Commitment Model	Dyer and Holder (1988) Inducement Model	Begin (1991) Professional EPS	Dunlop (1994) Short-Tier ILMs
'Stretch' objectives	Stretch goals		
Enriched jobs/teams	Narrow jobs	Flexible jobs	Narrow jobs
Employee participation	Few career options	Informal staffing/narrow promotion paths	Limited promotion opportunities
Extensive training	Minimal training	Minimal formal training, self-directed	Minimal training
Open communication	Some communication	Open communication	
Variable pay (gainsharing profit sharing)	Variable pay (very high risk/reward leverage)	High pay, extensive intrinsic rewards, individualized	Low pay, market driven
Skill-based pay			
Control based on shared goals	Control based on job design, pay	Control based on professional standards	
Minimum status differentials	Minimum status differentials	Minimum status	
Commitment to employment security	Commitment to employment security	Employment security for chosen few	No employment security
Mutuality in labour relations	Union avoidance, or conflict		

The four typologies share some common configurations (as Figure 2 shows). Walton's Control model is quite similar to Begin's Machine EPS. Walton's Commitment model is a lot like Dyer and Holder's Involvement strategy and Begin's Adhocratic EPS. Begin's Simple EPS and Professional EPS look much like Dunlop's Small Enterprises and Technical and Professional Amalgams, respectively. Such commonalities are to be expected. Each probably reads the other's literature. And, as Osterman (1994b) points out, internal labour markets have come to be defined broadly enough to essentially represent organizational human resource strategies.

Nonetheless, a couple of fundamental differences exist between the two perspectives when it comes to developing typologies. Students of internal labour markets, for example, tend to look at large and small organizations in both the public and private sectors, whereas human resource strategists show a distinct bias toward large, private sector corporations. But, as Dunlop (1994) shows, such firms (what he calls Multitier Internal Labour Markets) employ only about 14 percent of the U.S. labour force, which is a not so subtle reminder of the need for theorists (and researchers) to specify the boundaries of their particular typologies.

Further, typologies deriving from internal labour market analyses sometimes (although certainly not always) include elements of organizational governance in their models. Begin (1991), for instance, bases his typology not only on the content of human resource activities (which everyone does), but also on the nature of what he calls the authority distribution: this, basically, has to do with where in the organization human resource decisions are made, and by whom. To some extent this difference simply reflects the predispositions and traditions of management scholars on the one hand and institutional economists on the other. But, it also suggests a potential enrichment from a cross-fertilization of ideas (if not ideology).

While typologies abound, only a few attempts have been made to derive taxonomies of human resource strategies. To cite one example: using a cluster analysis of survey data obtained from 30 steel minimills in the United States, Arthur (1992) derived six identifiable 'industrial relations systems' which he subsumed under two labels based on the systems' primary goals: Control or Commitment (after Walton 1985). The former consisted of three systems: Pure Cost Reducers (very similar to Walton's Control model and Begin's (1991) Machine EPS), Conflicters (all unionized and characterized by low trust and high conflict), and Inducers (after Dyer and Holder (1988)—see Figure 3). The latter also consisted of three systems: Collective Bargainers (high skill, high wages, and high involvement in decision making through collective bargaining), Involvers (after Dyer and Holder), and Pure Commitment Maximizers (very similar to Walton's Commitment model and Begin's Adhocratic EPS). While this study lends some credence to parts of the typologies mentioned, the resulting systems reflect less internal fit and logic than do the configurations of the judgmentally derived typologies.

Clarifying Constructs: Organizational Environment

There is little convergence on the key dimensions of organizational environment. Some of the more commonly mentioned dimensions are depicted in Figure 4. For discussion purposes, they are grouped into three categories: strategic, sociopolitical, and stakeholders. (For a somewhat different configuration, see Kochan and Osterman 1994, 89.)

Figure 4
Components of the Organizational Environment

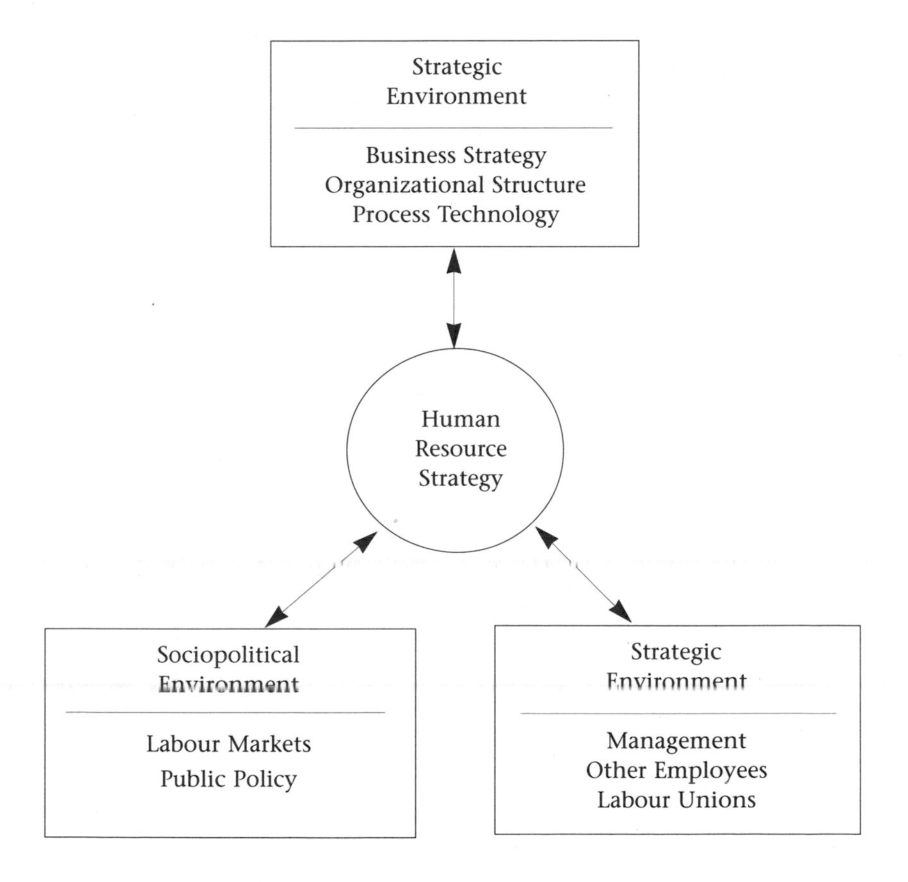

The Strategic Environment

The Strategic Environment consists of business strategy, organizational structure, and process technology. (Some—e.g., Begin (1991)—also include product-market characteristics such as stability, complexity, diversity, and hostility; the more common viewpoint, supported by some evidence, e.g., Huselid (1993), is that what really matters in terms of human resource strategies is how businesses respond to these characteristics, that is, what business strategies, structural arrangements, and technologies they choose to employ.)

The significance of business strategy is unquestioned among human resource strategists for whom the need for, and virtues of, a tight linkage or integration between business strategy and human resource strategy is gospel (e.g., Walker 1992). The reasoning is straightforward: since different business strategies require different types of, and behaviours from, employees and since different human resource strategies elicit different types of, and behaviours from, employees, it follows that much can be gained from matching strategies to attain a high degree of congruence between requirements and actualities (Cappelli and Singh 1992; Jackson, Schuler, and Rivero 1989; Schuler 1992; Schuler and Jackson 1987; Wright and McMahan 1992).

The same line of reasoning can be (although it usually is not) applied to organizational structure and process technology. (Some authors—e.g., Lawler (1986, 1992)—deal with this by incorporating one or both of these factors into their strategies rather than the organizational environment.) Increasingly, the literature stresses the need for congruence among strategies, structures, and techologies (Hammer and Champy 1993; Quinn 1992). Thus, as is suggested in Figure 4, the nexus of these three components, rather than business strategy alone, may give rise to critical staffing and behavioural requirements to which human resource strategies must be matched (Bamberger, Bacharach, and Dyer 1990).

The Sociopolitical Environment

The two dimensions here are labour markets and public policy. Both are more often cited as facilitators of, or constraints on, rather than driving forces behind, human resource strategies. As will be discussed later, there is some reason to believe that both the effectiveness and diffusion of certain types of human resource strategies can be (and are) affected by limited supplies of requisite skills and values in the labour market and by extant legislation and regulations. It is probably rare, however, for the impetus to adopt a particular human resource strategy to emanate from these sources (Kochan and Osterman 1994; Osterman 1994b).

The Stakeholder Environment
Frequently mentioned stakeholders in this context are top management, middle management, employees, and labour unions. A human resource strategy which fits both the Strategic and Sociopolitical Environments may nonetheless founder, or indeed fail to get off the ground, if it runs afoul of the values and beliefs of powerful stakeholders. Conversely, the preferences or needs of powerful stakeholders may lead to attempts to implement or, perhaps more likely, unduly perpetuate particular human resource strategies, even when they are inappropriate given extant Strategic and Sociopolitical Environments (Begin 1991; Kochan and Osterman 1994; Lawler 1992; Osterman 1994b).

Relationships from the Outside In: Multiple Model Theorists (MMTs)

MMTs approach Figure 1 from the outside in. They build (or borrow) characterizations of organizational environments, on the one hand, and typologies of human resource strategies, on the other, and then, using observation and logic, systematically study or postulate patterns of external fit (e.g., Begin 1991; Dyer and Holder 1988; Schuler and Jackson 1989). A previously uncited example, taken from the well-known work of Miles and Snow (1988), is shown in Figure 5. Characteristically, their emphasis is on the Strategic—not the Sociopolitical or Stakeholder—component of the organizational environment (product-market strategy, organizational structure and control, and process technology) and on human resource goals and activities—not governance structures. Also characteristically, their results are represented as both descriptive of the way things are and prescriptive of the way things ought to be for maximum organizational performance (at least within the domain of interest).

Others who approach human resource strategy from the outside in include students of human resource planning and advocates of the currently hot topics of total quality management (TQM) and process re-engineering. The former urge and instruct human resource planners to systematically examine elements of their organizational environments (especially business strategies) to uncover critical human resource issues and then, to devise human resource strategies to deal with these issues (see, e.g., Walker 1992). If followed, this process would perforce result in tighter linkages between the two strategies. Award criteria for the Malcolm Baldrige National Quality Award focus heavily on the Strategic component of the organizational environment, but 150 of a possible 1000 points pertain to a prescriptive concept of human resource strategy (United States Department of Commerce 1993). Hammer and Champy (1993), perhaps the best-known champions of re-engineering, illustrate how the changes they

Figure 5
Miles and Snow's Configuration

Environment and strategy	Defender	Prospector
Organizational Environment		
Product market strategy	Limited stable product-line growth through market penetration	Broad, changing product line, growth through product development
Organizational structure	Functional, centralized	Divisional, decentralized
Process technology	High volume, low cost	Customized and prototypical
Human Resource Strategy		
Basic thrust	Building human resources	Acquiring human resources
Staffing	Closed system, promotion from within	Open system, recruiting at all levels
Training	Extensive	Limited
Performance appraisal	Process-oriented, developmental	Results-oriented, administrative
Compensation	Position-based, internally consistent, hierarchical differences	Performance-based, market-driven, extensive use of incentives

Source: Adapted from Miles and Snow (1984).

advocate in organizational design, business processes, and information technologies are (or should be) accompanied by systemic changes in human resource strategy. Thus, while both TQM and re-engineering basically adopt an outside-in point of view, the prescriptive nature of the organizational environments envisioned limits the range of options with respect to human resource strategies. (Interestingly, the TQM approach generates divergent evaluations; Pfeffer (1994, 208), for example, sees the Baldrige criteria as setting 'the right conceptual tone for managing the employment relation[ship],' while Appelbaum and Batt (1994, 131) see them as 'slighting human resource criteria' because of 'several notable omissions central to employee well-being: employment security, wage growth, promotions, due-process guarantees, conflict resolution procedures, [and] employee voice.')

Relationships from the Inside Out: Dominant Model Theorists (DMTs)

DMTs approach Figure 1 from the inside out. The emphasis is on the promulgation of a particular human resource strategy (not all, however, favour the same one, as will become clear). From this starting point, the trail diverges. One concentrates on the model of choice, extolling its virtues and explaining and illustrating, often in great detail, its specific features and the necessary steps for its successful implementation. Lawler's (1986, 1992) propagation of the so-called High-Involvement model is a premier (although certainly not the only) example of this approach and will be used here to illustrate it. The other branch is relatively less preoccupied with the details of the preferred model and rather more concerned with its diffusion, and more specifically with showing how certain factors in the organizational environment (or beyond) block diffusion and why and how these factors should and can be overcome or changed. Two recent, but in many ways different, examples of this approach, again used here for illustrative purposes, are Pfeffer (1994) and Kochan and Osterman (1994).

The Models

Key features of the selected models are shown in Figure 6. While these brief statements, and the material which follows, fail to convey the full richness of the models, they do provide a flavour of their major similarities and differences.

Similarities of content include the following: top management commitment and support; high levels of employee participation, involvement, or empowerment at the workplace level, primarily through enriched jobs and/or self-managed work teams; high selection standards; extensive investments in training and development; opportunities for high levels of earnings through skill-based and/or performance-based pay schemes; a free flow of information up as well as down the organization; and stability of employment. All also emphasize the need for mutual trust and cooperation throughout an organization.

Lawler's and Kochan and Osterman's models also include effective voice for employees in organizational governance and strategy-making through labour unions or other forms of employee representation (which may include, as Pfeffer suggests, employee ownership). Lawler's and Pfeffer's models include egalitarianism and long-term career development (based on a policy of promotion from within),

Figure 6
Three Dominant Models

High Involvement (Lawler 1986, 1992)	Best Practices (Pfeffer 1994)	Mutual Gains (Kochan and Osterman 1994)
	Strategic Level	
Top management commitment	Long-term perspective	Supporting business strategies
	Overarching philosophy	Top management commitment
Cooperative union-management relations, involvement of unions in business strategy, egalitarian policies and practices	Employee ownership, symbolic egalitarianism	Effective voice for employees in strategy and governance
	Functional Level	
Stability of employment, flexibility of hours	Employment security, promotion from within	Staffing based on employment stability
Investment in training and development	Investment in training and development	Investment in training and development
Person- (not job-) based pay, performance-based pay, flex-benefits	High wages, incentive pay, wage compression	Contingent compensation
	Workplace Level	
Selection based on ability to grow	Selectivity in recruitment	High standards of selection
Involving work, organizational improvement groups	Job redesign, teams, cross-utilization	Broad task design and teamwork
Participation and involvement	Participation and empowerment	Employee involvement in problem-solving
Open information channels	Information sharing	Climate of cooperation and trust
Supportive supervision	Measurement of practices, feedback	
Justice and due process		
Sure and swift discipline		

and Lawler's also incorporates the following facilitative 'management practices': supportive supervision, flexible work arrangements, flex-benefits, justice and due process procedures, and sure and swift discipline. Pfeffer stresses the need for measurement and feedback. (Kochan and Osterman's supportive business strategies dimension will be taken up later.)

Internal Fit

Lawler's (1986, 1992) High-Involvement model, as suggested, is fully developed and extensively articulated as an integrated package of policies and practices. Pfeffer (1994) describes 16 practices used by 'effective firms,' pointing out that while 'the reader should not expect to find many organizations that do [them all], it is useful to grade one's organization against the overall list' (28). He specifies many of the interrelationships among the practices, but also leaves many 'to the reader to assess' (31). Kochan and Osterman (1994) adopt a middle ground; their Mutual Gains model consists of an integrated package of 'generic principles' organized into three tiers—those applying at the strategic, functional, and workplace levels. They also state that 'there is no single set of best practices for implementing these broad principles.'

These differences in emphasis may explain the variations in firms recurringly mentioned by these authors as exemplars of their particular approaches. AT&T, Hewlett-Packard, Xerox, Motorola, and Donnelly are frequently cited by Lawler and Kochan and Osterman, but not Pfeffer. Lincoln Electric and NUMMI are popular with Pfeffer and Kochan and Osterman, but not Lawler. Otherwise, Lawler alone features W.L. Gore, Herman Miller, and Nucor Steel; Pfeffer alone gives frequent mention to Advanced Micro Devices, Solectron, Southwest Airlines, Walmart, and Nordstrom; and Kochan and Osterman alone feature Cummins Engine, Saturn, Hewlett Packard, and Polaroid (as well as replicating mini case studies prepared by the Office of the American Workplace on Magma Copper, Federal Express, Chaparral Steel, Shenandoah Life Insurance, and Rohm & Haas).

External Fit

Lawler (1992, xiv) states, but does not dwell on, the point that the High-Involvement model 'is not necessarily the right management approach for all environments and all societies.' Kochan and Osterman adopt the position that while the principles of the Mutual Gains model are widely, but not universally, applicable, the practices through which they are implemented will (and should) vary depending on extant organizational environments. Pfeffer (1994, 65) is a bit more ambivalent; in his words, 'there is an important distinction between the contingent nature of the *implementation* of these [sixteen] practices, which everyone would agree is necessary, and the idea that the practices themselves do not provide benefit in many, if not most, situations' (italics in original).

All three models are touted as particularly in tune with today's dominant Strategic Environment: high value-added business strategies (based, for example, on quality, service, speed, flexibility, and innovation rather than low costs—a key generic principle in Kochan and Osterman's Mutual Gains model), flexible organizational structures and forms (a key piece of Lawler's High Involvement model), and sophisticated process technologies which support these high value-added business strategies and flexible organizational stuctures. All are also offered as being more suited than alternative models (particularly the Control model) to the economic and psychological interests of today's employees. The basic argument, as laid out by Kochan and Osterman is as follows:

> [C]hanges in markets and technologies have increased competitive pressures on firms to make a choice as to how to compete in today's markets, and one choice, i.e., the one that emphasizes productivity, product quality, and innovation, can best be achieved and sustained over time by investing in human resources and implementing appropriate variants on these mutual gains principles. . . . [M]ovement to these principles is the only way to achieve improvements in the social and economic conditions of employment for workers in a world where labour costs vary greatly and competitors can undercut the wages and benefit levels most people expect in an advanced economy and democratic society. In short, broad-scale adoption and diffusion of these principles and strategies are required if we are to achieve and sustain truly *mutual* gains for individual firms, shareholders, and employees, and the overall economy and society. (1994, 76, italics in original)

But, then there are the rhetorical questions. Lawler (1992, 323): 'If [the High-Involvement model] is so great, why doesn't everyone do it already?' Pfeffer (1994, 89): '[C]hange is occurring. The questions [are], why so slowly, particularly in the United States, and why with such difficulty?' Kochan and Osterman (1994, 11): 'If the ideas presented in this book are so terrific, why will the market not diffuse them? What will prevent these developments from occurring on their own?' The fact that these questions are raised (even rhetorically) and demand answers suggests that there are elements of organizational (or broader) environments to which these models may not be suited. This is an important point to which we will return after reviewing what is going on in actual practice.

Practice

To what extent does the accumulating theoretical work reflect what is actually going on in American and Canadian companies? How broadly are the concepts diffused? What is their staying power? What factors seem to facilitate or hinder their diffusion and sustainability? It is to these questions that attention is now turned. The discussion illustrates significant differences between the approaches and perspectives of the MMTs and the DMTs.

The Outside-In Perspective

Bottom-line, little is known about the diffusion (and hence the sustainability) of internally and externally congruent human resource strategies. There are case studies (many used for typology construction, as noted above) describing showcase examples. But, there are no broad-scale surveys, and no accumulation of more narrow surveys which might help determine how representative these showcase examples are, what industries are involved, and so forth.

Examples of what might be done are provided by a recent survey of 714 firms covering four industries in Canada (Betcherman, McMullen, Leckie, and Caron 1994) and by the previously cited survey of steel minimills in the United States (Arthur 1992). The Canadian study collected data pertaining to (among many other things) the use of 12 human resource practices (basically consistent with the Involvement model). Cluster analysis uncovered three types of human resource strategies, labelled traditional (characterized by relatively low usage of all the practices), compensation-based (characterized by relatively high usage of all the practices except formal job design and employee participation), and participation-based (characterized by relatively high usage of formal job design, employee participation, vocational and cultural skills training, and work-family programs, as well as a high degree of integration of human resources into formal business plans). Just over half the firms in the sample fell into the traditional cluster; the rest were about evenly split (23 and 24 percent, respectively) between the other two clusters. While there was some degree of association between business strategy and human resource strategy, no systematic attempt was made to assess the degree of external fit, or to indicate how many firms were characterized by such an external fit.

Arthur (1992) employed a more limited sample, but more relevant data analysis. He found human resource strategies in the minimills to be about evenly divided between the two broad types noted earlier: Control (Pure Cost Reducers = 27 percent, Conflictors = 13 percent, and Inducers = 13 percent) and Commitment (Collective Bargainers = 30 percent, Involvers = 7 percent, and Commitment Maximizers = 10 percent). Some subtypes (particularly Pure Cost-Reducers, Conflictors, and Commitment Maximizers) were found to be more statistically coherent than others. As for external fit, the Cost-Reduction or Control strategies were used by about 90 percent of the mills with a cost-based business strategy, while the Commitment strategies were used by about 60 percent of the mills following a business strategy based on differentiation. This represents a fair degree of external fit with this particular element of the organizational environment. To what extent the human resource strategies of the 'off-quadrant' cases (about 25 percent of the total sample) might fit with other elements of the organizational environment is unknown.

In a preliminary analysis, Arthur (1990) found that mills with a high degree of fit between their business strategies and their human resource strategies had higher levels of both productivity and quality than mills with a low degree of fit between the two. Because of data problems and the small sample size, however, the relationships failed to meet traditional levels of statistical significance. In a reanalysis, Arthur (1994) dropped the contingency notion. Across all mills (irrespective of business strategy), a comparison of Control and Commitment human resource strategies showed the latter yielding higher levels of productivity and quality (as well as lower levels of employee turnover), with all differences being statistically significant. Arthur (1994, 682-83) noted that 'these results support observations made by Walton (1985) and others concerning the effectiveness of commitment-type human resource systems, *at least in the context of manufacturing plants using technologically intensive and relatively integrated continuous production processes*' (emphasis added). At a minimum, this suggests that future studies of the MMT perspective should include process technology as well as business strategy in assessments of external fit and its performance effects.

Clearly, a good deal more research is needed to ascertain not only the extent of diffusion of various types of human resource strategies but also the nature of the forces that shape the choices of these strategies and of the organizational and individual outcomes which result (Huselid 1993).

The Inside-Out Perspective

Diffusion and sustainability are of greater concern to DMTs than to

MMTs, so the research is a bit more extensive here, although it, too, falls far short of overwhelming. Again, the evidence comes from both case studies and surveys.

The case studies provide notable examples of the preferred models (as indicated above), but there are no surveys which look at the overall picture. Rather, there are numerous surveys which focus on just one or two of the human resource practices associated with a particular type of human resource strategy (see Kochan and Osterman (1994) and Pfeffer (1994) for extensive reviews). In a particularly relevant example, Osterman (1994a) surveyed 875 establishments to ascertain (among other things) how many were engaged in five types of 'flexible work organization' (also referred to as 'workplace innovations') central to the Involvement and Mutual Gains models: teams, quality circles, job rotation, and TQM (in terms of communication, feedback, and teamwork). Seventy-eight percent of the respondents reported using one or more of these practices among at least one group of core employees; 64 percent reported that the practices involve 50 percent or more of the employees in the core group. Using tighter criteria (i.e., at least 50 percent of a firm's core employees had to be involved in two or more of the practices), Osterman concluded that only about one-third of the firms in the sample could be classified as 'significant users' of the practices of interest. His data are basically consistent with those obtained through other surveys (e.g., Lawler, Mohrman, and Ledford 1992). Osterman also concluded that only 13 percent of the significant users of these practices would have been so classified five years earlier. This may, as others (Betcherman and Verma 1993; Drago 1988; Goodman 1980) have suggested, reflect the difficulty of sustaining these types of workplace designs over long periods of time.

Surveys such as Osterman's (1994a)—whether focusing on workplace design, training, compensation, employment stability, or other components of human resource strategies one or two at a time—are helpful in establishing outside parameters with respect to the diffusion of relevant types of strategies. For example, the use of teams, quality circles, and the like is a necessary condition for engaging in an Involvement or Mutual Gains human resource strategy, but it is not a sufficient condition. A fair number of firms that use these practices probably do not also use all or even most of the other practices associated with these particular strategies. Osterman's (1994a) data, for example, show that participative workplace designs are more likely to survive and diffuse when integrated with such other human resource practices as cross-training, pay for skill, and gainsharing or profitsharing (but not necessarily formal off-the-job training or, surprisingly, given the centrality of this variable in all DMT models, employment security). But, he also notes that 'there is no HRM practice that is uniformly associated with the presence or absence of flexible work organization. Hence the notion of distinct clusters is not necessarily appropriate' (184, n. 29).

Anecdotal data from various sources support this view. On the one hand, firms with business strategies aiming to attain world-class levels of productivity, quality, service, speed, flexibility, or innovation are experimenting with redesigned work systems, extensive training efforts, various forms of contingency-based pay, and the like. On the other hand, some of these same firms (as well as others), under pressure from Wall Street and elsewhere to produce short-term profits, are turning to repeated rounds of downsizings, extensive use of contingent employees, minimal career commitments, and compensation schemes designed more to share risks with than to enhace the motivation of employees (Downie and Coates 1993; Dyer 1993). A recent Delphi study looking toward Workplace 2000 indicated a continuance of the bifurcated approaches with predictably poor results in terms of both employee performance and employee psychological and financial well-being (Dyer and Blancero 1994).

Once again, the general conclusion is that not much is known about the diffusion, let alone sustainability, of the DMT models. A reasonable conclusion seems to be that while there is widespread experimentation with certain key components of these models, there are relatively few truly integrated efforts underway (and some of the efforts may in fact be quite contradictory). Many of the integrated efforts are found in relatively small organizations or are rather limited applications in larger firms (e.g., just one or two locations, often start-ups or so-called greenfield sites) (Kochan and Osterman 1994; Lawler 1992).

What seems to be holding back the diffusion of the DMT models? This is, as noted earlier, a question which the various theorists have tackled, and, with due apologies for missed nuances, the following are some of the answers they provide (organized around the elements of the organizational environment shown in Figure 4). All agree, as indicated previously, that the current Strategic Environment makes their models particularly relevant and necessary, but that various components of the Stakeholder and Sociopolitical Environments serve as deterrents to adoption. With respect to the Stakeholder Environment, the problem, as the DMTs see it, is that in the United States economy the providers of capital (especially Wall Street and large institutional stockholders) and top managements wield all the power, while employees and, increasingly, labour unions have very little or none. This creates a situation in which short-term pressures for profits take precedence over longer term investments in innovative human resource strategies (often characterized as costs). This is a situation which fosters adversarialism and distrust between favoured and disfavoured stakeholder groups, a climate which is antithetical to the development of Involvement and Mutual Gains models.

The Sociopolitical Environment provides little help. Current government policy does little to enhance the diffusion or power of labour unions, let alone other forms of employee representation in firm governance. It also leaves it pretty much up to individual firms to provide training and employment security for employees, two essential features of the Involvement and Mutual Gains models. Market failures then lead to underinvestments in these areas because no firm can count on recouping their payoffs rather than losing them to competitors. And, in today's economy, no individual firm can realistically commit to providing employment security for its employees anyway. Finally, with respect to the Sociopolitical Environment, in the United States particularly, high unemployment rates combined with inadequate systems of public and vocational education provide an oversupply of unskilled labour which encourages the continuance of Control rather than Involvement or Mutual Gains models of human resource management.

Such analyses lead DMTs to advocate not only further research into, and proselytizing of, their models, but also fairly significant reforms with respect to labour relations and firm governance, backed by major changes in government policy. Positions vary, of course, especially with respect to public policy, but they tend to favour the enhancement of the government's role as a catalyst for change through such mechanisms as: providing information and technical support, eliminating legal and other barriers to employee involvement, providing incentives for firms to provide employee training, developing or fostering alternative forms of employability (versus employment) security, and the like. Kochan and Osterman (1994) advocate the formation of a 'mutual gains coalition' to include line and human resource managers, employer associations, employees, labour unions, professional associations, governments at various levels, and academics to diffuse the Mutual Gains model within and across firms.

The Role of Human Resource Organizations

If the strategic perspective of human resource management is taking hold in theory and, to a lesser extent, in practice, what are the implications for human resource organizations and for the executives, managers, and professionals who run them? The obvious prescription is for them to become more strategic in thought and deed. But what does this mean? To what extent does it reflect reality? What are the prospects for the years ahead?

Defining the Strategic Business Partner Role

Most current commentators place primary responsibility for strategic human resource management in the hands of top line executives (CEOs, their direct reports, the heads of various divisions or business units, and the like). The recommended role for human resource organizations is that of strategic business partner. Basically, this means that top corporate and divisional or business-unit human resource executives and managers should assume equal positions with other line and functional (e.g., marketing, finance) managers on top management teams when strategic issues, human resource-related and otherwise, are on the table. Envisioned activities for the strategic business partners include the following (Dyer and Holder 1988; Walker 1992):

- Working with their line counterparts to formulate and, from time to time, review the organization's broad human resource strategies (Control, Commitment, Mutual Gains, or whatever).
- Taking the lead in (but not the sole or even primary responsibility for) formulating the specifics of human resource strategies that are appropriate to particular corporate and business-unit strategies, as well as to other relevant aspects of the organizational environment; and, when necessary, taking the lead in challenging business strategies which appear to be infeasible or undesirable from a human resource point of view.
- Working closely with their line counterparts to assure that human resource and business strategies, once agreed upon, are adequately implemented.
- Assuring that their own departments are managed strategically; that is, that they have strategic plans which lay out goals and priorities, direct the allocation of resources, and guide the work of the function's managers and professionals.

This strategic business partner role and its attendant activities are envisioned as additions to, and not replacements for, other more traditional roles and activities performed by the human resource organization (e.g., program design and administration, operational assistance for line managers, policing adherence to policies and programs, and employee advocacy). The new role is to be used to bring business relevance and synergy (external and internal fit) to traditional activities, thereby contributing directly and noticeably to organizational effectiveness.

> The simple question to ask about the human resource function is this: Is it adding value, is it solving problems, is it serving the organization's strategic business needs? If the answer is no, then perhaps management would do well to turn its denizens loose on the competition to do their damage elsewhere. If the answer is yes, then the function can serve as an important partner in making changes designed to help the organization achieve greater productivity and performance. In any case, the smart general manager will make sure he or she knows what the situation is and whether human resources will be an ally or an obstacle to change. (Pfeffer 1994, 251)

Obviously, the strategic business partner role requires of its practitioners a set of competencies not always associated with human resources work. Some of the more commonly mentioned include: a business, as well as human resource, perspective; a generalist, rather than specialist, perspective; knowledge of business dynamics, issues, and vocabulary; knowledge of developments in relevant areas of the organizational environment (whether internal or external to the firm); diagnostic skills; consulting skills; and a willingness to take risks. (For more complete enumerations of the requisite competencies, see Ulrich, Brockbank, and Yeung (1989), and Blancero, Boroski, and Dyer (in press).)

Diffusion of the Strategic Business Partner Role

How widespread is the strategic business partner role? The short answer (again) is that no one knows for sure. But the available evidence suggests a modest and growing diffusion, notwithstanding some rather formidable obstacles.

The limited diffusion of human resource strategies within and across organizations, noted earlier, suggests a correspondingly limited diffusion of the strategic business partner role as well. This view is supported by a fairly recent world-wide survey of nearly 3,000 line executives and human resource executives, managers, consultants, and academics (40 percent of whom were from the United States) (Towers-Perrin/IBM 1992). As shown in Figure 7, only about one-quarter of the respondents to this survey characterized today's human resource organizations as proactive (versus responsive) and strategic (versus operational), and only about 40 percent saw them as partners with line managers regarding human resource issues (as opposed to taking primary responsibility for these issues). These (and related) findings led the study's authors to conclude that the 'respondents don't believe that [today's] human resource functions are fully capable of addressing a new, more business-oriented agenda for HR' (Towers-Perrin/IBM 1992, 20).

Much the same view emerged from a recent round of intensive interviews with a small number of senior Canadian human resource executives (Downie and Coates 1993). The results suggested that while the strategic business partner role was gaining ground in Canada, especially among larger, leading-edge firms, full diffusion and equal influence with line management within and beyond these companies was probably still a long way off.

Will the apparently upward, if slowly moving, trend continue? Yes, in the view of the Towers-Perrin/IBM respondents (again, see Figure 7). Looking forward to the year 2000, the percentage which anticipated that the human resource function would be primarily proactive and strategic was between 70 and 75 percent (triple the

Figure 7
Current and Future Status of the Strategic Business Partner Role

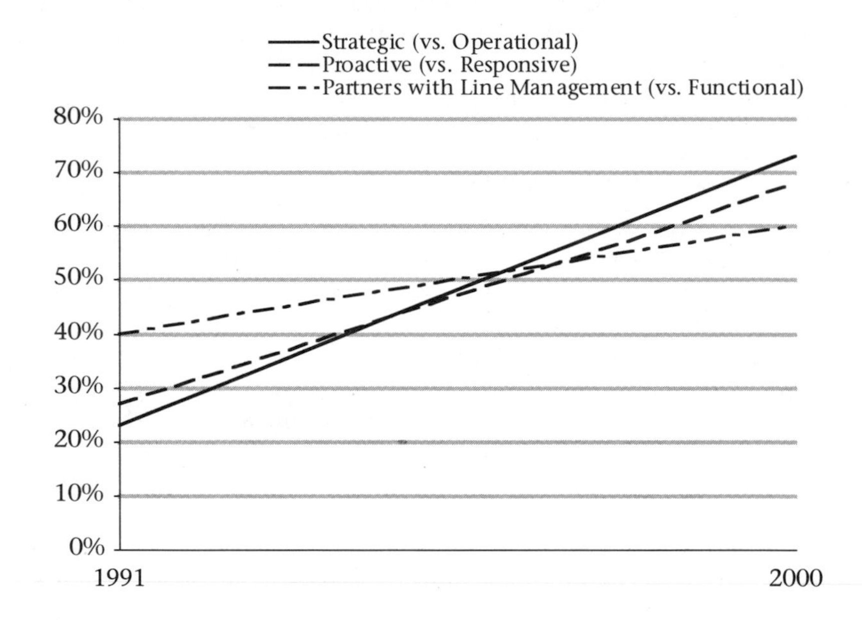

Source: Adapted from Towers-Perrin/IBM (1992), 21, exhibit 7.

1991 numbers), while the percentage which foresaw a full partnership with line management in human resource matters was 60 percent (about double the 1991 figure). As might be expected, movement in these directions was envisioned by a greater percentage of human resource executives and managers than of line executives, consultants, or academics, although the trend lines were similar for all four groups. (Interestingly, though, U.S. respondents were reported to be less likely than those from other countries to anticipate this kind of movement.)

Several factors are fueling diffusion of the strategic business partner role: intensifying searches for sources of sustained competitive advantage and related pressures on human resource people to show 'value-added' for their activities; accumulating evidence (cited above) that a strategic approach to human resource management can result in sustained competitive advantage; a steady stream of exhortatory literature extolling the virtues of a strategic approach to human resource management—and calling into question the professionalism of those not on board; and a seemingly endless supply of conferences and workshops purporting to develop the competencies required to play the strategic business partner role.

But, there are some obstacles as well. The low-hanging fruit has probably been plucked; most of the human resource practitioners who are going to be pulled by their bosses or colleagues into the strategic business partner role probably have been already. So, tough resistance can be anticipated from the remaining line executives and managers whose natural proclivities, talents, and, perhaps, organizational circumstances lean against the adoption of such a role. Indeed, two leading business periodicals, *Business Week* (Tough times 1991) and *The Wall Street Journal* (Torrent of job cuts 1991), recently reported that so-called culture-building CEOs are being systematically replaced by hard-driving executives whose primary talents lie in cutting costs and delivering short-term profits, not in investing for the longer term. Further, thus far unmoved human resource executives, managers, and professionals are undoubtedly the ones who lack, and are disinclined to develop, the competencies and risk-taking propensities required to tackle the strategic partner role. Their views may be reinforced by ongoing cutbacks in human resource budgets and staffs, a situation which is hardly conducive to taking on a new role.

How this tug and pull will balance out is anybody's guess. Our own is that movement will be slow. Some human resource people, under pressure to become more strategic—or more specifically, to contribute to the bottom line—have retreated into a rather narrow definition of what that means. Frank Doyle, senior vice president at

G.E. and one of the U.S.'s most influential and respected human resource executives, recently characterized many of his counterparts as 'perfect agents.' By this he meant that they are quite adept at carrying out top line executives' orders to downsize or cut health-care costs, but, he feared, less inclined to challenge or question these executives on human resource matters which are seen as inimical to the long-term interests of their companies, let alone their companies' employees (Doyle 1993). The Canadian study cited earlier uncovered a tendency, also noted elsewhere, among some human resource people to attempt to shift responsibility for human resource matters to their line counterparts and, then, to seek security in an advice and counsel role (Downie and Coates 1993). And there are the inevitable diversions—a plethora of recent articles and workshops on reengineering the human resource function, for example, are serving to turn the attention of human resource people inward on their own operations, rather than outward toward the broader business environment (Greengard 1994).

Some see human resource organizations at a critical juncture, facing a fundamental choice between a full-bore shift to the strategic business partner role or a fairly quick demise (Schuler 1990). The reasoning is as follows. Failure to embrace the new role will lead to its preemption, along with associated operational decisions, by line managers and external consultants. Meanwhile, automation and outsourcing will continue to eat away at the function's administrative and policing roles. And the employee-advocate role will continue to wither, lacking the unlikely resurgence of government or labour union pressures. What, then, will be left for a human resource department to do?

A Question of Influence

Others go so far as to suggest that even if the strategic business partner role is widely embraced by human resource executives, managers, and professionals, this does not necessarily mean that human resource issues will receive their just due in strategic business deliberations (Kochan 1994; Kochan and Dyer 1993; Kochan and Osterman 1994; Pfeffer 1994). This argument rests on the legacy of the function's traditionally low status and power position coupled with the nature of the strategic business partner role itself. The initial burden is on human resource people to build partnerships by gaining the confidence and commitment of more powerful top and line managers. This situation may well foster ingratiation rather than the assertion of a forceful stance giving voice and stature to human resource issues (Freedman 1990; Towers-Perrin/IBM 1992).

Historically, the argument continues, significant gains in the power and influence of human resource departments have come in concentrated periods coincident with external jolts: wars, social crises, union threats, and major changes in government policy (Baron, Devereau, and Dobbin 1988; Jacoby 1985; Kochan and Cappelli 1981). External pressures may be required this time around as well. Thus, success and, perhaps, survival for human resource people may rest on their willingness and ability to join in a coalition with like-minded colleagues, labour leaders, government policy-makers, and academics to formulate and implement a national agenda to: (1) strengthen the influence of employees as stakeholders in corporate governance and strategic decision making and (2) encourage and assist the building of a national infrastructure for diffusing human resource innovations which produce benefits not only for individual firms but also for the broader economy and society. Relevant policy initiatives might include: incentives which encourage employers to invest in new technologies, but only if they simultaneously invest in the human resource practices required for the successful implementation of these technologies; revised labour laws ensuring the right of employees to effective representation in organizational decision making which could come through traditional labour unions but might also come through experimentation with works councils and the like; legislation which provides adequate protection for employees while at the same time avoiding the 'one-size-fits-all' mentality by granting the parties involved flexibility with respect to standards and enforcement (as is done in some cases through the Voluntary Protection Program administered by the Occupational Safety and Health Administration); and meaningful investments in research on the effectivenes of human resource innovations in varying circumstances and in the dissemination of the results to facilitate the diffusion of appropriate human resource strategies within firms and across the economy (Kochan 1994).

Future Directions

Where does this leave us? On the one hand, it is clear that the strategic perspective has taken hold among a fair number of human resource theorists, researchers, and practitioners. Indeed, it may well have surpassed the operational and programmatic perspectives to become the dominant paradigm of the field. On the other hand, even devotees share considerable confusion, and sometimes outright disagreement, about basic constructs, key components, and future directions. While this ferment holds great promise for the academic and practical development of the field, it must be constructively channelled. Following are some suggestions along these lines, looking first at human resource strategy and later at the role of human resource professionals.

Human Resource Strategy

Additional work—more empirical than conceptual—is needed to clarify basic constructs. For example:

- To what extent do the many typologies of human resource strategy reflect actual practices? Additional theory-based taxonomic research would be most helpful in answering this important question.
- What are the key components of the organizational environment which shape decisions about human resource strategies? More theoretical work might be in order here. But particularly important are in-depth studies of strategic decision making processes: Who is involved? What factors are considered? What roles do these factors play in shaping the human resource strategies which emerge? Little is to be gained from additional studies which simply examine relationships between types of business strategies and types of human resource strategies. It may be interesting to know that X percent of firms with, say, differentiation business strategies employ, say, Commitment or Mutual Gains human resource strategies. But what really matters is: What took these firms in this direction, and, perhaps even more important, what took the rest in other directions? Hypotheses suggest that certain characteristics of the Strategic Environment stimulate certain types of human resource strategies but that these may or may not be reinforced by forces in the Sociopolitical and Stakeholder Environments (Kochan and Osterman 1994; Osterman 1994b). Is this the way it really works?

And, in the end, what difference does it make? Which types of human resource strategies work best under what environmental circumstances? Relevant evidence is beginning to accumulate (e.g., Arthur 1990, 1994; Ichniowski, Shaw, and Giovanna 1993; MacDuffie and Krafcik 1992; Macy and Izumi 1993), but several refinements are in order. Two, suggested above, are first, to continue to sharpen definitions and measures of human resource strategies and second, to move beyond business strategy to incorporate additional dimensions of the organizational environment as contingency variables. It would be helpful if this research considered a broader range of outcomes than has heretofore been the case. Thus far, the focus has been on productivity and quality; but other organizational outcomes—service, speed, flexibility (adaptability), and innovation—are becoming increasingly important sources of competitive advantage. Further, consideration should be given to the financial and psychological payoffs for employees, particularly in the face of mounting evidence that enhanced corporate competitiveness in many cases is coming out of employees' hides (Kochan and Osterman 1994). Finally, the effectiveness research needs to study samples other than blue-collar workers in manufacturing environments (Osterman, for example, found that workplace 'innovations' were actually more prevalent among professional/technical and service employees than among their blue-collar counterparts—see Kochan and Osterman 1994, table 4-3).

This analysis has focused on the United States and, to a lesser extent, Canada. But, there is much to be learned from experiences in other countries, too, particularly with respect to governance. To what extent do legislative and other arrangements which enhance the power of employees as organizational stakeholders in Japan and various European countries facilitate or restrict the diffusion of certain types of human resource strategies? What are the long-term effects in terms of important organizational, individual, and societal outcomes? Are these experiences culture bound, or do they also hold potentially useful lessons for North American firms and public policy makers?

The Roles of Human Resource Professionals

Much remains to be learned about: the extent to which the strategic business partner role has actually permeated human resource organizations in the U.S. and Canada, the extent of power and influence wielded by those who have adopted the role, and the factors which help and hinder both the diffusion and the power position of the role.

Again, what difference does it make? Writers today often imply that the keys to diffusing the strategic perspective within and across corporations lie in the diffusion of the strategic business partner role, accompanied by a continuing accumulation of salutary evidence. But others question this, arguing that human resource people will never on their own attain a level of power necessary to assure that human resource considerations receive their just due at the highest levels of corporate decision making. Rather, they suggest, human resource managers and professionals would be wise to join with other relevant parties in a mutual gains coalition to promote public policies which move in this direction. Which position is right? Part of the answer lies in learning more about the human resource role in strategic decision making.

But, part of it may also lie in questioning the very models that shape the thinking of people in our field. Perhaps it is time for those interested in human resource strategy to shift some of the theorizing and research from questions of competitive advantage, internal and external fit, and the power and influence of human resource executives and managers to broader issues of corporate governance and relationships between human resource decisions at the firm level and the dynamics of public policy making and policies at the national level, and even beyond.

References

Applebaum, Eileen and Rose Batt. 1994. *The new American workplace: Transforming work systems in the United States*. Ithaca, NY: ILR Press.

Arthur, Jeffrey. 1990. Industrial relations and business strategies in American steel minimills. Ph.D. diss., Cornell University.

———. 1992. The link between business strategy and industrial relations systems in American steel minimills. *Industrial and Labor Relations Review* 45:488-506.

———. 1994. Effects of human resource systems on manufacturing performance and turnover. *Academy of Management Journal* 37:670-87.

Bamberger, Peter, Sam Bacharach, and Lee Dyer. 1990. Human resource planning in high technology entrepreneurial startups. *Human Resource Planning* 13(1):37-44.

Baron, James, P. Devereau Jennings, and Frank Dobbin. 1988. Mission control? The development of personnel systems in U.S. industry. *American Sociological Review* 53:497-514.

Begin, James. 1991. *Strategic employment policy: An organizational systems perspective*. Englewood Cliffs, NJ: Prentice-Hall.

Betcherman, Gordon and Anil Verma. 1993. Follow-up to the new technology survey. Paper presented to the Canadian Industrial Relations Research Association, June.

Betcherman, Gordon, Kathryn McMullen, Norm Leckie, and Christina Caron. 1994. *The Canadian workplace in transition*. Kingston, ON: IRC Press, Industrial Relations Centre, Queen's University.

Blancero, Donna, John Boroski, and Lee Dyer. In press. Transforming human resource organizations: A field study of future competency requirements. *Human Resource Management.*

Cappelli, Peter and Harbir Singh. 1992. Integrating strategic human resources and strategic management. In *Research frontiers in industrial relations and human resources*, edited by David Lewin, Olivia Mitchell, and Peter Scherer. Madison, WI: Industrial Relations Research Association.

Cutcher-Gershenfeld, Joel. 1991. The impact on economic performance of a transformation in workplace relations. *Industrial and Labor Relations Review* 44:241-60.

Downie, Bryan and Mary Lou Coates. 1993. *The changing face of industrial relations and human resource management*. Current Issues Series. Kingston, ON: IRC Press, Industrial Relations Centre, Queen's University.

Doyle, Frank. GE's Doyle urges HR to embrace a world of change. *Work in America* 18(3):3.

Drago, Robert. 1988. Quality circle survival: An exploratory analysis. *Industrial Relations* 27:336-51.

Dunlop, John. 1994. Organizations and human resources: Internal and external markets. In *Labor economics and industrial relations: Markets and institutions*, edited by Clark Kerr and Paul Staudohar, pp.375-400. Cambridge, MA: Harvard University Press.

Dyer, Lee. 1993. *Human resources as a source of competitive advantage*. The Don Wood Lecture in Industrial Relations. Kingston, ON: IRC Press, Industrial Relations Centre, Queen's University.

Dyer, Lee and Donna Blancero. 1994. Workplace 2000: A Delphi study. Cornell University. Draft.

Dyer, Lee and Gerald Holder. 1988. A strategic perspective on human resource management. In *Human resource management: Evolving roles and responsibilities*, edited by Lee Dyer, pp.1-46. Washington, DC: Bureau of National Affairs.

Freeman, Audrey. 1990. *The changing human resource function*. New York: The Conference Board.

Goodman, Paul S. 1980. Quality of work life projects in the 1980s. In *Proceedings of the 1980 spring meeting of the Industrial Relations Research Association*. Madison, WI: IRRA.

Greengard, S. 1994. New technology is HR's route to reengineering. *Personnel Journal* (July):32C-32O.

Hammer, Michael and James Champy. 1993. *Reengineering the corporation*. New York: Harper Collins.

Huselid, Mark. 1993. The impact of environmental volatility on human resource planning and strategic human resource management. *Human Resource Planning* 16(3):35-51.

Ichniowski, Casey, Kathryn Shaw, and Giovanna Prennushi. 1993. The effects of human resource management practices on productivity. Columbia University, Graduate School of Business. Draft manuscript.

Jackson, Susan, Randy Schuler, and J.C. Rivero. 1989. Organizational characteristics as predictors of personnel practices. *Personnel Psychology* 42:727-86.

Jacoby, Sanford. 1985. *Employing bureaucracy managers, unions, and the transformation work in American industry*. New York: Columbia University Press.

Jones, Gareth and Patrick Wright. 1992. An economic approach to conceptualizing the utility of human resource management practices. *Research in personnel and human resource management* 10:271-99.

Kochan, Thomas. 1994. Principles of a post-New Deal employment policy. In *Labor economics and industrial relations: Markets and institutions*, edited by Clark Kerr and Paul Staudohar, pp.646-71. Cambridge, MA: Harvard University Press.

Kochan, Thomas and Peter Cappelli . 1984. The transformation of the industrial relations and personnel function. In *Internal labor markets*, edited by Paul Osterman, pp. 133-62. Cambridge, MA: MIT Press.

Kochan, Thomas and Lee Dyer. 1993. Managing transformational change: The role of human resource professionals. The *International Journal of Human Resource Management* 4:569-90.

Kochan, Thomas A., Harry C. Katz, and Robert B. McKersie. 1986. *The transformation of American industrial relations*. New York: Basic Books.

Kochan, Thomas and Paul Osterman. 1994. *The mutual gains enterprise*. Boston, MA: Harvard Business School Press.

Lawler, E.E. 1986. *High involvement management: Participative strategies for*

improving organizational performance. San Francisco: Jossey-Bass.
Lawler, E.E. 1992. *The ultimate advantage: Creating the high involvement organization*. San Francisco: Jossey-Bass.
Lawler, Edward E., Susan A. Mohrman, and Gerald E. Ledford, Jr. 1992. *Employee involvement and total quality management*. San Francisco: Jossey-Bass.
MacDuffie, John Paul and John Krafcik. 1992. Integrating technology and human resources for high-performance manufacturing: Evidence from the international auto industry. In *Transforming organizations*, edited by Thomas Kochan and Michael Useem, pp.209-26. New York: Oxford University Press.
Macy, Barry and Hiroaki Izumi. 1993. Organizational change, design, and work innovation: A meta-analysis of 131 North American field studies—1961-1991. In *Research in organizational change and development*, Vol. 7, pp.235-313. Greenwich, CT: JAI Press.
Miles, Raymond and Charles Snow. 1988. Designing strategic human resources systems. In *The strategic human resource management handbook*, edited by Lloyd Baird, Craig Schneier, and Richard Beatty, pp.42-52. Amherst, MA: Human Resource Development Press.
Milliman, John, Mary Ann Von Glinow, and Maria Nathan. 1991. Organizational life cycles and strategic international human resource management in multinational companies: Implications for congruence theory. *Academy of Management Review* 16:318-39.
Osterman, Paul. 1994a. How common is workplace transformation and who adopts It? *Industrial and Labor Relations Review* 47:173-88.
———. 1994b. Internal labor markets: Theory and change. In *Labor economics and industrial relations: Markets and institutions*, edited by Clark Kerr and Paul Staudohar, pp.303-39. Cambridge, MA: Harvard University Press.
Pfeffer, Jeffrey. 1994. *Competitive advantage through people*. Boston, MA: Harvard Business School Press.
Quinn, James Brian. 1992. *Intelligent enterprise*. New York: The Free Press.
Schuler, Randall S. 1990. Repositioning the human resource function: Transformation or demise? *Academy of Management Executive* 4(3):49-60.
———. 1992. Strategic human resource management: Linking the people with the strategic needs of the business. *Organizational Dynamics* 22 (summer):18-31.
Schuler, Randall S. and Susan Jackson. 1987. Linking competitive strategies with human resource management practices. *Academy of Management Executive* 1:207-19.
———. 1989. Determinants of human resource management priorities and implications for industrial relations. *Journal of Management* 15(1):89-99.
Tichy, Noel, Charles Fombrun, and Mary Anne Devanna. 1982. Strategic human resource management. *Sloan Management Review* 23(2):47-61.
Torrent of job cuts shows human toll as recession goes on. 1991. *Wall Street Journal*, 12 December, p.1.
Towers-Perrin/IBM. 1992. *Priorities for competitive advantage*. New York: Towers-Perrin.
Ulrich, David, Wayne Brockbank, and Arthur Yeung. 1989. HR competencies in the 1990s: An empirical assessment of what the future holds. *Personnel Administrator* 34 (November):91-3.
Ulrich, David and Dale Lake. 1990. *Organizational capability: Competing from*

the inside out. New York: John Wiley.
U.S. Department of Commerce. 1993. *Malcolm Baldrige National Quality Award, 1993 award criteria*. Gaithersburg, MD: National Institute of Standards and Technology.
Walton, Richard. 1985. From control to commitment in the workplace. *Harvard Business Review* 63 (March-April):77-84.
Walker, James. 1992. *Human resource strategy*. New York: McGraw-Hill.
Wright, Patrick and Gary McMahan. 1992. Theoretical perspectives for strategic human resource management. *Journal of Management* 18:295-320.

7 Barriers, Challenges, and Future Directions

Bryan Downie and Mary Lou Coates

The purpose of this chapter is to pull together the major themes that emerged during the conference, based on both the papers and the discussion. The chapter highlights the areas of consensus and divergence, the challenges, future directions, and agendas for change. The chapter is divided into four sections. The first discusses the new human resource management and the need for change. The second section looks more closely at what has actually been taking place in terms of the nature and extent of the diffusion of high-performance workplace practices, the barriers to change, the sustainability of human resource innovations, the role of unions in workplace innovation, and the effect of human resource practices on firm performance. The third section examines the challenges facing human resource management practitioners. In the last section we sum up and set forth some suggestions for future directions that were made at the conference.

The Need for Change in Human Resource Management

An overarching issue at the conference was whether transformed workplace practices and high-commitment/high-participation work systems are rhetoric or reality. Like much of the contemporary literature, conference speakers and participants seemed to agree that there is a need for change. In today's fiercely competitive environment, the compelling business need for flexibility, efficiency, quality, and productivity is driving organizations to seek more flexible workplace practices and to move to new high-performance work systems. Traditional systems of organizing and managing work are often not able to deliver the productivity and quality improvements, cost control, flexibility, and adaptability that many organizations require to remain competitive. Indeed, as other sources of competitive advantage (e.g., technology, regulated and protected markets, access to financial resources, and economies of scale) become less important than they once were, 'what remains as a crucial, differentiating factor is the organization, its employees, and how they work' (Pfeffer 1994, 14).

The consensus at the conference was that, based on both organizational and employee needs, a new human resource management system which emphasizes employee involvement, commitment, and flexibility is required. Today, more than ever before, organizations are realizing that if they are to become more competitive and improve organizational effectiveness, they need a greater focus on human resource issues and the effective utilization of employees. Both Jeffrey Pfeffer and Edward Lawler have advocated this perspective. Gordon Betcherman and Ken Delaney raised the issues of diversity in the work force and work and family responsibilities as particular challenges that need to be addressed in the workplace.

Betcherman, in his conference paper and other recent work (Betcherman et al. 1994), outlined the *implications for workers* of a continued reliance on traditional work systems. He noted that traditional work systems contribute to a high degree of employment insecurity in the labour market, high turnover, short job tenure, and inadequate investment in training, particularly in workplaces where there is a large proportion of nonstandard jobs (e.g., part-time, short-term, and contract work) which in some companies may intensify labour market polarization. Lee Dyer and Thomas Kochan also pointed out that some of the recent literature (Kochan 1994; Kochan and Dyer 1993; Kochan and Osterman 1994) has linked human resource strategies to the goal of improving living standards as well as enhancing competitiveness.

Despite the pressure and the apparent desire to move away from traditional to more high-performance work systems, conference speakers raised some concerns with respect to the new human resource management system (e.g., Appelbaum and Delaney). These are discussed later.

Many organizations are taking a strategic perspective, that is, they do see people as a central source of competitive advantage, and they see that human resource management (HRM) should be an essential part of business strategy. In a recent study it was found that the most successful manufacturing organizations had a greater focus on their work force and used more work-force empowerment, training, and team-related practices (Gordon and Wiseman 1994). Pfeffer and Lawler had somewhat different views on strategic human resource management. Pfeffer talked about the competitive advantage of human assets in terms of the systems in the organization and the structures that are created, whereas Lawler argued that it is the organizational capabilities that are developed which provide competitive advantage today.

Overall, the literature and conference presentations and discussions indicate that in addition to a growing realization of the need for change, a number of significant developments in the management of human resources are occurring. As discussed later, there is some debate on whether these are innovations or experiments. There are also clear barriers to change, and the diffusion of innovative human resource practices is slow. Nevertheless, something is happening, and a set of best practices may be emerging.

Several of the speakers referred to components of this new HRM or various practices or principles that should apply to managing the work force (see Figure 1). Some of these so-called 'best practices' include employee participation, information sharing, work teams, training, employment security, alternative rewards systems (e.g., variable compensation, skill-based pay, performance-based pay, employee stock ownership plans), problem-solving groups, the elimination of status differences, job redesign, job rotation, and multiskilling, flattening hierarchies, and decentralization.

One area of divergence that arose during the conference centred on whether or not the adoption of these human resource management practices was a necessary and sufficient condition for a move towards high-commitment/high-performance workplaces. Pfeffer and Lawler (this volume) and Kochan and Osterman (1994) take a more normative approach. They argue that a human resource strategy comprised of certain practices or components should be applied within and across firms. Human resource strategies that are integrated and mutually reinforcing (i.e., have 'internal fit') are held to be even more effective. For example, Pfeffer (1994) unambiguously lays out 16 practices that, he argues, are effective in achieving competitive advantage through managing the work force. Although similar for the most part, there are variations in what constitutes this set of 'best practices' (see Figure 1). This approach does acknowledge that the same human resource system is not equally effective in all situations and that these 'best practices' are not universally applicable. The general course of action with this approach is to make the particular human resource strategy work in the environment and to focus on how any barriers to diffusion can be overcome.

Randall Schuler, on the other hand, argued that adopting a 'best practices' approach applied in a non-contingent manner may be too ambitious and premature at this point in time. He was also uneasy with prognostications that if human resource practitioners were

Figure 1
'Best Practices' for Managing the Work Force

Kochan and Osterman	Lawler	Pfeffer
Top-management commitment; supporting business strategies	Top-management commitment	Long-term perspective; overarching philosophy
Effective voice for employees in strategy and governance	Cooperative union-management relations; involvement of unions in business strategy; egalitarian policies and practices	Employee ownership; symbolic egalitarianism
Staffing based on employment stability	Stability of employment; flextime	Employment security; promotion from within
Investment in training and development	Investment in training and development	Investment in training
Contingent compensation	Performance-based pay, person- (not job-) based pay, flexible benefits	High wages; incentive pay; wage compression
High standards of selection	Selection based on ability to grow	Selective recruiting
Broad task design and teamwork	Involving work, organizational-improvement groups	Job redesign; teams; cross-utilization of people
Employee involvement in problem solving	Participation and involvement	Participation
	Sharing of information; suggestion system	Information sharing
Climate of cooperation and trust	Supportive supervision	
		Measurement of human resource policies
	Justice and due process; sure and swift discipline	

Source: Table 1 in Pfeffer's paper, p.15 above and Figure 6 in Lee Dyer and Thomas Kochan's paper, p.144 above.

unable to carry out the changes demanded of them, they would be replaced by non-HR professionals and in their hands, these 'best practices' would become an 'elixir.' Dyer, too, stated that there are no 'best practices' and he argued that there is no strong evidence, as some claim, that shows the validity of those 'best practices.'

Instead, Schuler and Dyer take the view that there are many different human resource strategies and different environments. They both pointed to the conundrum of organizations which have different human resource practices but are equally successful (e.g., Federal Express and United Parcel Service). There can be organizations which are successful but do not do a good job of managing people and, conversely, organizations that do a good job of managing people but are not successful. Eileen Appelbaum also alluded to this when she argued against a 'one-size- fits-all kind of organizational framework.' Ellen Glanz pointed out that in her experience with benchmarking excellent human resource practices in different companies, the differentiators were not the practices but certain underlying principles. One of those underlying principles was line managers actually having accountability for managing and developing their people.

Therefore, rather than advocating a 'best practices' approach, Schuler and Dyer argued that the basic course of action is to match the human resource strategy to the environment in order to enhance organizational effectiveness. Human resource strategy is approached from the outside in, and attempts should be made to identify the key elements in the organizational environment which human resource strategy ought to fit.

The 'external fit' perspective raises the question of whether any particular human resource policy can be characterized as a 'best practice' or whether such practices can 'only be determined within the context of a particular firm's strategic and environmental contingencies' (Huselid 1995). Gordon Betcherman, in his paper, stated that '[t]he particular features of a successful [human resource management] approach will depend on the characteristics of the firm, its history and culture, as well as its environment.' As a human resource management practitioner, Louise Piché pointed out that changes in human resource management have been externally driven, that is, changes in the marketplace and changes in management and culture have had the most significant impact on human resource management policies and practices in her organization.

We can conclude by saying that there will be a continuing debate on whether or not there is a certain set of 'best practices' that should be implemented. It is even less clear how many of these practices should be applied and what their configuration should be in any particular organization.

Given that the type, complexity, and strategic importance of human resource issues has increased, what is happening to the role of the human resource management function? Traditionally, it has been seen as a bureaucratic, isolated, and specialized staff function which has played a reactive or 'firefighting' role with little influence on corporate business strategy. Today, it is clear that new demands are being placed on the role, structure, and responsibilities of the human resource management function within organizations. The human resources manager is required to have a much broader range of expertise, to understand the business needs of the organization and assume a higher corporate profile, to be more of a coach and enabler, to play a greater strategic role in business decision making and a more proactive role in integrating employee needs and business objectives in order to meet the goals of the organization.

Several of the papers presented at the conference examined the role of human resource managers and, in particular, their role as strategic players within organizations in the implementation of new high-performance workplace practices. It was clearly indicated that here too, there was a need for dramatic changes. Edward Lawler's paper emphasized the dualities that exist for the human resource practitioner. It will be recalled that by this he meant that in addition to being a strategic partner, the human resource practitioner still needs to carry out some of the more traditional staff support activities. Louise Piché spoke of the difficulties and frustrations she faces in managing that dual role. The role of the human resource management function and the challenges facing the human resource management professional are discussed in a later section.

Based on the papers and discussions at the conference, the reality is that whether it is accomplished through the adoption of a set of human resource management 'best practices,' internally consistent and integrated human resource practices, and/or through the alignment of human resource management practices with the organization's competitive business strategies, there is a need for change and a move away from the traditional workplace approaches and to high-performance work systems. Furthermore, there seems to be a consensus that if human resources are going to be a source of competitive advantage and improved firm performance, important changes are necessary for the human resource management function.

The Reality of the New Human Resource Management

As noted above, the conference made it clear that the new human resource management practices have moved beyond rhetoric. What is less clear is whether there are limitations on the use of these high-performance workplace practices and how pervasive they are within and across organizations. This section highlights the conference discussions relating to the nature and extent of diffusion, the barriers to change, and the sustainability of new forms of work organization. There is also a discussion of the role of the union and the effect of human resource practices on firm performance.

The Diffusion of High-Performance Workplace Practices

Based on the evidence presented at the conference, we can conclude that the amount of innovation in the workplace is considerable. For example, Ken Delaney of the United Steelworkers indicated that in more than 60 percent of workplaces he studied, 'something was happening.' Nevertheless, there was a consensus at the conference that the transformation in workplace practices and the adoption of high-commitment/high-performance work systems are diffusing only slowly.

In the United States, Paul Osterman found that in 1992, about 35 percent of private sector establishments with 50 or more employees were making significant use of flexible work organization practices (Osterman 1994). In the paper presented at this conference, he indicated that despite the fact that organizations are moving toward high-performance work systems, there is a difference between the use of these practices and the level of *penetration*. At first glance, the use of flexible work organization practices is quite widespread, but when looking at only those practices which involve at least 50 percent or more employees, the occurrence of each practice drops off sharply. One notable exception to this is the use of self-directed work teams, which was fairly extensive. Therefore, although quite a bit is happening, it is not necessarily taking place on a large scale within organizations or across organizations. There are very few firms embracing all the so-called high-performance workplace practices and few that use a set of practices across the entire organization. Kochan and Osterman (1994) found that firms tend to adopt these practices either singly or in diverse mixtures or patterns.

Furthermore, there seems to be a fair amount of experimentation occurring, and practices are often dropped after a certain period of time. Based on her field work in the U.S. apparel industry, Eileen Appelbaum found evidence of 'compromise innovations' or 'hybrid' types of work organizations. These are practices which are in existence but are not being fully reflected at the shop floor level; that is, there is a gap between the firm's policies and its actual practices.

Findings provided by Gordon Betcherman on what is happening in Canada reveal that, as in the United States, only about 30 percent of organizations are following some type of high-performance human resource management system.[1] Betcherman also found that there is a great deal of experimentation with high-performance workplace practices but that these never got beyond 'frill' status.

As will be discussed later, the conference also shed light on developments taking place in the human resource management function. These changes, too, suggest that at least large firms are attempting to change the way human resources are utilized. For example, Prem Benimadhu reported that research conducted by the Conference Board of Canada indicated that the human resource function was shifting away from the technical side and developing stronger ties with chief executive officers (CEOs) in managing change and creating high-performance organizations. The human resource executive is required to make a business contribution to the organization and in some cases, the function is becoming a business unit. A majority of human resource executives now report to the CEO, denoting a higher corporate profile for the human resource management function in organizations. In addition, there has also been increased line involvement in human resource activities, indicating that closer links between business strategy and human resource strategy are being formed.

Clearly, some organizations are moving toward high-performance workplace systems. However, the transformation has been neither speedy nor pervasive. As several speakers at the conference also noted (Osterman and Betcherman, for example), the sustainability of high-performance workplace practices is in question. In the discussion, Betcherman used the term 'carousel effect' to describe some of the 'flavour-of-the-month' experimentation that has gone on in some firms with high-performance workplace practices.

Barriers to Change

Given the need for change, why has there been a relatively slow diffusion of high-performance workplace practices? Most of the speakers at the conference discussed various barriers to change (see Figure 2). There was general agreement that capital and financial markets were a barrier. Jeffrey Pfeffer explained that one of the fastest ways to drive stockholder value up was to announce a massive layoff. He and others also criticized the overemphasis on 'denominator manage

1 Betcherman suggests that the degree of workplace change may be slightly greater in the United States than in Canada because of the higher incidence of small firms in Canada, which are less likely than larger firms to have moved toward high-performance work systems.

Figure 2
Barriers to the Diffusion of High-Performance Workplace Practices

Social-psychological processes, e.g., controlling management behaviour, monitoring employees (Pfeffer)

The social environment, e.g., resistance from line managers, executives (Pfeffer; Osterman; Dyer)

Capital and financial markets (Pfeffer; Osterman; Delaney; Dyer)

A lack of supportive government policy (Pfeffer; Osterman; Dyer)

A lack of linkages between organizations seeking to build high-performance workplace practices and those engaged in such practices (Pfeffer)

A short-term orientation (Piché)

An emphasis on cost reduction and downsizing (Pfeffer; Lawler; Appelbaum; Piché; Betcherman)

A lack of resources and/or knowledge by small- and medium-sized firms (Osterman)

Governance structures that focus on shareholder interests and extend limited influence to employees or unions (Pfeffer; Osterman; Betcherman; Delaney)

A lack of information on implementing and sustaining high-performance workplace practices (Betcherman)

Institutional and policy obstacles, e.g., educational, unemployment insurance and collective bargaining systems, employment standards regulations, underinvestment in training (Betcherman; Dyer)

The human resource management function, e.g., cautious managers, reluctant to share knowledge and expertise, nonplayers on strategic issues (Lawler; Glanz; Dyer)

ment'[2] (downsizing), the short-term focus on internal financial controls that promote 'making-the-numbers' behaviour, and the use of

2 Hamel and Prahalad (1994) explain the phrase 'denominator management.' Return on investment (ROI) has two components: a numerator (net income) and a denominator (investment assets, capital employed or, in a service industry, head count). They argue that for many company executives who are under pressure for quick ROI improvement, the tendency has been to cut the denominator through downsizing, delayering, and divesting as an alternative to the tougher approach of raising net income.

financial measures that stress results and ignore processes and organizational capabilities that produce those results, particularly in the long run. Pfeffer also pointed out that financial reporting systems do not differentiate between expenditures that do and do not build competency and skill in the organization, factors that both Edward Lawler and Ellen Glanz saw as critical in achieving competitive advantage. As a result, when financial performance diminishes, investments in human assets and capabilities often become the first expenses to be cut.

Lee Dyer also commented that 'short-term pressures for profits take precedence over longer term investments in innovative human resource strategies (often characterized as costs).' Louise Piché spoke of the barriers associated with a strong focus on becoming more efficient and driving costs down, a short-term orientation, and operating in a crisis environment.

In addition to governance structures which focus on shareholder and not employee interests, government policy was also criticized for failing to enhance the power of labour unions or other forms of employee representation in firm governance (Pfeffer; Osterman; Betcherman; Delaney). High unemployment rates, inadequate educational systems, an underinvestment in training, and current institutions and policies such as employment standards regulations, and the unemployment insurance system were also felt to be disincentives to high-performance workplace approaches. For example, Gordon Betcherman stated that the unemployment insurance system, which allows employers to use layoffs as an adjustment mechanism without assuming the additional costs arising from the further unemployment created is a barrier to the diffusion of high-performance workplace practices.

The traditional collective bargaining system, with its emphasis on management rights, the separation of employer and employee interests, adversarialism, and conflict and distrust, was viewed as a barrier to the adoption of innovative human resource practices (Pfeffer; Betcherman). To date, much of the literature seems to indicate that unions have a role to play in the diffusion and sustainability of workplace innovation (Eaton and Voos 1994). A study of Canadian manufacturers revealed that the most successful plants were, on average, slightly more unionized and unionization 'did not seem to be a barrier to broad-based success' (Gordon and Wiseman 1995, 9). The findings of Osterman and Betcherman presented at the conference seem to run contrary to the prevailing view. The role of unions is discussed in a later section.

Several speakers did note that in some situations, the introduction of new work arrangements has met with opposition from unions. In addition to unions, resistance has also come from lower- and middle-level line managers and those executives who have taken less of a culture-building perspective and more of a hard-line, cost-cutting approach.

One of the more intriguing barriers discussed during the conference were the social-psychological processes that restrict implementation of high-performance workplace practices. Pfeffer presents the argument that by examining the psychological dynamics underlying the control exercised or administered by managers and supervisors, one gains a clearer understanding of why ineffective practices have persisted. For example, surveillance and control by supervisors may create low performance by reducing motivation and effort and increasing stress. In turn, this may justify the need for continued or closer monitoring thereby creating a reinforcing cycle of behaviour which perpetuates excessive or unwarranted levels of supervision and controlling management behaviour.

In some organizations, the human resource function was held responsible for the lack of diffusion of a high-performance model. For example, Lawler argued that too often, the human resource function has been a 'nonplayer' and one with a vested interest in existing systems and not in making needed changes. In some cases, there has been a lack of understanding by the human resource management function of the business and as a result, the function has not been able to design human resource systems that are aligned with the business strategy and other parts of the organization. Dyer also pointed out that in terms of moving to a more strategic business partner role, human resource people may have been too cautious. He also states that most of the human resource practitioners who are going to be pulled into a business partner role by their bosses or colleagues are involved in this more strategic role by now. Therefore, resistance can be expected among remaining line executives and managers who are not prepared to embrace such a role. As a result, future activity on this front may be much less likely. Ellen Glanz stated that there has been a reluctance for HR to share their knowledge and expertise across different parts of the organization.[3] Osterman also found that in organizations where the human resource department is a nonplayer in strategic policy making, workplace innovations are less likely to be sustained.

3 The tendency of human resource practitioners to cling to their special knowledge was also discussed in a study on the integration of corporate strategy and human resource management at a major U.S. manufacturing firm. It was stated that by 'demystifying' and 'giving human resource management away' (involving line management more), the process of human resource management is strengthened (Angle, Manz, and Van de Ven 1985, 63). However, some human resource managers and/or line managers may be unwilling to embrace this 'new partnership.'

Aside from these barriers, a fundamental reason why we are not seeing more workplace innovation may revolve around issues of implementation. As many of the conference speakers noted, organizational transformation is a difficult, costly, and risky process. There are a number of so-called 'best practices' that characterize a transformation to high performance work systems. However, given their complexity, organizations with very traditional human resource management systems and/or small or medium-sized firms may face a very arduous task in implementing them.

Sustainability of High-Performance Workplace Practices

Two important factors were emphasized in terms of the sustainability of high performance practices—employment security and the role of the union.[4] In the empirical research Osterman conducted for the United States, he actually examined whether employment security commitments were important in sustaining new forms of work organization. Surprisingly, he found that firms with employment security policies did not have higher rates of innovation or more sustained innovation than firms that did *not* provide some form of employment security.

This finding has important implications for the debate on whether the extensive restructuring and downsizing that has been taking place sabotages or makes it impossible to implement high-performance work systems. Employment security had been held to be a necessity for high-performance work systems (for example, see Figure 1, above). However, there seems to be some shifting away from what has traditionally been meant by 'job' or 'employment security.' As one speaker noted, 'in today's economy, no one firm can realistically commit to providing employment security for its employees' (Dyer). Prem Benimadhu stated that due to fierce competition, shifts in the world economic order, and turmoil in the markets, there has been a 'shattering of the employment contract.' The whole notion of employment security has changed from the concept of 'jobs for life' to one of providing 'the experience or skills necessary to improve the general employability of most workers' (Betcherman). In the words of the chairman and CEO of a major Canadian company which changed the way it viewed the implied employment contract,

> [t]he idea replaces the traditional view that an employee has the right to stay on the payroll until retirement. Instead, we now

4 Osterman also found that human resource practices such as training and development and the compensation and reward system were significantly related to the sustainability of workplace innovation.

maintain that the job is only there as long as the employee's function itself meets the needs of the corporation, and as long as the corporation remains competitive and healthy. (Stacy 1993, 45)

A study of Canadian organizations also indicated that the notion of job or employment security was changing (Downie and Coates 1994).

The issue sparked an interesting debate during the conference around the compatibility of cost-reduction strategies, downsizing, employment security, and the adoption of high-performance workplace systems. One of the issues that arose in discussions was the extent to which companies were pursuing cost reductions under the guise of high-performance work systems and whether high-performance workplace practices were just another way of coming at the problem of trying to remain cost-competitive in today's environment.

Edward Lawler cited two recent studies (Lawler, Cohen, and Chang 1993; Bureau of National Affairs 1994) that revealed that the focus of most human resource functions was on cost control. Gordon Betcherman also found that 60 percent of organizations in Canada in his sample were following a cost-reduction strategy. During the discussion, Jeffrey Pfeffer decried the 'obsessive' focus on cost. Edward Lawler pointed out that aside from the cost side of the business equation, human resources also account for a high proportion of the revenue side, that is, without effective human resources, firms cannot generate much, if any, revenue.

It was also argued that it is impossible to pursue both downsizing and high-performance/high-commitment work systems. Eileen Appelbaum discussed the 'myths' of downsizing—that it does not necessarily reduce the number of workers nor does it always produce the desired results, such as improved productivity. She also concurred with Jeffrey Pfeffer's view that much of it is Wall Street-driven. Other studies have also found only a temporary improvement in business as the result of restructuring (Hamel and Prahalad 1994).

Gordon Betcherman also felt that firms that embark on a strong cost-reduction strategy on the one hand are going to have a difficult time successfully introducing high-performance work systems on the other hand. It has been stated that '[t]he employment stability issue is really the Achilles' heel of the employee involvement approach' (Dyer 1994, 4). Despite his own evidence that indicated employment security was not important in explaining sustainability, Paul Osterman doubted that a firm that continues to lay off and 'devalue' its work force would be able to implement high-performance work systems successfully. He suggests that one explanation for why firms have been able to pursue both restructuring and the introduction of high-performance work systems is that the level of fear of job loss in the economy is so high that employees are willing to participate in work reorganization despite the great uncertainty and lack of security.

The Role of Unions

It has been argued elsewhere that the effectiveness of new forms of work organization depends on the presence of strong unions (Eaton and Voos 1992, 1994; Kelley and Harrison 1992). Some of the findings presented at the conference contradicts this evidence. Both Osterman's findings for the United States and Betcherman's evidence from Canada indicated that union involvement is unrelated to the sustainability of high-performance workplace practices. However, it was recommended that not too much be read into this. Betcherman suggests that the apparently unimportant role of unions in sustaining workplace innovation indicates that intangible factors such as commitment and trust are critical. Osterman, too, states that the quality of union-management relationships is important and there is not a pervading 'union effect' on the innovation process. Nevertheless, their findings indicate a clear need for additional research in this area.

Workplace change has been a double-edged sword for many unions and the conference addressed the dilemma that organized labour has faced and the controversy that exists even within its own ranks. Unions have responded to management-led work reorganization initiatives in two ways: passive acceptance or opposition and rejection (Betcherman; Delaney). There has not been a solidarity of response to workplace change by labour, and different unions have taken different approaches.

High-performance workplace systems offer both opportunities and risks to organized labour. On the one hand, as Ken Delaney from the United Steelworkers stated, unions have a vested interest in companies that are pursuing high-performance workplace strategies because of what this system offers workers in terms of the potential gains from greater training, autonomy in the workplace, and increased quality of work. On the other hand, the introduction of high-performance systems can also pose threats to workers, particularly if employers choose to follow a low-wage as opposed to high-wage strategy (United Steelworkers 1991; Parker et al. 1994). For example, based on research conducted for the Steelworkers, Delaney found little evidence of an increase in discretionary authority by workers and, in many cases, high-performance systems were also associated with work intensification, that is, an increased pace of work and/or job enlargement.

As an alternative to passive acceptance or outright rejection of workplace redesign initiatives, Delaney proposed that unions follow a 'good-jobs strategy' which focuses on improving the nature of jobs and the quality of work (e.g., it focuses on health and safety, training, skills development). He also advocated a bargained approach to workplace reorganization and discussed Algoma Steel as a case where there have been both increases in the quality of work and productivity improvements. In the early 1990s, a serious financial crisis at Algoma Steel led to a restructuring initiative which created a new worker-owned enterprise. In return for wage and benefit reductions and a reduced work force, employees signed a collective agreement that contained a number of employee participation initiatives (Nishman 1995). From the union perspective, a key human resource issue in involving unions in workplace redesign is meeting the needs of this 'good' jobs agenda.

Performance Gains

One of the issues that was discussed by the conference participants related to sharing the gains derived from the introduction and development of high-performance workplace practices. Ken Delaney finds that there has been a limited sharing of efficiency gains. He also stresses the need to look at workplace redesign as a means to make jobs better for workers and not only to increase productivity. Eileen Appelbaum also expressed concerns with how performance gains, especially those that are unrelated to productivity, should be shared. She gave the example of new team production systems in the apparel industry that make it possible to guarantee perfect quality to retailers. Some of the retailers will pay a premium for this. The system has become more efficient, but she poses the question: Who does the premium belong to? Rather than a narrow focus on labour productivity, she suggested, there should be a broad range of performance gains that are shared with workers. This, too, is an issue which needs to be examined more extensively.

This discussion raises the question of how the new human resource management workplace practices are related to firm performance. Research results have shown that there may be a link between human resource practices and firm performance and that high-performance work systems perform better than traditional systems (Betcherman, this volume; Delaney and Huselid 1995). The evidence is clearly mixed, and depends on the various measures of performance outcomes. For example, Betcherman found that in terms of such shop floor indicators as quits, layoffs, accidents, and unit labour costs, high-performance workplaces outperformed establishments with traditional workplace systems. However, there was no statistically significant relationship with such financial performance indicators as profitability, market share, and sales.[5]

A recent report by the U.S. Conference Board revealed that two-thirds of organizations had made significant progress in getting employees to focus on quality and one-half reported increases in productivity and employee awareness of customers' needs. However, only 30 percent of major U.S. and European companies who significantly changed their corporate strategy, organizational structures, and work forces over the last five years reported any major gains in market share and only one-third were successful in increasing employee commitment and workers' adaptability to change (*HR Planning Newsletter* 1995). Therefore, this, perhaps more than any other issue, needs more research.

Challenges Facing Human Resource Management Professionals

Although there has definitely been a move toward high-performance workplace systems and new workplace practices, traditional approaches to organizing, utilizing, and managing work prevail. The human resource management professional has been faced with the challenge of making a transition from the traditional to the new.

Human resource management is evolving. If human resources are an important source of competitive advantage, the human resource manager encounters a number of challenges in developing, maintaining, and sustaining this advantage and these systems. Conference speakers, discussants, and participants offered insight into what we need to know about organizations and the challenges and future prospects and directions for today's human resource management professional.

George Smith, a human resource management practitioner and chairperson of one of the conference sessions, stated, 'We are living in a dynamic, complex, and ambiguous time.' He sees the human resource manager being at the forefront of change, helping organizations to see their way through the chaos and turbulence. Several other speakers (Schuler; Glanz; Dyer) also talked about the diagnostic approach that human resource managers need to take in implementing many of the new workplace practices.

Along the same lines, according to Lee Dyer, the key ingredient that the human resource person brings to the table is the ability to

5 Betcherman offers two explanations for his findings. First, financial gains do exist but the data and methodology were not able to capture them. Second, the firm's human resource practices may not be describing what is actually taking place in the workplace.

diagnose the environment, to identify important human resource issues, and to provide a perspective to those who are planning business strategy changes or reorganizations on what the potential human resource implications of those changes might be. Randall Schuler stressed that this diagnostic framework needs to be in place because different environmental conditions warrant different human resource practices. Ellen Glanz also discussed the diagnostic skills required in the human resource manager's role as business partner—in translating from business issues to human resource approaches and then providing or brokering the necessary services.

Edward Lawler, too, proposed that the human resource management function can become more of a strategic partner by focusing on its potential to identify, develop, and maintain organizational capabilities and by taking on more responsibility for organizational effectiveness. Instead of being an opponent of change, the human resource function has to become a business partner in strategic change. Lawler identified a number of changes in the human resource management structure and responsibilities that are required if the function is to assume a new course of action. The human resource manager needs to become part of the senior management team with access to strategic discussions and decision making. Individuals should be rotated between the human resource management function and line management in order to increase the business knowledge of the human resource manager and to better integrate business strategy and human resource management policies and practices. Forming cross-functional teams across all levels of the organization and from a variety of functions also enables human resource managers to expand their business knowledge and fosters the development of an 'organization-wide ownership over human resource systems.' Lawler also suggests that other ways to provide administrative services such as payroll and benefits be examined (e.g., outsourcing, creating regional or national processing centres).

Ellen Glanz agreed with Lawler's view that there is a need for the human resource management function to build capabilities. However, she argued that there is a need to ensure that integrated human resource processes are also in place to harness employee capability and commitment and enable organizations to utilize individual resources effectively and make the kinds of changes that are needed. Prem Benimadhu spoke of the 'disconnect' in organizations today between the vision that the CEO is promoting and the human resource policies and practices that are needed to support the vision.

In fairness to the human resource practitioner, there are clear limits to what can be expected of a human resource manager. For example, Lawler, Dyer and Kochan, and Ellen Glanz cautioned that in transforming itself into a more strategic player, the function cannot abandon its traditional administrative and human resource management activities. Instead, the human resource manager in the 1990s and beyond has to manage a set of 'dualities' in the role (depicted in Figure 5 of Lawler's paper). Louise Piché also spoke of how this notion of strategic partnering is really a double-edged sword. Not only does the human resource management function need to help develop and implement business strategies but also, at the same time, the role of the human resource function is very much influenced by the business strategies of the organization. In her view, 'cutting-edge HR will only be found in cutting-edge organizations.' In addition, she spoke of the difficulties and frustrations she faces in managing the dual role that Edward Lawler discussed and her concern that she should be moving a lot faster.

Moreover, conference participants were also warned of the danger in underestimating the technical expertise that human resource professionals bring to the table. Louise Piché expressed concern that the rhetoric associated with making human resource management a line responsibility may reinforce the notion that anyone can be a good manager of people and, therefore, a good human resource practitioner.

While the evidence indicates that the role of the human resource management function is changing, these changes are happening only slowly (Downie and Coates 1994; Towers Perrin 1992). There has not been a transformation of the human resource management function, and the discussion at the conference indicated the limits and pressures faced by the human resource practitioner.

Future Directions and Issues

Aside from emphasizing the need for human resource practitioners to become more proactive and seize the opportunities to be change agents in organizations, the conference papers and discussions called on researchers, academics, and public policy makers to facilitate workplace reform. Jeffrey Pfeffer advocated a complementary research agenda to better understand the barriers limiting the adoption and diffusion of high-performance workplace practices in order to overcome problems of implementation. Dyer and Kochan also called for 'meaningful' research and the dissemination of results on the effectiveness of human resource innovations.

Several of the speakers indicated that government policy has not been friendly to high-performance workplace systems. It was recommended that governments develop a better understanding of workplace issues, particularly of how public polices can better support high-performance strategies and that, as major employers, they examine the applicability of high-performance practices in their own workplaces. Lee Dyer and Thomas Kochan suggested that human resource practitioners join in a coalition with labour leaders, government policy makers and academics to develop a national agenda to strengthen the influence of employees and to create a national infrastructure for diffusing innovative human resource practices that benefit individual firms as well as the economy and society.

Among the various public policy initiatives recommended were training grants and technical assistance programs to help introduce new technology, new production processes or quality initiatives; labour law reform and alternative collective bargaining systems to give workers a strong, independent, and effective voice; legislation to provide employees with adequate protection; and public acknowledgement of firms pursuing high-performance work systems to encourage the emulation and diffusion of these practices and to legitimatize such changes.

As noted earlier, several issues and questions remain unresolved. Paradoxically, there are organizations which are undergoing aggressive restructuring and are downsizing their work forces at the same time that they are striving to implement high-performance/high-commitment workplace practices. Are the two strategies compatible? Also, there is no strong evidence on how high-performance human resource practices are related to various measures of performance at the shop floor level and to overall financial indicators such as profitability and market share. And if there is a link between high-performance work systems and firm performance, how should performance gains, particularly those unrelated to productivity, be shared? A final question that remains is, what role do unions and collective bargaining play in moving towards a high-performance work system? These are issues that clearly must be addressed in the future.

In summary, the following points are worth reiterating.

- In both Canada and the United States, there is a significant amount of experimentation with human resource innovation in the workplace. However, high-performance workplace practices are being implemented in a piecemeal fashion and on an incremental basis. They are not pervasive either within firms or across firms.
- The diffusion and sustainability of high-performance workplace practices still remain major problems. There are significant barriers clearly limiting a broader-based application of new work systems.
- There are differences of opinion on whether or not there is a 'best

practices' approach or whether the appropriate human resource strategies depend on the environment within which the firm operates.

- There appears to be a shift in opinion with respect to the need for employment security guarantees as a foundation for new approaches to human resource management. Instead of a traditional notion of employment security, the position that now seems to be taken centres more on the need to provide workers with the skills and experience that enhance their employability.
- The human resource management function is clearly undergoing change, and the expectations for the role of human resource managers within organizations are rising.
- Human resource managers not only face new challenges but, more than ever before, they are encountering opportunities to carve out a new role in today's organization. How successful they are will very much depend on their ability to manage dual roles (the traditional role and that of the strategic partner).
- Unions, too, are faced with both challenges and opportunities and difficult choices on whether and how to respond to new workplace practices. Some unions have passively accepted workplace changes while others have vehemently opposed them.
- It was suggested in the conference that unions can play an effective role by negotiating changes and ensuring that in moving to new work systems, issues such as training, health and safety, and improved quality of work remain on the agenda.

The conference covered a great deal in terms of the nature and scope of changes that are occurring in the economy and in the workplace, the barriers to change and its diffusion, and the impact these changes are having on organizations, unions, employees, and the human resource management function. Nevertheless, the impression that conference speakers and discussants left with us is that there will be much more change in the future. Clearly, the need to understand, adjust, control, and proactively manage change will continue. For human resource practitioners, their role is to move beyond being simply implementors of change. The goal posts seem to have shifted. Today, they are being asked to be managers and leaders of change.

References

Angle, Harold L., Charles C. Manz, and Andrew H. Van de Ven. 1985. Integrating human resource management and corporate strategy: A preview of the 3M story. *Human Resource Management* 24(1):51-68.

Betcherman, Gordon, Kathryn McMullen, Norm Leckie, and Christina Caron. 1994. *The Canadian workplace in transition*. Kingston, ON: IRC

Press, Industrial Relations Centre, Queen's University.
Bureau of National Affairs. 1994. *SHRM-BNA Survey No. 59*. Washington, DC: Bureau of National Affairs.
Delaney, John T. and Mark A. Huselid. 1995. The firm-level impact of high-performance work practices in for-profit and nonprofit organizations. *Academy of Management Journal*. Under review.
Downie, Bryan and Mary Lou Coates. 1994. *Traditional and new approaches to human resource management*. HRM Project Series. Kingston, ON: IRC Press, Queen's University.
Dyer, Lee. 1994. *Business strategies and human resource policies*. Interview by Mary Lou Coates. Kingston, ON: IRC Press, Industrial Relations Centre, Queen's University.
Eaton, Adrienne E. and Paula B. Voos. 1992. Unions and contemporary innovations in work organization, compensation, and employee participation. In *Unions and economic competitiveness*, edited by Lawrence Mishel and Paula B. Voos, pp.173–215. Armonk, NY: M.E. Sharpe.
———. 1994. Productivity-enhancing innovations in work organization, compensation, and employee participation in the union versus the nonunion sectors. In *Advances in industrial and labor relations,* edited by David Lewin and Donna Sockell, pp.63–109. Greenwich, CT: JAI Press.
Gordon, John and Joe Wiseman. 1994. *Best plant practices: The human resource factor*. Kingston, ON: IRC Press, Industrial Relations Centre, Queen's University.
Hamel, Gary and C.K. Prahalad. 1994. *Competing for the future*. Boston, MA: Harvard Business School Press.
HR Planning Newsletter. 1995. 15(6).
Huselid, Mark A. 1995. The impact of human resource management practices on turnover, productivity, and corporate financial performance. *Academy of Management Journal* 38:635–72.
Kelley, Maryellen R. and Bennett Harrison. 1992. Unions, technology, and labor-management cooperation. In *Unions and economic competitiveness,* edited by Lawrence Mishel and Paula Voos, pp.247-86. Armonk, NY: M.E. Sharpe.
Kochan, Thomas A. 1994. Principles of a post-New Deal employment policy. In *Labor economics and industrial relations: Markets and institutions,* edited by Clark Kerr and Paul D. Staudohar, pp. 646-71. Cambridge, MA: Harvard University Press.
Kochan, Thomas A. and Lee Dyer. 1993. Managing transformational change: The role of human resource professionals. *The International Journal of Human Resource Management* 4:569-90.
Kochan, Thomas and Paul Osterman. 1994. *The mutual gains enterprise*. Cambridge, MA: Harvard Business School Press.
Lawler, Edward E., S.G. Cohen, and L. Chang. 1993. Strategic human resource management. In *Building the competitive work force,* edited by P. Mirvis, pp.31–59. New York: Wiley.
Nishman, Robert F. 1995. *Worker ownership and the restructuring of Algoma Steel in the 1990s*. Kingston, ON: IRC Press, Industrial Relations Centre, Queen's University.
Osterman, Paul. 1994. How common is workplace transformation and how can we explain who adopts it? *Industrial and Labor Relations Review* 47:173-88.

Parker, Mike and Jane Slaughter, with Larry Adams et al. 1994. *Working smart: A union guide to participation programs and reengineering*. Detroit, MI: Labor Notes.

Pfeffer, Jeffrey. 1994. *Competitive advantage through people: Unleashing the power of the work force*. Boston, MA: Harvard Business School Press.

Stacy, Don T. 1993. Empowerment: Beyond lip service to bottom-line responsibility. *Canadian Business Review* 20(1):44-5.

Towers Perrin. 1992. *Priorities for competitive advantage*. New York: Towers Perrin.

United Steelworkers of America. 1991. *Empowering workers in the global economy: A labour agenda for the 1990s*. Toronto, ON: United Steelworkers of America.

Appendix A

Conference Program 22–23 September 1994

Welcome, Bryan Downie
Director, Industrial Relations Centre/School of Industrial Relations

Session One

Chair, James Nininger
President & CEO, The Conference Board of Canada

Speaker, Jeffrey Pfeffer
Stanford University

Managing Human Resources for Competitive Advantage: Barriers to Change

Session Two

Chair, Judith Maxwell
Executive Director, Queen's-University of Ottawa Economic Projects

Speaker, Edward Lawler III
University of Southern California

Strategic Human Resource Management: Building Organizational Capabilities

Discussants
Ellen Glanz, Senior Consultant, Conceptual Systems Inc.
Louise Piché, Vice President, Quality and Human Resources, Canadian National Railways

Session Three

Chair, Michael McDermott
Senior Assistant Deputy Minister, Human Resource Development Canada

Speaker, Paul Osterman
Massachusetts Institute of Technology

Workplace Transformation in the U.S.: Policies and Practices

Discussants
Eileen Appelbaum, Associate Research Director, Economic Policy Institute
Randall Schuler, Research Professor, New York University

Session Four

Chair, James Cameron
Director of Labour Relations, General Motors of Canada

Speaker, Gordon Betcherman
Queen's University

Workplace Transformation in Canada: Policies and Practices

Discussants
Prem Benimadhu, Vice President, Human Resources Research Group, Director, Compensation Research, Conference Board of Canada
Ken Delaney, Research Director, National Office, United Steelworkers of America

Session Five

Chair, George Smith
Vice President, Industrial Relations, CP Rail

Speakers, Lee Dyer and Thomas Kochan
Cornell University and Massachusetts Institute of Technology

Is There A New HRM?: Contemporary Evidence and Future Directions

Appendix B

Conference Participants

Mark Alexander
Toronto East General Hospital

Eileen Appelbaum
Economic Policy Institute

David Arrowsmith
Queen's University

Michel Audet
Laval University

Keith Banting
Queen's University

Julian Barling
Queen's University

Gerald Barsalou
SNC Lavalin Inc.

Reg Basken
Energy & Chemical Workers Union

Prem Benimadhu
Conference Board of Canada

Gordon Betcherman
Queen's-University of Ottawa Economic Projects

Jean Boivin
Laval University

Ian Bovey
Northern Telecom Ltd.

Donald Brown
Canada Post

Mary Byczok
Great Atlantic & Pacific Co. of Canada Ltd.

James Cameron
General Motors

Robert Canuel
Kraft General Foods

Don Carter
Queen's University

Bill Cheshire
National Trust

Mary Lou Coates
Queen's University

Carol Cox
Dylex Limited

Gordon Crowther
Livingston Group Inc.

Ken Delaney
United Steelworkers of America

Bryan Downie
Queen's University

Linda Duxbury
Carleton University

Lee Dyer
Cornell University

Gord Fry
Great Atlantic & Pacific Co. of Canada Ltd.

Paul Gardiner
Ministry of Labour

Ellen Glanz
Conceptual Systems Inc.

David Glue
Canadian General Insurance Group

John Gordon
Queen's University

Morley Gunderson
University of Toronto

Joanne Harack
Connaught Laboratories Ltd.

Ian Hay
Federal Express Canada Ltd.

Ian Hendry
Richardson Greenshields

John Holmes
Queen's University

Timo Hytonen
Queen's University

Andrew Jackson
Canadian Labour Congress

Lorne Kenney
The Premier's Council

Tom Knight
University of British Columbia

Harvey Kolodny
University of Toronto

Pradeep Kumar
Queen's University

Andre Lamarche
Avenor Inc.

Edward Lawler III
University of Southern California

Harvey Lazar
Human Resources Development Canada

Joanne Lechasseur
Confédération des Caisses Populaires et d'Économie

Deborah Leighton
Queen's University

Heino Maeots
Coca-Cola Beverages Ltd.

Jody Manley
Queen's University

Bohdan Marmash
Royal Lepage Limited

Jean-Paul Martineau
Kraft General Foods Canada

Judith Maxwell
Queen's-University of Ottawa Economic Projects

Michael McDermott
Human Resources Development Canada

Jerry Meadows
Ministry of Labour

Greg Murtagh
Sectoral Skills Council

Keith Newman
Communication, Energy & Paperworkers Union

Keith Newton
Industry Canada

James Nininger
Conference Board of Canada

Shawn O'Connor
Canadian Labour Market and Productivity Centre

John O'Grady
John O'Grady Consulting

Sandra Oliver
Canada Malting Company

Shawna O'Grady
Queen's University

Paul Osterman
Massachusetts Institute of Technology

Jane Parr
Ault Foods

Emma Pavlov
Imperial Oil Limited

Robert Peacock
Bell Canada

Jeffrey Pfeffer
Stanford University

Steve Phinney
Ault Foods

Louise Piché
Canadian National Railways

Derwyn Sangster
Canadian Labour Market and Productivity Centre

Randall Schuler
New York University

Iain Scott
William M. Mercer Limited

Andrew Sharpe
Canadian Labour Market and Productivity Centre

Judy Shuttleworth
B.C. Telephone Company

Georges Simard
Ontario Hydro

Deborah Smith
Xerox

George Smith
CP Rail

Kelly Speck
Government of British Columbia

Akivah Starkman
Human Resources Development Canada

Douglas Stephens
Kodak Canada Inc.

David Sudbury
Honda Canada Inc.

Denis Sutton
Manitoba Telephone System

Mike Ternovan
Union Gas Limited

Thomas Thayer
Queen's University

Anil Verma
University of Toronto

Richard Weatherdon
Queen's University

Caroline Weber
Queen's University

Anna Whitley
Canadian Broadcasting Corporation

Arlene Wortsman
Canadian Labour Market and Productivity Centre

Lorna Wright
Queen's University